Unofficial
CHINA

About the Book

This original and provocative text presents an absorbing view of social life in China today. Through a diverse set of case studies, the contributors—a superb group of historians, literary critics, sociologists, and political scientists—introduce readers to a wide range of issues facing Chinese society as a whole. The underlying theme of state-society ties successfully captures the dynamic interplay that helps shape both popular and official culture. The book's rich discussions of different methods for studying contemporary China will be especially valuable as a tool for introducing students to the study of popular culture.

Unofficial
CHINA

Popular Culture and Thought
in the People's Republic

EDITED BY

Perry Link
Princeton University

Richard Madsen
Paul G. Pickowicz
University of California–San Diego

WESTVIEW PRESS
Boulder, San Francisco, & London

Copyright © 1989 by Westview Press, Inc.

Published in 1989 in the United States of America by Westview Press, Inc., 5500 Central Avenue, Boulder, Colorado 80301, and in the United Kingdom by Westview Press, Inc., 13 Brunswick Centre, London WC1N 1AF, England

Library of Congress Cataloging-in-Publication Data
Unofficial China : popular culture and thought in the People's
  Republic / edited by Perry Link, Richard Madsen, Paul G. Pickowicz.
    p. cm.
  Includes bibliographical references and index.
  ISBN 0-8133-0923-9. ISBN 0-8133-0924-7 (pbk.).
  1. China—Social life and customs—1976–   . 2. China—Intellectual
life—1976–   . 3. China—Popular culture. I. Link, E. Perry (Eugene
Perry), 1944–   . II. Madsen, Richard, 1941–   . III. Pickowicz,
Paul.
DS779.23.U56 1989
951.05'8—dc20   89-36440
                                                                                    CIP

Printed and bound in the United States of America

⊗   The paper used in this publication meets the requirements of the American National
    Standard for Permanence of Paper for Printed Library Materials Z39.48-1984.

10   9   8   7   6   5   4   3   2   1

Contents

Acknowledgments   ix

1   Introduction, *Perry Link, Richard Madsen, and Paul G. Pickowicz*   1

PART ONE
LITERATURE, THE CINEMA, AND AUTHORITY

2   Hand-Copied Entertainment Fiction from the Cultural Revolution, *Perry Link*   17

3   Popular Cinema and Political Thought in Post-Mao China: Reflections on Official Pronouncements, Film, and the Film Audience, *Paul G. Pickowicz*   37

PART TWO
MARRIAGE AND THE FAMILY

4   "How Come You Aren't Divorced Yet?" *Zhang Xinxin*   57

5   Love and Marriage in North Chinese Peasant Operas, *R. David Arkush*   72

6   My Mother's House, *Deborah Davis*   88

PART THREE
RELIGION, ETHNICITY, AND PROPRIETY

7   The Catholic Church in China: Cultural Contradictions, Institutional Survival, and Religious Renewal, *Richard Madsen*   103

8   Recycling Rituals: Politics and Popular Culture in Contemporary Rural China, *Helen F. Siu*   121

9   Pride and Prejudice: Subei People in Contemporary
     Shanghai, *Emily Honig*   138

10   The Persistence of Propriety in the 1980s,
     Ellen Johnston Laing   156

PART FOUR
SOCIAL CURRENTS

11   Guerrilla Interviewing Among the *Getihu,*
     Thomas B. Gold   175

12   Value Change Among Post-Mao Youth: The Evidence
     from Survey Data, *Stanley Rosen*   193

Chronology   217
Suggested Reading   223
About the Editors and Contributors   225
Index   227

Acknowledgments

This book was made possible by financial support from the American Council of Learned Societies (ACLS); a Pacific Rim Research Grant provided through the Graduate School of International Relations and Pacific Studies at the University of California (UC)–San Diego; and the Pacific Rim Research Center at the University of California–Los Angeles (UCLA). We are grateful to Jason Parker at the ACLS, Peter Gourevitch and Richard Attiyeh at UC–San Diego, and Lucie Cheng and Philip Huang at UCLA for arranging the funding.

For help with the translation of Zhang Xinxin's essay, we are indebted to Bai Xiaodong and Judith Rosselli.

We are grateful to Sue Brennecke, who helped with typing and many other practical details in the preparation of this book.

Perry Link
Richard Madsen
Paul G. Pickowicz

Unofficial
CHINA

1

Introduction

PERRY LINK, RICHARD MADSEN,
AND PAUL G. PICKOWICZ

Few foreigners anticipated the Beijing Spring of 1989 and the massacre of protesting workers and students that so tragically ended it. Western sinologists were not generally aware that many citizens of China were so profoundly discontented with their government. China scholars did not expect the student protesters to be so determined and well disciplined. Nor did foreign observers predict how vicious would be the Chinese government's repression of the protests. The Beijing Spring taught us how little we knew about the most important aspects of life in China.

In many ways, of course, our knowledge of China has vastly improved in the past decade. As a result of the opening to the West initiated by Deng Xiaoping in the late 1970s, foreign sinologists have enjoyed vastly improved access to data. Impressive advances have been made in the field of history with the gradual opening of central and local Chinese archives. Political scientists can know much more about power structures, both formal and informal, and about the nuances of policymaking processes. Despite some setbacks, anthropologists and other fieldworkers have been gaining access to China's villages. In fields such as economics and demography, the flood of new information has sometimes constituted a methodological problem in itself as scholars accustomed to the detective work of studying fragmentary information have suddenly had to learn "macroprocessing."

Despite this new access, one of the most important parts of life has remained essentially unprobed: contemporary Chinese popular culture. What do people think about? How do they view life? We know much more about administrative structures than about the ideas of the people who staff them and the feelings of the people who are subject to them. We know much more about economic production than about the motivations of producers and consumers.

Our lack of knowledge about this realm of ideas, feelings, and motivations inhibits us from understanding momentous events such as those of the Beijing Spring. For instance, unless we understand more deeply how people in different situations in China think about the tensions between hierarchy and equality and between social order and chaos, we will never comprehend why the students and workers who participated in the demonstrations demanded democracy so fervently and why some political leaders suppressed those demands so brutally. Unless we have a more subtle understanding of economic motivations, we will not understand why the workers of China have been so profoundly discontented despite an undeniable rise in their material standard of living during the past decade.

The purposes of this book are to probe this large and elusive area of popular culture, including not only cognitive ideas but also feelings, emotions, and moral and aesthetic values, and to offer theoretical and methodological suggestions to scholars interested in continuing this kind of research.

Like so many works of scholarship, this book sprouted from the union of a little money and a few vague ideas. In early 1985, the American Council of Learned Societies (ACLS) sponsored a small brainstorming session at Ann Arbor, Michigan, to help generate ideas on priorities for funding and development of Chinese studies. Participants agreed that one underdeveloped but important area for new research on contemporary China was popular culture. Paul Pickowicz, who was present at the session, volunteered to ask Perry Link and Richard Madsen to join him in a committee to explore this topic. Jason Parker of the ACLS promised some seed money.

The project grew and the ideas became clearer. The committee began tentatively to formulate the theoretical and methodological issues involved and organized an expanded planning session with Matthew Chen, Sherman Cochrane, Deborah Davis, Gail Kligman, and Alexander Woodside. The resulting workshop (sponsored by research grants from the University of California–San Diego and UCLA) eventually led to the publication of this book.

The book's title came from a discussion about the manuscript with some intellectuals in Beijing during the fall of 1988 as the storm clouds that led to the outbursts of the Beijing Spring were already beginning to gather. Someone raised the question, What would be the best Chinese word to describe the manuscript? After a lively discussion, the Beijing scholars narrowed the choice to two terms: *wuguanfang*, literally meaning "unofficial," and *buzhengtong*, meaning "unorthodox," with a connotation of "deviant." It was interesting to learn how closely related in the Chinese universe of discourse are the unofficial and the deviant. This linguistic connection reflects a political system in which government officials consider anything outside their control to be unorthodox and deviant. The courageous advocates of democracy in China have been trying to create a system in which the unofficial would not ipso facto be held suspect but would be respected as the source of China's creativity. We hope that in some small way *Unofficial China* will help foreign readers to better appreciate the cultural challenges that the citizens of China face in their search for political reform.

THEORETICAL CONSIDERATIONS

Our project had a fertile intellectual environment in which to grow, based on a conjuncture of two sets of developments—in the West and in China. In the United States and Europe,

> popular culture studies have, [in the words of Chandra Mukerji and Michael Schudson] undergone a dramatic change in the last generation—from an academic backwater, all too often a superficial pursuit of the trivial, to an intellectual hotbed, a theoretically rich and empirically expansive new focus in a variety of disciplines. Anthropologists, historians, sociologists, and literary scholars have mounted impressive intellectual challenges to basic assumptions in their own fields that had previously barred close attention to popular forms.[1]

In China, the "opening to the West" has given Western scholars access to data that allow them to join the ferment in their disciplines by doing meaningful research on popular culture in China. And the reforms in China are producing important new cultural phenomena for both Chinese and foreigners to ponder.

The principal challenge we faced as we cultivated this project was to make connections between the best ideas being discussed in theoretical studies of popular culture and the actual practice of doing research about China. For instance, we had to develop working definitions of our primary terms that could fit the kinds of information we could gather about life in China and that would speak to some of the most salient issues in contemporary Chinese society. For the purposes of this book, then, what do we mean by "culture"? What do we mean by "popular"? What, for that matter, do we mean by "China"?

In our planning sessions and in the workshop, we had lively discussions about all of these topics. Were we to define culture as "mental life," "consciousness," "values," "feelings," "aesthetic understandings"? Was culture something subjective—ideas and/or feelings in people's minds—or objective—symbolic resources like language and ritual or literary texts and dramatic performances that people make use of in the process of thinking and feeling? In the growing theoretical literature on popular culture one can find a confusing array of arguments for defining culture in any of these various ways. For China scholars at this stage of China's history and at this stage of the field's development, which are the best alternatives?

The chapters in this volume represent no simple consensus on these issues. At some level, of course, all would assume that culture has both an objective and subjective dimension: that it consists of shared symbolic resources possessed by communities, handed down by tradition, and embedded in the fabric of institutions; that these resources are constantly being reinterpreted, refashioned, and regenerated by the individuals who make up these communities, participate in these traditions, and live within these institutions; and that the goal of our research should be to capture some sense of the dialectical interplay between these objective and subjective dimensions of culture. However, the chapters here represent different approaches to the questions of which dimension to emphasize and how to accomplish a sense of the interplay between them.

Some of our authors emphasize the subjective side of the equation. By using participant-observation and depth interviewing, they try to convey a rich sense of how particular individuals under different circumstances subjectively understand common cultural predicaments. They attempt to achieve an insider's knowledge of contemporary Chinese culture. The author who succeeds most fully in this, of course, is Zhang Xinxin—she *is* an insider, and she describes, sometimes in stream-of-consciousness fashion, the feelings of young intellectuals like herself who are going through divorce. But even Zhang Xinxin's chapter is not devoid of a sense of detachment from the subjective understandings of her interviewees. To give perspective to her interviews, Zhang sketches in a broad, if rather impressionistically defined, backdrop of the external constraints—social class relations, mobility opportunities, laws, and traditional mores—that shape Chinese marriage relations.

Zhang Xinxin emphasizes the subjective dimension of the culture of family life in China; David Arkush emphasizes the objective dimension. His account of Chinese ideas about love and marriage, based on a study of the texts of local operas performed in Ding County half a century ago, stands outside of Chinese culture in time as well as place. Yet by conveying an impressionistic sense of how these operas came to be written and produced and how audiences responded to them, even Arkush's chapter manages to suggest how Chinese people subjectively perceived the social rules for family life.

Both Zhang Xinxin's intimate, subjective understanding and David Arkush's detached, objective analysis of Chinese culture have strengths and weaknesses. For a working China scholar, however, a choice between these approaches depends not merely on theoretical desiderata but also on practical necessities. One has to make the best possible use of the resources available to explore a topic. Both Zhang Xinxin's and David Arkush's chapters are commendable because they demonstrate their authors' respective strengths. And together, they provide intellectually provocative, complementary perspectives on Chinese family life: Zhang Xinxin's modern, urban intellectuals are enacting what David Arkush's traditional peasants sometimes fantasized about. Did the old fantasies somehow pave the way for the new realities?

If Zhang Xinxin's and David Arkush's chapters on marriage and family life represent dialectically opposite poles in the tension between the objective and subjective dimensions of cultural analysis, Deborah Davis's chapter represents a kind of synthesis. It conveys a vivid sense—a sense perhaps possible only to an outsider not numbed by constant exposure to the routine of ordinary life in China—of the external constraints imposed on contemporary urban family life by the limitations of housing space. This chapter also shows how individuals, especially women, subjectively perceive these limitations and try partially to overcome them by meaningfully organizing their living space. With varying emphases, most of the other chapters in this book attempt such a synthesis between external and internal, between objective and subjective understandings of contemporary Chinese culture.

Although these chapters represent, at least implicitly, a variety of ways to approach an understanding of "culture," they also represent a variety of ways to define "popular." In our conference and its antecedent planning sessions, we introduced one another to distinctions between such categories as folk culture and mass culture, high culture and low culture, hegemonic culture and counterhegemonic culture. Where do we locate our working understanding of popular culture among these galaxies of ideas?

Each of these distinctions has its origin in different ways of understanding the most basic problems of modern society. The distinction between folk culture and mass culture revolves around the problems posed by the destruction of traditional ways of thinking and living, for example, the erosion of folk religion by the ideas conveyed in modern mass media such as advertising and political propaganda. The distinction between high culture and low culture calls attention to the conflicts between aristocratic groups— people with "good breeding" and superior educations—and the democratic aspirations of ordinary people. The distinction between hegemonic culture and counterhegemonic culture reflects Marxian concerns for understanding the possibilities of class consciousness and class conflict.

The chapters in this book define popular culture in a way that centers around the most salient problem in modern China—the tension between state and society. Again, our chapters represent a variety of approaches within a broadly defined consensus. All of our chapters at least implicitly define popular culture as distinct from official culture, that is, the official ideology of the Chinese state. Popular culture, as the term is used here, consists of ideas, beliefs, and practices that have origins at least partially independent of the state. Each author portrays his or her topic as something that the government has wanted to suppress or sought to discourage (religious practice, described in Helen Siu's and Richard Madsen's chapters; divorce, discussed by Zhang Xinxin; underground literature, studied by Perry Link; and ethnic prejudice against the Subei people, described in Emily Honig's chapter), or pretended to ignore (the private sphere of family life analyzed by Deborah Davis and the aesthetic preferences described by Ellen Laing), or warily tried to co-opt (the new private entrepreneurship, studied by Thomas Gold; the creation of politically critical movies, discussed by Paul Pickowicz; and the use of survey analysis among social science professionals, described by Stanley Rosen). Popular culture, as used in these chapters, includes any kind of culture that has its origin in the social side of the tension between state and society.

However, there are also other kinds of tension in China: tensions between traditional ideas and modern ideas, between the different self-images of ethnic groups, between the mores of cosmopolitan intellectuals and those of "workers, peasants, and soldiers." Individual chapters also deal with different aspects of these tensions and can speak to scholars who are interested in the study of popular culture from these various perspectives.

Besides pondering long and hard what we meant by popular culture, we devoted considerable effort to construct a working definition of China!

Having defined popular culture as nonofficial culture, we were faced with the problem of how to conceive of the unity and diversity of China. Outside of the government and its ideology, which embrace the whole of China, are there any commonalities of experience, thought, values? Or are there many Chinas, many social worlds, defined by particular, idiosyncratic cultures? Many of the chapters deal with small subgroups within the large political entity called China. We do not assume that the pieces of popular culture we study are widely shared. The Chinese Catholics of Richard Madsen's chapter comprise less than 1 percent of the Chinese population, and less than 10 percent of the population (though "fully half" of Zhang Xinxin's college classmates) get divorced. Is there any way meaningfully to think of the ideas and practices of these small segments as a part of larger patterns of thought and practice shared by almost all Chinese? The chapters in this book do not offer clear answers to this question. Most of the authors are careful not to generalize beyond the particular groups whose culture they study. But implicitly, at least, many suggest that the particular fragments of culture they discuss gain meaning and significance from their relationship to a larger whole. For instance, some of the most idiosyncratic twists of plot in Perry Link's hand-copied novels still reflect, if only in mockery, widely accepted Chinese idioms, as in the story of the soldier who is handed a ticking time bomb and has to call in an official report to his superior before disposing of the bomb! Though framed by the particular experiences of specific groups, our chapters all point beyond themselves, offering windows into Chinese culture as a whole. Even when—perhaps especially when— they offer perspectives different from those of the most powerful members of the society or the most numerous segments of the population, these windows onto the culture may show us much of significance about that culture's basic dynamics.

Drawing broadly on the theories about popular culture that come out of our various academic disciplines, we have tried to adapt these ideas to the special requirements of understanding contemporary China. We hope that our work will in turn enrich the theoretical discourse of our disciplines. Recent Chinese history offers a host of paradoxes, anomalies that do not easily fit standard academic theories of culture. The most notable among these perhaps is the extraordinary resistance of traditional forms of thought to modernization, as exemplified in the ability of religious practices to revive after being systematically suppressed by a Marxist government for longer than a generation. Notable, too, is the resurgence of aristocratic culture in a society that has publicly propagated extreme egalitarianism. Efforts to explain such paradoxes adequately will surely lead to important innovations in academic theories of popular culture. Scholars interested in popular culture theories should therefore take careful note of developments in China, which are too important to be left to China specialists.

METHODOLOGY

To fulfill its scholarly promise, a project such as ours faces enormous difficulties, of course. With a population as huge and diverse as China's one must always take care to specify which part of it one is speaking of. Moreover, aspects of popular culture do not only vary with objectively measurable variables such as age, sex, education, locale, ethnicity, occupation, and official status. They can vary as well from public to private contexts (as when a propaganda official criticizes a short story at the office, but supplies it to his daughter at home), and even with the varying moods to which all human beings are subject. Finally, typical ideas and feelings, whether of groups or individuals, can change over time. As a first step to addressing these complex questions, the editors asked each author to identify, insofar as possible, the group whose culture he or she is dealing with.

Even when one's subjects have been reasonably well identified, there remains the larger problem of how, put bluntly, to get inside other people's heads. This is, of course, a theoretical problem for any culture at any time. Fundamentally, it is the philosophical problem of "other minds." You can observe my behavior, but how can you know with certainty what thought accompanies it? You can listen to what I say about my thought, but by what standard can you check the accuracy of my description, which may be misleading whether I intend it to be or not? Such questions, which are only compounded when one deals with foreign cultures, may seem sufficiently daunting as to recommend simple agnosticism about what happens inside the minds of others. Why not simply content ourselves with objective descriptions of speech and overt actions, without trying to plumb to the level of subjectivity?

First, it must be clear that we are *not* assuming in this book that speech and action are somehow separate from thought, nor that they should, as it were, be bypassed as we try to discover what thought really is. Quite to the contrary, what people say and do—as the chapters here show—form the bulk of the evidence for what they think and feel. The extremely complex interplay of thought, speech, and action are theoretical questions beyond our present scope; we employ here only the minimal assumption that a full and satisfying account of life is possible only if *all three* are considered. Everyone has had the experience of acting on an idea without talking about it, of expressing a thought in words without doing anything about it, or of thinking one thing while saying and doing either something else or nothing at all. These simple reflections, added to the safe assumption that human beings in China are no different from human beings elsewhere, should make it plain that the effort to account for thought is worthwhile.

We posit four levels of thought in everyday Chinese life:

1. *Official ideals.* These are the public propaganda goals that are announced by the party leadership and held up for public assent. They are pervasive, relatively uniform, and protected from overt dissent (e.g., "Strive for the Four Modernizations").

2. *Thought as expressed.* Ideas and values expressed in words include official ideals, but also extend far beyond them, especially in private contexts: "Peanut oil is too expensive!" How congruent verbal expressions may be with inner thought is, of course, open to question. The statement, "Since peanut oil is too expensive, we must strive harder for the Four Modern-

izations!" could easily spring from thoughts other than those expressed in the surface meaning.

3. *Thought as acted upon.* Ideas and values that govern behavior may coincide with official ideals or verbal expression, but also may not: high officials sending their children for study in the bourgeois West.

4. *"Silent" thought.* One must always assume, especially in a society with a tradition of state control of expression, the possible existence of thought and feeling that are neither expressed nor acted upon. Research of such thought is inevitably frustrating, limited, as it must by definition be, either to earlier times (about which people *now* may talk) or to speculative extrapolation into the present based on other times or places. Nevertheless, recent history in China has shown that the more accessible aspects of thought—those tied to speech and action—are better appreciated if this silent category is also borne in mind.

The positing of these four categories does not imply that every thought falls neatly into one of the four. Obviously an idea can be both expressed and acted upon—and in accord with official ideals as well. The present project aims to skip over level 1 and look at levels 2, 3, and (where possible) 4. We choose this "unofficial" emphasis not from a bias that unofficial China is the only real China, or that official ideology is merely superficial; we view both official and unofficial thought as fully real, and indeed complexly interrelated.

The chapters that follow explore unofficial thought in a wide variety of ways. Scholars from several disciplines (history, literature, art, sociology, anthropology, political science) use various materials and methods (field observation, interviews, surveys, fiction, film, painting, opera) to explore ways in which contemporary popular thought can be discovered and studied.

Although each chapter will speak for itself, we can offer some general observations on the efficacy of our several methods, which can be organized roughly into four categories: (1) interview and field observation, (2) inference from cultural artifacts, (3) inference based on continuities with earlier times, and (4) use of surveys.

Interview and Field Observation. Most of our chapters use interview and observation to some extent; those by Honig, Siu, Davis, and Gold use it primarily. The strengths and weaknesses of the interview method for the China field are well known, having been intelligently discussed by earlier researchers such as Martin Whyte,[2] Andrew Walder,[3] Anita Chan,[4] and Anne Thurston.[5] One problem widely discussed in the past has been whether émigré interviews in Hong Kong adequately reveal life in the People's Republic of China (PRC). The reopening of China eliminates that question only superficially. The two basic worries that underlay the question of Hong Kong interviews—representativeness and reliability—remain as problems.

The researcher still needs to estimate how representative a particular view is, and among what group. This requires, fully as much as it did in Hong Kong, that one consider the background and viewpoint of the interviewee, and that one cross-check differing accounts. While direct access to China allows greater immersion in the details of a specific location, and hence greater confidence about it, the danger grows commensurately that one's conclusions will not be generalizable to other places. There remains a need for careful delineation of the populace of whom one speaks.

The question of reliability—sometimes called veracity—persists as well. How does one know when a respondent is offering a "correct" answer rather than a frank opinion?[6] How does one gauge the biases that can arise because an interview might be audited by others, or because of its formal context, or because the interviewer is a foreigner?

Theoretically, it is always possible to doubt an answer on such grounds, just as it is possible—theoretically—to say that blood is actually green and is only perceived as red when viewed by the human eye. But, unless one espouses such extreme skepticism, there are reliable signs by which to recognize candor and escape excessive doubt. For example, Anne Thurston was able to note points at which interviewees switched unmistakably from "recitation of the prevailing orthodoxy" to detailed accounts of "their own personal stories."[7] Thurston and Andrew Walder, both advocates of an open-ended interview structure, found stories that popped up unexpectedly, bristling with concrete detail, to be not only beyond reasonable doubt but persuasive enough to induce them to alter and refine their research questions.[8] Thurston and Anita Chan both were able to dispense with much doubt after developing personal relationships that made their informants into friends.[9] Chan even found defensiveness and embarrassment—normally barriers to frankness— to be interpretable data in their own right.[10]

In short, when one knows an informant long and well enough to observe him or her in various moods and contexts, systematic doubt about sincerity becomes unsustainable. Can a person continue to dissemble when angry? Exhilarated? Frustrated? Exhausted? To do so would require nearly super-human efforts, and at some point the burden of proof must shift to the skeptic who imagines such efforts to be at work. What might be called contextually rich interviewing has become much more possible with the opening of China, and with it suspicions of artificial answers must also diminish.

Moving farther along a spectrum that begins with the highly structured interview and proceeds to open-ended and contextually rich interviews, one comes to actual field observation and participation. Thomas Gold, in his research on individual entrepreneurs in Shanghai, used a method of participant-interview whereby he listened and asked questions while actually employing the services of the people he sought to understand. Cantonese-speaking Helen Siu, in the Guangdong delta, was able to use methods both of trained ethnographer and daily-life participant. Zhang Xinxin, whose chapter on divorce is based on cases she knows well from her own life context, represents, in a sense, the unstructured extreme of a spectrum of interview methodologies.

Inference from Cultural Artifacts. This method is exemplified in the chapters by Ellen Laing, David Arkush, Paul Pickowicz, and Perry Link, although each author uses other methods as well. It is important to understand this method in precise terms; failure to do so can cloud both the substance of the results and the confidence one has in them.

Two fundamentally different approaches are available when using cultural artifacts (fiction, drama, film, etc.) to study popular thought. One, which we might call author centered, takes the creator of a work as a reliable informant. If there is reason to trust the vision and sincerity of an author (or playwright, filmmaker, etc.), then his or her cultural work can be taken as a mirror for reality, including the reality of how people think and feel about things. For example, we can read Zhang Xinxin and Sang Ye's literary reportage called *Chinese Profiles* and learn much about the lives, feelings, and thoughts of people in various social stations. To do so we need to trust the authors; we do not need to know anything about readers.

The other approach, which we might call appeal centered, is based on a work's appeal to readers or viewers. If we know that a work is popular (or at least well-liked within a certain group), we can then look at that work, imagining ourselves as the audience, and begin to appreciate the values and ideas contained within it that presumably explain its appeal. There is, of course, a danger in assuming that a Westerner will see in a cultural artifact the same concepts and values that a Chinese will see; no observer can be free of his or her own cultural assumptions. But in many cases (and especially for *popular* arts), the salient cognitive and moral points in a work are too obtrusive to be easily mistaken; it would be difficult to imagine a reader or viewer feeling attraction to a work and *not* accepting its emphatic viewpoints and values. It would be far-fetched, for example, to imagine a viewer being attracted to *The legend of Tianyun Mountain* (one of the films studied by Pickowicz) if he or she felt that intellectuals have been treated justly in China or that party bureaucrats are generally fair and sincere. In case of lingering doubts about interpretation, it is possible, when using contemporary materials, to check one's conclusions through interviews.[11] For media such as film and drama, it can also be useful to sit among Chinese audiences, who can be wonderfully animated at times, and note immediate responses.

These two methods, author centered and appeal centered, are not only different but quite opposite in key respects. For the first method it is crucial to know the author, in order that we have a basis for trusting his or her report. For the second, the author is unimportant, and indeed can be entirely unknown; what we do need to know is that the work had appeal and among roughly what kind of audience the appeal was felt. Similarly, in the first method, the *accuracy* of the author's report is crucial; without accuracy, there can be no claim of truly reaching to the popular culture we seek to study. But in the second method, the accuracy of the cultural material is irrelevant; only its *authenticity* need be verified. A flamboyantly imagined ghost story, so long as we know it had a genuine audience, can tell us something about the mental life of that audience.

The chapters by Laing, Arkush, Pickowicz, and Link employ the appeal-centered method; the inclusion of Zhang's paper can be viewed as the editors' use of the author-centered method.

Inference Based on Continuities with Earlier Times. Any seasoned China-watcher knows that social reality does not—indeed could not—fluctuate as rapidly as social policy has. Beginning in 1949, there has hardly been a period of even four or five years in which the outside world was not asked to believe that, once again, a wholly "new" China was emerging. For many years Western observers were only too ready to accept these successive policy statements as descriptions of new realities. But the reopening of China after Mao has allowed us to appreciate much better the importance of continuities in Chinese life. Indeed, the twists and turns of social policy can now be seen more clearly as attempts, whether misguided or not, to affect a social reality that itself has changed much more slowly. Life and thought in the 1980s appear crucially related not only to the 1950s and 1960s, but also to the early twentieth century and earlier times.

In the present book, Richard Madsen begins his conceptualization of Catholicism in China with the Rites Controversy of the eighteenth century; Ellen Laing shows how contemporary notions of propriety are continuous with ideas of Qing times; Emily Honig traces prejudice against Subei people in Shanghai to the formation of that city in the late nineteenth century; David Arkush uses village opera from the 1940s to study basic themes in peasant thought; Helen Siu illuminates peasant uses of ritual in the 1980s by using comparisons with the 1950s.

There is, of course, a theoretical problem in assuming continuity, namely, that change exists as well. No continuity is ever perfect. But then, how can one measure continuity and assume it at the same time? The assuming would seem to make the measuring impossible.

In these chapters we do not assume continuity in this strict (almost mathematical) sense. We use it, rather, as a base for raising questions about the contemporary empirical record. Such an approach provides a needed antidote to the former habit of using ephemeral policy statements as starting points for the raising of questions. Moreover, we always employ other methods in tandem, checking the patterns that continuity would suggest with, for example, contemporary observation, interviews, or cultural artifacts. The value of looking for continuities is generally confirmed as our encounters with the contemporary record become ever richer.

Use of Surveys. In the early 1980s China began to publish a large number of attitude surveys on a wide variety of topics. The formidable volume of this publication has been accompanied by equally formidable problems in how to use and evaluate it. Stanley Rosen, who has done as much as any Western scholar to collect and examine this survey material, offers in this book an analysis of the methodological problems as well as an indication of what, despite the problems, the surveys can be useful for. Rosen includes a considerable methodological discussion within his chapter; the reader is referred there for more detail.

*   *   *

None of the above methods—or any others—can be flawless. Part of the excitement we have felt in the present project has been precisely the effort to explore the question of method. The editors asked each contributor to include explicit comments on method wherever it may not be clear by example.

In most cases we cannot get, nor should we expect, definitive answers of the sort, "Percentage X of the Chinese populace believes Y." Even saying that most or many in a designated group feel or think a certain way can be hard to sustain. Yet even if we discover only what the salient *issues* are in popular culture, we still learn something very valuable. Emily Honig's excellent chapter, for example, does not attempt to give us any percentage on the prejudices of Shanghainese against Subei people; it does give us a clear and lively sense of the issue involved and a rich appreciation of the many contexts in which it can be relevant. Regardless of what one or another Shanghainese might feel, we learn about a salient and pervasive issue in Shanghai life.

We also make no prior assumptions that the popular culture we find will be substantively either the same as or different from official culture. Prejudices against Subei people (Honig) and the practices of independent Catholicism (Madsen) not only depart from official ideology but have sometimes been in conflict with it. Home as the mother's space (Davis) or the propriety of living-room centerpieces (Laing) generally apply in spheres quite separate from official culture—neither supportive of it nor, except in extreme times, considered to be opposed. Underground fiction (Link) can, on the one hand, be strongly opposed by officialdom, but, on the other, reveal concepts (such as attitudes toward authority) that are fully congenial with official ideology.

Finally, we do not expect our results to form some kind of composite mosaic that will suggest an overall picture of contemporary Chinese thought. It is doubtful that such a vast, complex, and changing field could ever be adequately portrayed in any case. Our more modest aims have been to point out that the whole area of contemporary popular culture in China needs and awaits scholarly attention and to indicate some of the ways in which the field can be approached. Accordingly, as editors we have placed a higher priority on the demonstration of research method than on synthesis of our sample results. We hope that there are enough seeds of theoretical and methodological insight here to allow, with proper cultivation, a garden of at least a hundred flowers to grow.

NOTES

1. Chandra Mukerji and Michael Schudson, *Rethinking Popular Culture: Contemporary Perspectives in Cultural Studies* (Berkeley and Los Angeles: University of California Press, forthcoming).

2. Martin Whyte, *Small Groups and Political Rituals in China* (Berkeley and Los Angeles: University of California Press, 1974), pp. 237–263.

3. Andrew Walder, *Communist Neo-Traditionalism: Work and Authority in Chinese Industry* (Berkeley and Los Angeles: University of California Press, 1986), pp. 255–269.

4. Anita Chan, *Children of Mao: Personality Development and Political Activism in the Red Guard Generation* (Seattle: University of Washington Press, 1985), pp. 2–6.

5. Anne Thurston, "Victims of China's Cultural Revolution: The Invisible Wounds, Part I," *Pacific Affairs*, vol. 57, no. 4 (Winter 1984–1985): pp. 601–604.

6. "Correct" can mean politically correct, as defined by party policy, but it can also mean, in a broader cultural sense, "the right thing to say," especially in formal contexts, as, for example, when high school students say *Dream of the Red Chamber* is their favorite novel even though they have not read it.

7. Thurston, "Invisible Wounds," pp. 602–603.

8. Ibid., p. 602; Walder, *Communist Neo-Traditionalism*, p. 256.

9. Chan, *Children of Mao*, p. 3; Thurston, "Invisible Wounds," p. 602.

10. Chan, *Children of Mao*, p. 3.

11. Although interviews can be used to probe one's materials more deeply, the views of an informant must not be held sacrosanct. Just as a foreign researcher can fail to perceive culturally relevant points because of unfamiliarity, so can a person inside a culture overlook things because of a certain *over*-familiarity. (Americans who met Tocqueville did not always perceive what he did.)

PART ONE

Literature, the Cinema, and Authority

2

Hand-Copied
Entertainment Fiction from
the Cultural Revolution

PERRY LINK

Most of the scholarship on artistic life during the Cultural Revolution emphasizes its one-dimensionality, often leaving the impression that ordinary people were exposed to nothing but the monotonous models of revolutionary art. Perry Link, professor of East Asian languages and cultures at Princeton, argues that the state's monopoly on literature was not as complete as it may seem. His study of hand-copied, underground entertainment fiction shows that during the Cultural Revolution there was a lively audience among urban youth for detective stories, spy thrillers, romances, knight errant fiction, triangular love stories, and pornography. Virtually all these genres surfaced after the Cultural Revolution and enjoyed considerable aboveground popularity. The values conveyed in most of these works were hardly revolutionary; on the contrary, in stylistic and thematic terms they had much in common with the popular fiction produced in Qing and early Republican times. The popularity of these works shows that the range of popular thought far exceeded what was acknowledged in official sources. Still, this fiction should not be regarded as dissident literature; in general it was apolitical, accepted traditional notions of hierarchy, relegated women to an inferior status, and regarded the outside world with suspicion.

—Eds.

During the years of the Cultural Revolution, one of the many puzzles for foreign scholars of Chinese literature was the question of who could possibly be reading the boring and repetitive stories being published. Were we to believe that the masses really enjoyed reading about one exemplary hero after another, be it Lei Feng, Ouyang Hai, or Gao Daquan, each about as pure-hearted as he was simple-headed? Could the natural interests of millions of readers actually fall within such narrow bounds?

After Mao, we have had a much fuller (but still far from complete) view of reader interests in China. We also have had, retrospectively, a better view of where those interests went during the Cultural Revolution. Along with the officially published literature of 1966–1976, there also existed widely circulated entertainment fiction in the form of hand-copied volumes (*shouchaoben*). These stories of beauties, seductresses, spies, detectives, traitors, corpses, and wizards of the martial arts, as well as of China's top leaders informally described, are powerful testimony that a much fuller picture of the thoughts and tastes of the popular readership in China remains to be discovered. This does not mean that the officially approved political fiction was completely absent from people's thoughts, only that it was but one part of a much larger and more variegated reality.

HAND-COPIED VOLUMES

Hand-copied volumes were produced and circulated surreptitiously. Authors would begin by pilfering a supply of stationery from their own or someone else's work unit,[1] and then would find a secret place to begin writing—typically using flashlights under blankets, if we are to believe the standard cliché. Most hand-copied volumes were only 10 or 20 pages long. When they were longer, those doing the copying would sometimes divide the task among several people. For example, a 142-page hand-copied version of Wumingshi's *Woman in the tower* (*Tali de nuren*) clearly shows that the copying was shared about equally among eight different people, the last of whom pointedly wrote "copying finished" (*chao wan*) at the end.[2]

Once a story had been written down, the pages were bound with string and passed around among friends. If truly popular, the story would be passed from one person to another until it became a "flying book" (*feishu*) that never found its way home. This would oblige the original author, if he or she desired a personal copy, to begin again. Zhang Yang, whose story *The second handshake* (*Di'erci woshou*) eventually "flew" the length and breadth of China, had to re-begin his work a total of seven times.[3] At one high school in Guangdong, authorities responded to a sudden wave of hand-copying by calling a public meeting of students and parents to suppress the activity and to uncover its backstage ringleaders. But no ringleaders could be found; the contagion had been produced purely by the enthusiasm of students.[4] There is no evidence of financial motives in the spread of hand-copied volumes; the forces that drove them seem to have been purely the thirsts of readers.

The initiative and liveliness involved in producing hand-copied volumes belies its truly dangerous aspects. The author of *The second handshake* was arrested in 1975, charged with "opposing Chairman Mao's revolutionary line," and sent to prison, where he almost died of tuberculosis and pleurisy.[5] Such danger explains why authors and re-copiers of hand-copied volumes never appended their names to their work and clearly did whatever else they could to avoid detection. Sometimes they would not even tell their own families. One young author described himself as a "guerrilla," writing on the move as opportunity permitted.[6] Many of the writers seem to have been educated youth sent by the state to live in the countryside ("sent-down" youth), where looser surveillance made hand-copying more possible than it was in the more tightly controlled cities.

The material of hand-copied volumes also spread orally. Moreover, with the advent of audiocassettes, oral narrations could be recorded and copied electronically.[7] This was not only easier than re-copying by hand, but had the additional advantage of being easier to hide should a self-appointed guardian against spiritual pollution or bourgeois liberalism happen by. After all, a homemade, hand-copied volume on a shelf next to Marx or Shakespeare is identifiable at a glance. But an audiotape looks the same whether it contains Beethoven, the party secretary's latest speech, or an underground horror story.

Not all hand-copied volumes contained entertainment fiction. Some were political statements, some were personal philosophies, still others were poetry;[8] Christians are said to have harbored hand-copied versions of the Bible. All indications, however, are that these other kinds of hand-copied volumes were far less popular than the entertainment fiction, which included (1) original creations, (2) re-copyings of pre-Liberation works, and (3) translations, or retellings, of foreign works (such as Arthur Conan Doyle's stories of Sherlock Holmes or Jules Verne's science fiction). Of the samples in my possession, those containing entertainment fiction are the most soiled and tattered.[9] This chapter considers only the entertainment fiction, concentrating on works from the Cultural Revolution rather than works of foreign or prerevolutionary origin.

To whose thoughts do we gain access in studying these materials? In China the stock answer to the question "Who reads hand-copied volumes?" is "high school students." Cliché though it be, this answer seems basically accurate. The only formal survey on the question was done in Shanghai in 1983, and it asked only about pornography, not about the wide variety of other themes in hand-copied fiction. The survey found that 66 percent of students in "work-study" schools (i.e., schools for delinquents) were readers of pornographic hand-copied volumes. Of these, more than half also listened to audiotapes and one-fifth participated in hand-copying.[10] Although the readership rate was, in all likelihood, abnormally high at these special schools in Shanghai, there are other reasons to believe that hand-copied volumes of many kinds were widely read among several categories of urban youth, including young workers, those "waiting for work," and college students. In Guangzhou, for example, university students in 1980 were able to supply me with hand-copied love and horror stories from their dormitory drawers, while the *Guangzhou Evening News* complained that hand-copied volumes were easily available "to young workers" on the streets downtown.[11]

There are three good reasons for assuming that hand-copied volumes provide access to the minds (on certain topics, at least) of very large numbers among the urban population, as well as among sent-down youth in the countryside (but not peasants).

First, some volumes are known to have circulated very widely. *A maiden's heart* and *The second handshake* were known in all parts of China, seemingly to everyone. When *The second handshake* was published aboveground in 1979, within a few months it sold 3.3 million copies (the most in the post-Mao period for any book of literature), and was also made into a radio drama, a cartoon strip, a film, and several dramatic and operatic versions.[12]

Second, there is obvious continuity between the appeal of Cultural Revolution hand-copied fiction and that of aboveground post-Mao fiction, whose popularity is much easier to establish. That *The second handshake* could be immensely popular in both contexts clearly illustrates this continuity. In other cases, thematic similarities, such as the exposure of abusive pow-erholders,[13] and technical similarities, such as far-fetched coincidence and twisting plots, provide additional evidence of the continuity. The appearance in the post-Mao period of unofficial (but not underground) tabloids, sold on the street and filled with beauties, corpses, and "inside" political stories— the very stuff of hand-copied volumes—further confirms the continuity of basic popular tastes.

Third, there are also strong continuities between Cultural Revolution hand-copied fiction and *earlier* Chinese popular fiction, including the love triangles in mandarin duck and butterfly genre fiction, the adventures of "the Chinese Sherlock Holmes," Huo Sang, the muckraking fiction of late-Qing, and Chinese science fiction.[14] These continuities again demonstrate the strength and atavism of popular themes, and suggest that the basic values and attitudes expressed in hand-copied volumes may say something even about the older people who generally did not read them—but who once did read their generic predecessors, and did feel, at least at one time, in sympathy.

SOME EXAMPLES

Most hand-copied stories can be classified into one of several standard types whose roots lie variously in traditional fiction and/or Western influence. Below I list six important story types, and summarize an example of each.

Detective Story

Terrifying footsteps (*Kongbu de jiaobusheng*) is 25 pages long, copied in four or five different hands, and stapled (deceptively!) between colorful covers that read "Selection of Works from the Canton Exhibition of Artistic Photography." Set in nineteenth-century England, the story opens with an honest and hardworking, but poverty-stricken, university student of physics named Charlie (*chali*). One day Charlie's mother falls ill and needs £100,000 for emergency surgery. Desperate to help, Charlie answers an advertisement that promises precisely £100,000 to anyone who will spend a night in a mysterious haunted house.

It turns out that the haunted house is a trap into which a diabolic woman named Black Peony lures men and then has them clubbed to death by giant thugs from India. In a flashback we are told that Black Peony (who in fact is a gorgeous blonde) had begun well enough—as a professor's wife—but had gradually succumbed to the evil attraction of dancehalls. Eventually she was seduced by an Indian rajah, who then sold her into slavery and absconded. Furious for revenge, Black Peony traced the rajah to India, ambushed him, and showered him with bricks—only to discover, alas, that she had identified the wrong rajah. In fact the man who had tricked her had been no rajah at all, but a charlatan who had already been executed for other crimes. The real rajah was kind enough to listen to Black Peony's story and grant her request for 50 "toughs," 50 "braves," and 20,000 English pounds. With this fortification in hand, she returned to London to carry out the plan that would occupy the rest of her life: You see, the narrator tells us, the impact upon her psyche of all these events was so severe that she has sworn mortal revenge upon all the men of the world as her only avenue of release.

Charlie becomes Black Peony's ninety-seventh victim. His and the other corpses lie in a special glass room inside the mysterious house. When one of these corpses suddenly springs to its feet, we find that it was a clever disguise of Sai Lun, a famous London detective who has been working on the case with his partner (and adopted "younger brother") Sai Ying. Much of the storytelling describes how these two crack the case and bring Black Peony to justice. She is tried at "the international court" in Spain, convicted, and, although "her story deserves our sympathy," executed for the crime of murder.

Anti-Spy Story

The annihilation of the underground stronghold (*Dixia baolei de fumie*) is set during the 1953 "Resist America, Aid Korea" campaign.[15] It tells how Public Security operatives uncover and destroy a chemical laboratory run by the CIA to develop poisons of warfare that is located beneath a graveyard in Chongqing. The evil group consists of three Americans (who are not described) and a variety of Chinese accomplices (who are described at length): Huang Meifang is a sexy, westernized young woman who tempts police agents into deathtraps; Dr. Jiang tests U.S. poisons on Chinese subjects; Clerk Wang has been suborned to infiltrate Public Security for the U.S.; the Big Black Rogue (*hei dahan*) does muggings and other errands; an innocent-looking old lady wears a Rolex watch that in fact harbors a radio used for secret communications. The other radio in the two-way set is also inside a Rolex,[16] which in turn is inside a mysterious silver ball that only the craftiest person can figure out how to open.

The story is loosely constructed and introduces a variety of interesting incidental characters and subplots: fourteen shabby-looking but highly skilled artisans meet and vie to open the mysterious silver ball; a husband-wife pickpocket team accidentally becomes involved when they happen to swipe one of the Rolex radios; a shapely and promiscuous woman student of "physical education" is chosen by the Big Black Rogue to run one of his errands.

Modern Historical Romance

Contemporary China's oral network of "alleyway news" (*xiaodao xiaoxi*) frequently carries stories about the personal lives and factional jockeyings of top leaders. Some of these tales, well embroidered if not downright fictive, were put into hand-copied volumes during the Cultural Revolution. Their debt to Chinese historical romance (*lishi yanyi*) is obvious.

An example is *The case of the Nanjing Bridge (Daqiao fengyun)*.[17] Set in 1969, it purports to explain an assassination attempt by Lin Biao against Mao Zedong. Mao is traveling from Beijing to Shanghai on a train that is scheduled to cross the Nanjing Bridge one day at 5:03 P.M. Through a complicated ruse, the Lin Biao group gets an unwitting old lady to carry a "baby" (really a time bomb) onto the bridge at precisely that time. But the plot is discovered, the bomb is dismantled, and Mao returns safely to Beijing in an airplane personally despatched by Zhou Enlai. Zhou reasons that the plotters must be highly placed and well connected, or they could not have known the top-secret details of Mao's itinerary. Hence the Public Security police, who probably have been infiltrated by the villains, cannot be trusted on the case. The army, lacking detective experience, also will not do. Zhou decides to call on a personal contact, one Sun Dasheng ("Great Victory" Sun), a detective genius who has been doing labor at a Manchurian May Seventh school because of his former associations with the fallen general Luo Ruiqing.

Sun sets out by rail for Beijing to see Zhou Enlai, and then to Nanjing to work on the case. Along the way he employs clever disguises, jumping train several times in order to shake off tailers. He likes to smoke a pipe, because it "clears his head," and also because he can use its highly polished bowl as a convex mirror to observe people behind him.[18] He is met in Nanjing by Public Security personnel who in fact are in the Lin Biao clique and among the original plotters. They take Sun to a state guest-house, where they try to get him drunk so they can kill him. But Sun, perceiving everything in advance, feigns inebriation, kills the intended assassin, and escapes to the roof of the guest-house where he radios General Xu Shiyou (the Nanjing commandant loyal to Mao and Zhou) for help. Xu responds with a battalion of troops. Sun is rescued but the Lin Biao people escape through an elaborate maze of tunnels that lie beneath the guest-house. The details of the whole matter became clear, we are told, after the Lin Biao affair of 1971.

Modern Xia (Knight Errant) Story

Some hand-copied stories clearly echoed China's *wuxia* tradition. I have no pure example of this type, but one story, called *Strange encounter with a wandering brave (Liulanghan de qiyu)*,[19] does illustrate some of its important features.

Set in 1969, the story tells of a beautiful young woman named Fang Fang, who works as an accountant in a defense plant. All the young men at the plant covet her attention, but she remains aloof. One day she goes into town to draw the monthly wages for the entire factory. Having stuffed the cash into a travel bag, she then stops at a restaurant and orders two bowls of noodles. As she begins to eat, a big, rough, dirty beggar walks over, grabs one of the bowls, and wolfs it down. When she flees in panic this food-grabber (as such people were called) gobbles the other bowl of noodles, too.

Then he notices her travel bag, and opens it to find it stuffed with money. At first he is overwhelmed by his good luck. Then he realizes that such a large amount of money can only be public funds, and that this innocent girl will suffer a sentence of hard labor or worse if she loses it. His *xia*-like righteousness spurs him to chase after her, return the travel bag, and insist that she count the money to verify that not a penny is missing. He even refuses the reward she offers. But he does accept her name and address and promises that he will seek her out if he should ever really need help.

Some time later, wandering in the countryside, utterly destitute, he is forced to seek her help. He tells the gateman at her defense plant that he is her relative (the lie is necessary to gain admission). Fang Fang eagerly lends him 50 yuan, whereupon he turns and leaves. Shortly thereafter, the defense plant announces that it will be hiring 200 new workers, and that priority will go to the relatives of current workers. (The state reason for this policy is security, but really, the narrator tells us, it is simply a way to prettify use of the back door.) Fang Fang applies on behalf of her "cousin" the food-grabber. She asks for, and receives, the back-door assistance of a deputy party secretary. The food-grabber is hired, takes a bath, gets a haircut, dons new clothes, and turns out to be a strong and handsome young man named Li Chunsheng.

Now, it turns out that the deputy party secretary who helped Fang Fang has lascivious designs on her. She should have suspected as much, we are told, as he is a divorcé and well known as a dirty old man. Frantic for an excuse to avoid him, Fang Fang runs to Li Chunsheng and abruptly proposes that they marry. They do, and a year later have a baby. How strange, reflects the narrator, are the ways of the world! Who would have guessed that this gorgeous prize of a young woman would end up bearing the child of a grimy food-grabber?

Triangular Love Story

Many triangular love stories in twentieth-century China have followed a formula, in which a talented but unappreciated young man, the protagonist, chooses between: (1) a flashy, somewhat aggressive, westernized girlfriend, and (2) a relatively plain, deferential, traditional young woman.[20] The hand-copied story *Eternal regrets in love* (*Qingtian changhen*) shows that this formula persisted during the Cultural Revolution. The story is set in Hong Kong. Cai Minghui, an impecunious student, falls in love with Liu Manling, a beautiful classmate from a wealthy family. The girl's snobbish parents, who are opposed to Minghui because of his poverty, introduce their daughter to a cousin who is a superficial dandy. Minghui's pride is hurt, but Manling repeatedly assures him of her steadfast love.

Manling's parents give her an ultimatum when she graduates from high school: Either marry your cousin or leave Hong Kong and go to college in Europe. Manling chooses Europe, and Minghui swears to wait for her return, however long it might take.

Minghui seeks employment as a tutor in the house of Zhang Min, a high school principal. Zhang's daughter, Mengying, is a lovely and pure girl who unfortunately is sick with an inherited disease that keeps her at home. She falls in love with her tutor, Minghui, and urges that her father help him to attend university. Minghui does enter university, eventually graduates, and is invited by Zhang Min to teach at his high school. Although Minghui is very grateful to Mengying and her father, he remains faultlessly faithful to Manling. But then, one day he receives a letter from Europe with the shocking news that Manling has died in an airplane crash. Shortly thereafter, he decides to marry Mengying as a way to repay the kindness of the Zhang family.

After six months a telegram comes from Manling. She had miraculously escaped death in the airplane crash, and wonders why she has had no letters from Minghui. She returns to Hong Kong to take over as principal at (coincidentally!) the same school where Minghui teaches. She feels deeply resentful toward Minghui, but forgives him when she learns the truth about what has happened. Mengying, who now is dying, insists that the two lovers marry; Manling eventually agrees.

Pornographic Story

Probably the most widely circulated pornographic story from the Cultural Revolution is called *A maiden's heart* (*Shaonu zhi xin*). In a version published in Hong Kong under the title *The sexual experiences of a high school girl* (*Yige gaozhong nusheng de xing tiyan*), we meet Manna, a sixteen-year-old beauty who has just finished high school and is preparing to enter the Shanghai Physical Education Institute. Over the summer she meets her cousin Xu Xiaohua, a strong and handsome student at Fuzhou University; their sexual frolicking is described in vivid detail. But after about two weeks Xu suddenly gets a notice that he is being sent to the Soviet Union to study. The two young sex addicts vow to write letters, and do, but eventually neither letters nor self-stimulation can satisfy Manna. She meets a classmate named Lin Feng, who is also a splendid male specimen, and they marry. On their wedding night Lin becomes so aroused that he fails to notice that

Manna is not a virgin. This sets the stage for her to address her readers, at the end, with a little homily on the bliss and harmlessness of premarital sexual intercourse.

*   *   *

The quality of writing in hand-copied volumes is generally mediocre.[21] Incorrectly written Chinese characters and the use of nonstandard simplifications abound. The plots contain contradictions, non sequiturs, and glaring gaps. Some of these errors may arise from there being several authors (or copiers)—or even from something as simple as a torn-out page in an earlier version. But abrupt turns of plot are clearly literary characteristics of the genre. Designed to entertain, hand-copied volumes frequently sacrifice wholeness of plot to immediate pursuit of interest. For example, in *Terrifying footsteps,* when the narrator needs a big mansion to serve as Black Peony's haunted house, it is explained that the wealthy merchant who owned the house simply fell off a cliff one day—unfortunate for him, very convenient for the plot. In *The Nanjing Bridge,* when super-detective Sun Dasheng is met in Nanjing by Lin Biao's group, who are bent on killing him, why don't they just do it? The plot offers no logical reason for delay, but the imperatives of storytelling do: We have still to hear about the mysterious guest-house with its maze of tunnels and push-button trapdoors, Sun's dramatic escape to the roof, and much more.

Abrupt turns of plot also provide surprise, one of the favorite technical effects in these stories. Surprise can be generated when the reader is tricked into mistaken assumptions, as when the reader is told that 97 corpses are lying in a row, and then suddenly one "corpse" springs to its feet; or when Black Peony attacks a rajah and the reader later learns that it was the wrong rajah. Surprise is also generated when pertinent information is withheld through use of nonchronological narration. Black Peony's dastardly behavior, for example, is made all the more stupefying because there is no sign until the end, in one big flashback, of the life-story that led up to it. Yet another device for inducing surprise is far-fetched coincidence: When she returns from Europe, Liu Manling just happens to find work at the high school where her old flame is teaching; when Fang Fang goes desperately in search of her "wandering brave," she just happens to find him on a busy railway platform. Surprise also comes from strange juxtapositions, especially of things normally taken to be separate or incompatible. This effect is often explicitly labeled *qi,* or "marvelous." It is *qi,* for example, that a Rolex watch should double as a two-way radio, or that a famous beauty should end up married to a food-grabber.[22]

Why is surprise so important? Does its apparently great appeal to contemporary Chinese readers perhaps reflect (as it has in other cultural contexts) a boredom with daily life? One imagines a young urban worker, riding the same bus back and forth between the same factory and the same small flat at the same times each day, or the sent-down youth with nothing to look at but ricefields and the same mountain for several years.

OBSERVATIONS

That stories such as those summarized above even *existed* during the Cultural Revolution is a fact that at first can seem startling, and it is worth reflecting upon. We must, somehow, conceive these stories as organic parts of the same complex collage of popular thought that included the extremely different, formal political language that appeared in slogans, speeches, newspapers, and indeed almost everywhere. The existence of hand-copied volumes establishes that formal political language reflected only one level of everyday thought even during tightly controlled periods such as the Cultural Revolution; it further establishes that the range of such thought has far exceeded what has been acknowledged in official Chinese sources or very well known in the West. Between such disparate phenomena as *Terrifying footsteps* on one side and an official slogan like "Combat Revisionism" on the other, much, obviously, can be thought. We are challenged not only to probe this large space, but to re-evaluate the place of official thought within it.

What follows, under eight arbitrary headings, are some preliminary reflections on what can be learned from the hand-copied volumes listed in the bibliography at the end of this chapter.

Politics

Hand-copied stories seldom include the official political language at all, and when they do, it appears only incidentally, even somewhat artificially. In *The annihilation of the underground stronghold*, Chairman Mao is suddenly quoted as saying, "Defeated enemies are never happy with their defeat. They always have to make their last desperate efforts." Such phrases intrude artificially enough as to suggest that they may have been added as protection in case of discovery by the authorities. Similarly, the political tenet that workers are honest and good is observed in the labeling of incidental characters, who, for example, volunteer to wheel a wounded Public Security agent to a hospital on a pedicab. In no such case, though, is politics at all vital to the storytelling.

A more interesting fact is that heroes and villains are sometimes politically defined: The heroes of *Underground stronghold* are Public Security special-agents and the villains are CIA agents. Yet it is important to note that the appeal of the villains is not their politics but their dastardly derring-do, their underground weapons laboratory, their quick getaways, their two-way radios, etc. Similarly the Public Security police, although clearly the good guys, are not good because of their politics, which in fact are not mentioned at all. Nor are they quite as interesting as the bad guys, who generally outshine them in technique, and sometimes even make them seem like bumblers. In short, the identification of the "good" and "bad" characters as Public Security and CIA appears to be simply a convention of the storytelling—perhaps taken for granted as thoroughly as were cowboys versus Indians tales in the United States of the 1950s.

But in another way, the topic of politics does engage genuine interest, specifically in the "modern historical romances" and their fascination with high-level politics.[23] In *The Nanjing Bridge*, we see Mao Zedong jockeying against Lin Biao and Zhang Chunqiao, with General Xu Shiyou as a pawn in their game. In sharp contrast to the occasional sprinkling of political language described above, this kind of meaty reference to politics clearly was not done for the sake of protective cover—indeed, it was done at considerable risk. Mao Zedong is not always referred to as "Chairman Mao"; he is sometimes just "Mao," or even "the old man" (*lao touzi*). Part of the enjoyment is that the reader, as a kind of voyeur, can experience the sense of being elevated to a level of near-parity with these mighty historical figures.

Authority

Though official ideology is absent or merely incidental in hand-copied volumes, traditional attitudes about authority are powerfully present. Authority figures embody a combination of power and morality that resembles Confucian *de*. They consider all angles, reflect (with furrowed brow, typically) on what is right, and pronounce decisions that have moral force like that of a sage's. In *The Nanjing Bridge*, Mao Zedong considers what to do about Xu Shiyou's report that Mao's train was almost blown up on the bridge. He decides, first, that Xu Shiyou is a good person. Then he instructs Zhang Chunqiao and Yao Wenyuan, who are enemies of Xu Shiyou, to proceed to Shanghai and inform Xu's other enemies that he, Mao, personally says Xu is a good proletarian commandant. Zhang and Yao, who have no alternative before the power of Mao, obsequiously agree.

The connection between power and "face" is clear: Each supports the other. Mao's tremendous face gives him enormous power; in turn, he uses his power to preserve his face. For example, the investigation of the assassination attempt must be kept strictly secret because if rumors about it were to spread among the common people, these very rumors would harm Mao's prestige. That someone—anyone—would want to kill him detracts from his face and thus his power. (Note the interesting contrast with assassination attempts in the modern West: When President Ronald Reagan was shot, his popularity in the polls went up, not down.)

The attitudes of subordinates toward superiors provide even clearer evidence of authoritarianism. Indeed, the punctilious observance of bureaucratic form, in the context of thriller stories, can produce amusing results. In *The Nanjing Bridge*, a detective is crawling along the top of a speeding train, heading for the engine, with his pursuers constantly shooting at him from behind; when he reaches the engine he climbs into the cab, and, before doing anything else, presents his documents, including a personal letter from Zhou Enlai, to the panicked engineers. Similarly, if an underling does *not* have proper authorization, the first thing he does is seek it. The soldier who discovers the ticking bomb on the Nanjing bridge decides that, first of all, he had better call headquarters with a report. Only when this is done does he go back to dismantle the bomb. In *Underground stronghold*, Detective Shen, in hot pursuit of a CIA agent, is wounded and disappears. His two assistants, instead of continuing the chase on their own, look at each other in surprise and decide that "since there's nothing we can do (*meiyou banfa*), we'd better return to the precinct and report to the leadership on all that has happened."[24]

Women

The authoritarianism that defines the relationship between superiors and subordinates clearly conditions male-female relations as well. For example, in the husband-wife pickpocket team in *Underground stronghold*, the husband is clearly in charge and the wife obeys. Once, when they are lying in bed and hear mysterious footsteps outside, the husband tells the wife to get up and check things out.[25] The wife is also morally weaker. The two both know that picking pockets is wrong, but it is the woman who has relapses and occasionally lures the man back into the despicable practice. (This assumption, that wives tend to be more selfish and corrupt than husbands, is widely reflected in the aboveground literature of the post-Mao period as well.)[26]

The consignment of women to inferior positions is not consciously asserted by storytellers; it emerges from their implicit assumptions. The fact that this kind of implicit assumption appears in popular stories tells us something, presumably, about common attitudes in everyday life.

But there is a very different way, using these stories, to study popular ideas about women. Storytellers sometimes fashion images of women—quite consciously, in this case—that obviously are *not* typical of daily life, but still tell us much about popular stereotypes and persistent cultural myths. Black Peony, for example, is as unusual as she can be, not at all representative of daily life. Indeed, the reader's fascination with her depends on this fact. She and Huang Meifang in *Underground stronghold* are *femmes fatales* who lure men to their deaths. Although they clearly resemble the fox fairy of Chinese tradition, contemporary readers also insist that such characters stand for Jiang Qing, and that the popularity of reading about them during the Cultural Revolution sprang in part from the chance for vicarious expression of an otherwise forbidden loathing.

Another stereotype is the woman who has abandoned herself to sex. The shapely twenty-two-year-old in *Underground stronghold*, who is called Wild Rose, "makes friends indiscriminately" (*luan jiao pengyou*). The heroine in *Sister Xia* (*A Xia*) abandons herself to sex as a means of revenge upon her unfaithful boyfriend. Manna in *The sexual experiences of a high school girl* is simply overwhelmed by the pure pleasure of the act. But the point of view in describing all these young women is, interestingly, what I would call male, in the sense of being designed to satisfy male, not female, fantasies.[27] The same seems to be true of other pornographic media such as videotapes, playing cards, and ballpoint pens. (The latter, for example, feature nude women, not nude men.)

Foreign Lands

One of the most surprising aspects of hand-copied fiction from the Cultural Revolution period is how much it is concerned with foreign countries. During years when China has commonly been described, by Chinese as well as by foreigners, as sealed off or turned inward, it is most interesting to note how frequently underground entertainment fiction was set in foreign countries or otherwise involved with foreign cultures. Some hand-copied volumes, as noted above, were translations of foreign works, and those written in China only strengthen the impression of a popular fascination with the outside world. *Terrifying footsteps*, complete with a Charlie, a Herman, a blonde, and a rajah, is set in England. *Eternal regrets in love* is set in Hong Kong, and one protagonist goes to Europe for study. Similarly, *The second handshake* follows a young woman in her pursuit of medical education in the United States, where she lives in a southern mansion replete with white pillars, black servants, telephones, and automobiles. In *Long runs the Pearl River (Zhujiang shui chang)*, the bloody political feuding of two Cantonese families ends when a young man helps members of both families to sneak out to Hong Kong.[28] Even the straight pornography of *The sexual experiences of a high school girl* includes a touch of foreign interest, as the protagonist dons imported bikini underwear to set out for an evening of pleasure.

Such preoccupation with the outside world may surprise us, but it is explainable. Indeed, it may be precisely the "sealing off" of China that best explains popular curiosity about the outside world, as well as the necessity of seeking information through an illicit medium like hand-copied fiction. It is well known that when China reopened to the outside after Mao, some of the first questions (asked by many people, in various ways) were: What has been going on outside? What have we been missing? Viewed in the context of this post-Mao rush to explore the outside, the strong foreign component in hand-copied volumes seems quite natural.

Although much of the interest in foreign things can be understood as curiosity about what has been going on, there clearly are deeper concerns as well. Both *Eternal regrets in love* and *The second handshake* are triangular love stories in which a male protagonist chooses between two young women: one who is more active, well educated, strong-willed, and ready to journey abroad; the other who is more traditionally Chinese, preferring to stay at home and be domestic, deferential, and a bit boring, but always familiar and reliable. This kind of triangle, which has strong roots in prerevolutionary popular fiction,[29] can be read as allegory for a very fundamental cultural question: How much should China westernize, and how much traditional Chineseness should be preserved?[30] Which "girlfriend" should be China's future? When these kinds of questions persist in popular storytelling, it becomes apparent that the cultural problems of westernization are much deeper than the stylishness and curiosity that readily appear on the surface.

Evil, Spies, Secrecy, and Intrigue

Hand-copied stories are clear-cut in their distinctions between morally good and morally bad characters: The destitute vagabond in *Strange encounter with a wandering brave* is clearly a good person. Although forced by circumstances to be a food-grabber, his fundamental morality is beyond question because of his insistence on returning every penny of the travel bag stuffed with money.

But if the goodness of the good characters can be startling, the evilness of the bad ones is downright engrossing, and clearly an important source of entertainment. The temptresses are as alluring as they are lethal, the spies as spiffy as they are heinous. The symbolism of the color black is often used to capture this evil-but-alluring quality. Black Peony (who is actually blonde) is a good example. The Big Black Rogue in *Underground stronghold* wears all black clothes. Something like the wolf in *Little Red Riding Hood*, the rogue intercepts a little girl on her way to her grandmother's house, and, smiling through an unshaven, "black" face, tells her just to call him Uncle Black (*hei shushu*).

Good and evil in personal character are tied in patriotism and even national defense. Fang Fang in *Strange encounter with a wandering brave* works in a weapons plant. The villains in *One embroidered boot* (*Yizhi xiuhua xue*) are KMT spies who seek to blow up Chongqing. In both *Underground stronghold* and *The second handshake*, the villains are U.S. spies producing chemical weaponry. In short, there is plenty of evidence that traditional Chinese assumptions about the natural connection between morality and patriotism survive, not only in the public expressions of political leaders and intellectuals, but in unmonitored popular fiction as well.

Much of the appeal of spies and detectives has to do with their technique. We have noted how Sun Dasheng in *The Nanjing Bridge* uses his glossy pipe-bowl as a convex rearview mirror. He also ditches tailers by jumping off the front of a moving train, waiting until they jump off after him, and then leaping aboard the last car as the train rumbles on. Besides such cleverness of stratagem, which is reminiscent of both Zhuge Liang and James Bond, there is a cleverness of case-cracking, of making rational deductions that illustrate the scientific method of Sherlock Holmes (or his early twentieth-century Chinese clone, Huo Sang). For example, when an old lady asks a soldier on the Nanjing Bridge to hold a well-wrapped baby for a few minutes, explaining that the baby was put in her care by his fellow soldiers on behalf of their senior officer (*shouzhang*), the soldier immediately reasons that: (1) he and his fellow soldiers never use the term *shouzhang* for the two *lianzhang* of their company, and (2) neither of their two commanders is married, and therefore, (3) there is something suspicious about this "baby." He unwraps it to find a ticking bomb and, as noted above, hastens to file a report.

Many techniques involve secrecy and deception. These go beyond personal disguises, plentiful and imaginative though these are. Deception can be massive and multilayered, and considerable interest attaches to plumbing its depths. The denouement of the *The Nanjing Bridge*, for example, reveals a massive network of secret tunnels beneath a state guest-house. The villains escape through these tunnels, and a detective discovers them only when a guest-house cook tells him that a button on the wall behind a portrait of Mao opens a trapdoor at the base of the wall. After determining, through Holmesian deduction, that the cook must be telling the truth, the detective finds the button, pushes it, and descends through the trapdoor, where he discovers a maze so vast that he abandons the hope of chasing the villains and settles for dismantling a time bomb that he finds tied to a corpse.

Clearly it cannot be inferred that secrecy and deception in Chinese society match what is found in the flamboyant imaginations of popular storytellers. What we can say with some confidence is that readers of hand-copied volumes have found these ideas fun to think about. The ideas may reflect the obsession with secrecy that centers in China's Public Security bureaucracy, but, just as importantly, they may reflect a social context whose ordinariness and lack of privacy make huge secrets seem fun precisely because they are so impossible.

Science, Technology, and Gadgetry

Pure science is viewed as good in hand-copied volumes. Charlie in *Terrifying footsteps*, is a student of physics—a detail that helps to indicate that he is a stalwart, correctly directed young man. But more frequently, science and technology are mentioned as objects of curiosity, aspects of the wondrous, wide world of modern and foreign things. In *Underground stronghold*, a detective enters an apparently normal room and, with stylish savoir-faire, asks if it is soundproofed. The same sense of mystery attends the later appearance of the small silver ball that secretly harbors the Rolex watch that is also a two-way radio.

Heroes

A hero is both morally correct and technically skilled; that is, he knows the right ends and has the means to achieve them. His morality is measured by his ends, not by his means. Thus, the food-grabber grabs food (which might seem wrong) because he needs to live (which lets him do good). The same logic makes it quite all right for him to lie to get past the arrogant gatekeeper at Fang Fang's defense plant. In such matters, efficiency is his only concern. His morality, as we have seen, is stupendously established by his insistence on returning a travel bag stuffed with money.

Some heroes resemble the *xia* (knight errant) of traditional Chinese fiction. The food-grabber is actually referred to as a modern *jianghu qixia* or "strange roving knight." True to that image, his inner qualities are not apparent in his extremely shabby external appearance. The fourteen artisans in *Underground stronghold*, who meet to try to open the mysterious silver ball, recall the traditional *xia* even more vividly: All are shabby-looking but famous; each has prodigious skills; each has come to vie for the prize of showing that his skills are greatest; the thirteen who lose observe the ethic of withdrawing in deference to the greater *gongfu* of the one who succeeds.

Narrators of stories side with their heroes in moral terms, and either say or imply that readers should do so as well. This is true, amazingly, even in the unabashed pornography of *The sexual experiences of a high school girl*. The descriptions in this work are so explicit that the young woman narrator cannot assume the detached pose used by narrators in traditional Chinese pornography—that is, of warning readers against evil. Still, she manages to maintain the principle that, in telling her story, she is guiding readers for their own good. She does this by turning the warning against evil around, and frankly offering "advice" to the "lovable girls of the world" about how wonderful sex actually is.

Underdogs

The humble, the dispossessed, and the unappreciated are frequently elevated to respectability in hand-copied fiction. Charlie in *Terrifying footsteps* is penniless, and his mother is a washerwoman, yet he is a university student of physics. Cai Minghui in *Eternal regrets in love* is similarly penniless, and similarly a brilliant student. Like the *caizi* (man of talent) in traditional talent-and-beauty stories, he is worry-laden and somewhat sickly, and his brilliance is generally unappreciated by the world.[31] Both Sai Ying in *Terrifying footsteps* and Little Zhang, one of the junior detectives in *Underground stronghold*, were orphans, cast off by the world. Their talent goes unrecognized until they are "adopted" and trained by the senior detectives Sai Lun and Chief Sun, respectively. Coupled, sometimes, with the implication that the lowly are virtuous is the charge that those on top can be evil: The party secretary in *Sister Xia*, for all the propriety and morality in his outward demeanor, secretly funnels every pretty girl in his factory through his bedroom.

It seems likely that the popularity of these pro-underdog themes may arise from the need for self-respect among young readers. What does one do if one feels—as many educated youth during and after the Cultural Revolution apparently did—that one's talents have been wasted, that one has been insufficiently appreciated, and that less qualified people have been rewarded? What if one gets nowhere in protesting these things? Well, one can read stories about the talents of the penniless, the hidden potential of orphans, the immaculate morality of people who look like beggars, and the secret iniquity of those who appear respectable. Such reading can bring comfort in several ways. First, obviously, it helps to rationalize why one might not be doing so well: Sometimes the world is just upside-down. Second, it helps dispel the sense of solitary suffering by allowing identification with fictional characters who share one's plight. Third, a reader probably can, in many cases, actually stand above such fictional characters and derive comfort from the sense that, however bad things are, he or she is still doing reasonably well compared to those (equally talented) people who are, after all, beggars, orphans, and hand launderers.

Although this kind of pro-underdog ideology may seem to resemble democratic thought in certain ways, it is importantly different. It seems to accept hierarchy and authoritarianism entirely, merely protesting that people who truly deserve recognition do not get it. The continued acceptance of hierarchy can be seen in the just-mentioned cases of the two penniless orphans trained to be detectives: Both are taken on as the "younger brothers" of their senior partners (and saviors), to whom they remain unquestioningly subordinate. Similarly, the fourteen shabby artisans who match skills in cracking the silver ball implicitly accept the hierarchical principle that differences in skill should determine differences in rank among them. The underdog ideology does not offer new rules for society; in fact, it often underscores the old rules.

* * *

When I first discovered and began to read hand-copied volumes, I expected to find something different and perhaps distinctively Chinese. I suppose there were a few reasons for this. The materials were, after all: (1) illicit sources, (2) from the still-mysterious Cultural Revolution period, and (3) produced in a culture whose ways of thinking even in "normal" times are always interesting but not always fathomable. Some of what I have found, and analyzed above, may indeed seem especially Chinese—for example, the pronounced deference to bureaucratic authority, the notion of a contaminating allure in Western things, and the culturally allegorical triangular love stories. But it may also be that I write about such things because I enjoy finding Chinese phenomena.

From a larger perspective, it is worth observing that the basic content of hand-copied volumes is not unusual at all: crime, corpses, lovers, sex, intrigue, and other thoroughly ordinary least common denominators of what has interested human beings everywhere and at all times. Are the stories flamboyant? Yes. Far-fetched? To be sure. But exotic? Not at all. I find this solid evidence of the commonality of popular human interests, even in the most peculiar of social conditions, to be refreshing.

NOTES

1. Two originals in my possession are written, for example, on letterhead that reads "Zhanjiang District Revolutionary Committee" and "Revolutionary Committee of the Second People's Hospital of Kaifeng City," respectively.

2. Because hand-copied volumes could be reproduced indefinitely and at low cost, they did not develop black-market prices. But other, non-handmade materials that circulated with them did. A 1983 survey in Shanghai found sexually explicit pictorials for 10 yuan or more, ballpoint pens that displayed nudes for 20 yuan, and a pack of obscene playing cards for 50 yuan. See Fudan daxue zhexuexi qibaji diaocha xiaozu, "Zhongshi huangse shouchaoben dui zhongxuesheng de duhai" [Take seriously the pernicious influence of obscene hand-copied volumes on high school students], *Qingnian yanjiu*, May 1983, p. 51. I am grateful to Stanley Rosen for providing me with this survey report.

3. For details, see Perry Link, *Mandarin Ducks and Butterflies: Popular Fiction in Early Twentieth-Century Chinese Cities* (Berkeley and Los Angeles: University of California Press, 1981), pp. 237–239.

4. Ding Wangyi, "Zhongguo dalu de dixia wenxue" [Underground literature in mainland China], Part 2, *Haineiwai* (New York), February 1979, p. 30.

5. Wang Weiling, "Zai jiankuzhong molian, zai douzhengzhong chengzhang: Ji *Di'erci woshou* de xiezuo he zaoyu" [Tempered by hardships, raised in struggle: Notes on the writing and the fate of *The second handshake*], *Wenyi bao* (Beijing), no. 357 (September 1979), pp. 47–48; also interview by Perry Link at the China Youth Publishing House, October 8, 1979.

6. Ding, "Zhongguo dalu de dixia wenxue."

7. According to the Fudan University survey (cited in note 2), the pornographic story *A maiden's heart* spread widely on audiotapes in Shanghai. Pornographic videotapes have spread during the post-Mao years as well (see Xu Yihui, "Huangse luxiang dui qingshaonian de duhai" [The pernicious influence of pornographic videotapes on youth], *Qingnian yanjiu*, January 1986, pp. 47–48).

8. See Ding, "Zhongguo dalu de dixia wenxue," Part 3, *Haineiwai*, March 1979, pp. 18–20; Miriam London and Ta-ling Lee, "Two Poems from the Chinese Underground," *American Spectator*, November 1979, pp. 20–21. The editors of *Guangzhou wenyi* claim that their special column on Song poetry became a hand-copied volume in northwest China (interview by Perry Link, March 7, 1980).

9. The bibliography lists my personal collection of hand-copied volumes, plus those for which I have summaries. My five originals, which were given to me by friends in China, are certainly relatively mild in their content. No friend would have dared, for example, to give me pornography; my two pornographic examples (one in summary) are from the Hong Kong press.

10. Fudan daxue zhexuexi qibaji diaocha xiaozu, "Zhongshi huangse shouchaoben dui zhongxuesheng de duhai," pp. 52–53.

11. "Guangzhou juexin jiaqiang shehui wenhua guanli gongzuo," *Yangcheng wanbao*, May 30, 1980, p. 1.

12. Perry Link, interview of officials at the China Youth Publishing House, October 8, 1979; Gu Zhicheng, "*The Second Handshake*, a New Bestseller," *Chinese Literature* (Beijing), January 1980, p. 104.

13. Compare, for example, *Strange encounter with a wandering brave* (see Bibliography) with Jin Yanhua and Wang Jingquan, "Cries from Death Row" [Silaoli de nahan], *Guangxi wenyi*, January 1980, pp. 3–13.

14. See Link, *Mandarin Ducks and Butterflies*, pp. 22, 23, 30, 41, 42, 133–140.

15. The anti-spy (*fante*) genre in contemporary China has developed largely in imitation of Soviet anti-spy stories that were imported into China in the 1950s.

16. The stylishness of the Rolex brand, incidentally, seems to have survived the revolution as much as State Express cigarettes and Johnnie Walker Black Label scotch.

17. This work was published, after an undetermined amount of editing, in Hong Kong in 1979 (see Bibliography).

18. The pipe also suggests Sherlock Holmes, who is well known to the popular Chinese readership.

19. Published in Hong Kong; see Bibliography.

20. Prominent examples are Xu Zhenya's *Yuli hun*, Zhang Henshui's *Fate in tears and laughter*, and Zhang Yang's *The second handshake;* see Link, *Mandarin Ducks and Butterflies*, pp. 22–39, 40–54, 236–239.

21. An apparent exception is *Strange encounter with a wandering brave*, described above. My text of this story is from the Hong Kong magazine *Guanchajia*, whose editors may have repaired the work to some extent before publishing it. But it is unlikely they would have invented lively phrases in parallel style such as *lian zou dai pao* "ran headlong" or *bafang la guanxi, sichu zou houmen* "pulling strings in the eight places, going the back door in the four directions"; or that they would have worked up the marvelously vivid description of the beggar frantically boarding a bus, startling fellow passengers, and peering out in pursuit of Fang Fang. This text also employs traditional storyteller's conventions, such as opening an episode with *hua shuo* "we were saying"; introducing action with *zhi jian* "and then it was seen that"; and addressing readers directly with *ge wei* "all of you." The writer of this work, unlike those of most hand-copied volumes, must have been elderly, educated

before the revolution; indeed, he refers to himself at one point as a "sorry old man" (*zao laotou*).

22. The devices through which surprise is sprung are by no means peculiar to hand-copied volumes. They are thoroughly familiar in aboveground post-Mao fiction, and are well rooted in traditional Chinese storytelling as well. A few appear to be attributable to Western literary influences. Clarification of these various literary roots and connections would be a large task, beyond the scope of the present chapter.

23. One modern historical romance is called *Plum blossom party* (*Meihua dang*). I have not seen it, but according to Ding Wangyi ("Zhongguo dalu de dixia wenxue," p. 19), it is a panoramic saga of the revolution, tightly knit and well crafted. Apparently it accepts the official Cultural Revolution line sufficiently (calling Wang Guangmei a "head spy for the KMT," for example) that it was published *neibu* (for internal distribution) and became, according to Ding, the most widely circulated underground work during the Cultural Revolution.

24. This episode is reminiscent of an underground joke I heard in Guangzhou in 1980: A large house has three floors, one occupied by Vietnamese, one by Americans, one by Chinese. The house catches fire. The Vietnamese (cowards, of course) flee. The Americans run for buckets and ropes, splashing and shouting in a frenzy. The Chinese hold a meeting to summarize the current situation.

25. This works oppositely at my house in the United States.

26. Examples are: Qin Bo in Chen Rong's *Ren dao zhongnian* [At middle age], *Shouhuo*, January 1980, pp. 52–92; the general's wife in Bai Hua's *Yi shu xinzha* [A bundle of letters], *Renmin wenxue*, January 1980, pp. 24–40; and Deputy Secretary Kuang's wife in the film *Xiang qing* [Call of the countryside], Hu Bingliu and Wang Jin, dirs., Guangzhou: Pearl River Studio, 1981. The aboveground examples, including the three cited, tend to be set in well-to-do official families.

27. It is possible that the story *Sister xia* is an exception, but I cannot be sure because I have not read the original. According to a summary by Ding Wangyi ("Zhongguo dalu de dixia wenxue," Part 1, *Haineiwai*, January 1979, p. 19), the young woman called Sister Xia, after learning that her boyfriend has secretly taken an additional lover, reasons that if men can wantonly take their pleasure with women, why can't women similarly take their pleasure with men? As she sets out to act on this principle, one of her encounters is with the party secretary of her factory, who, she learns, has been bedding down with all the attractive women workers. This inspires her fantasy that, if someday she could become a woman party secretary, then she could have all the good-looking young men. Proto-feminist though this may seem, one would have to study the rhetoric of the fiction before drawing conclusions.

28. I have seen only Ding Wangyi's summary ("Zhongguo dalu de dixia wenxue," pp. 19–20), not the original, of *Zhujiang shui chang*. The topic of escaping secretly from China is obliquely referred to as well in Wang Jing's *In the archives of society* (*Zai shehui de dang'anli*), which was originally published in the unofficial journal *Fertile Earth* [*Wotu*], January 1979, and later in the official journal *Cinematic Creations* [*Dianying chuangzou*], October 1979. Generally, of course, stealing out of China is an extremely taboo topic in public discourse.

29. See Link, *Mandarin Ducks and Butterflies*, pp. 23–30, 41–42.

30. It is interesting that the fear of cultural pollution from the West appears in hand-copied volumes. Both Black Peony and Huang Meifang (see the section on women) operate from Western-style dancehalls, and such dancehalls are what originally drew Black Peony morally astray. Such facts show that concern with cultural pollution is by no means limited to ideological conservatives in the party like Hu Qiaomu and Deng Liqun.

31. For more information see Link, *Mandarin Ducks and Butterflies*, pp. 64–78.

BIBLIOGRAPHY OF HAND-COPIED VOLUMES

Originals (in Perry Link's Library)

Dixia baolei de fumie (The annihilation of the underground stronghold), 31 pp.
Kongbu de jiaobusheng (Terrifying footsteps), 25 pp.
Qingtian changhen (Eternal regrets in love), 29 pp.
Renxinglun (On human nature), 38 pp.
Tali de nuren (Woman in the tower). Wumingshi, 142 pp.

In Reprinted Form

Daqiao fengyun (The case of the Nanjing Bridge). "Organized" by You Kecun (pseud.).
    Guanchajia (Hong Kong), 1979.
Di'erci woshou (The second handshake). Zhang Yang. Beijing: China Youth Publishing
    House, 1979.
Gongkai de qingshu (Open love letters). Jin Fan (pseud.). *Shiyue* (Beijing), January
    1980.
Liulanghan de qiyu (Strange encounter with a wandering brave). Sha Tian (pseud.).
    Guanchajia (Hong Kong), 1979.
Yige gaozhong nusheng de xing tiyan (The sexual experiences of a high school girl).
    Xie zhen: Haiwaiban (Hong Kong), February 1987.

In Summary Form*

A Xia (Sister Xia)
Hong (Rainbow)
Meihua dang (Plum blossom party)
Meizhou bao shisan hao (American panther no. 13). A translation of a Soviet anti-
    spy story.
Xiangjiang hong (Xiang river's red)
Yizhi xiuhua xue (One embroidered boot)
Zhujiang shui chang (Long runs the Pearl River)

---

*The summary of *Yizhi xiuhua xue* is from several interviews. The other summaries are from
Ding Wangyi, "Zhongguo dalu de dixia wenxue," Part 1, *Haineiwai*, January 1979, pp. 18–20.

3

Popular Cinema
and Political Thought
in Post-Mao China
Reflections on
Official Pronouncements, Film,
and the Film Audience

PAUL G. PICKOWICZ

In the years immediately following the Cultural Revolution, cinema became the most popular cultural medium in China, with an estimated 10 billion viewers in 1982. Many genres were successful, but, following the rise of the Democracy Wall movement, the films enjoyed most by urban youth were serious political movies that criticized the party and state. Paul G. Pickowicz, history professor at the University of California– San Diego, asks why these films were so popular and what they reveal about the political concerns of their audience. By contrasting the political content of the films to major pronouncements issued by the authorities, he shows the considerable gap between the official view and popular perceptions. In the early 1980s, for example, official sources stressed the accomplishments of the party and state during the period from 1949 to 1965, presented the Cultural Revolution as an aberration perpetrated by a small group of conspirators, and asserted that the wrongs of the past had been righted after 1978. But the popular political films argued that the evils of the Cultural Revolution had systemic origins in the mid-1950s and that political abuses associated with the Cultural Revolution were still very much plaguing Chinese life in the 1980s. However, these popular demands for justice and accountability were cries for reform rather than expressions of outright opposition to party rule.

—Eds.

Students of popular thought pay relatively little attention to the proclamations of governing elites. The views found in official pronouncements, we assume, do not necessarily reflect the thinking of ordinary people. The chapters in this book contribute to our understanding of Chinese society by exploring the many realms of popular thought that have little to do with official politics or are generally ignored in official accounts of social life.

But our relative lack of interest in official statements does not mean that we seek to avoid discussions of politics or that we ignore the dynamic relationship that exists between elite and popular culture. The mental world of ordinary people, such as the educated young urbanites discussed in this chapter, obviously includes ideas and attitudes about high politics and state affairs. One of the challenges for scholars of popular thought is to throw light on the relationship between official political testimonies and popular political thought. We assume that the official and the popular are not identical, but does it follow that they are entirely different and do not interact with each other? In sorting out the relationship between what is official and what is popular it is crucial, first, to recognize that in the realm of elite culture there is tension between the official and the unofficial and, second, to consider the ways in which the unofficial political thought of elites interacts with the popular political thought of non-elites.

The purpose of this chapter is not to examine the entire spectrum of popular political views, but to focus specifically on popular attitudes toward the party and state. These topics were important in the early post-Mao years because the party and state wanted to be perceived as morally legitimate in order to win public support for the economic reform programs associated with Deng Xiaoping. Leaders did not want their ambitious plans to be sabotaged by a citizenry that harbored serious reservations about the moral rectitude of the state and party.

The post-Mao leadership, like its forerunners, spent considerable time and energy fostering the view that ordinary citizens revered and supported the authorities. It is extremely difficult, therefore, for scholars (either Chinese or foreign) to do systematic research on something as controversial and complex as the ways in which popular political thought criticized the state and party. Sources of information are scarce and, when available, pose many knotty methodological problems.

During my year of residence in Beijing in the early 1980s it occurred to me that feature films might be a useful, though hardly comprehensive, source of information on the elusive topic of popular political thought. The films produced in the 1950s, 1960s, and 1970s, had an official feel and, with few exceptions, glorified the state and party. But many of the most popular films of the early 1980s seemed different. I was especially interested in movies referred to by the audience as serious films (*yansu pian*). Produced by elite filmmakers, these melodramas were unusually popular and invariably included rare and frank criticisms of the party and state. I wanted to know why these serious films were so popular and whether they revealed anything about popular political thought. I wondered whether motion pictures made in the People's Republic at long last could be studied as illuminating expressions of popular political thought, rather than as manifestations of the official worldview or reflections of political sparring among the elites.[1]

The advantages of using popular films to understand popular thought are obvious. First, the size of the sample group is staggering. In 1982 the Chinese film audience was estimated to be 10 billion people, a number that is larger, I suspect, than the audience for fiction. In the early 1980s *Popular cinema* (*Dazhong dianying*) was the most widely read magazine in China, with a monthly readership of 10 million.[2] Furthermore, it seems logical to assume that the behavior of the film audience was not random, that it is possible to know why the most popular films were more appealing than the least popular films. Scholars of popular political thought have good reason to be intrigued by an audience that consistently demonstrated a strong preference for serious films, especially when those films repeat similar criticisms of the party and state.

But those who attempt to use popular film sources as a window on popular political thought must move with caution. For example, it is impossible to generalize about the entire Chinese film audience, which consists of many important subgroups such as children, young people, the elderly, minorities, urbanites, rural dwellers, men, women, factory workers, military personnel, educated people, and many others. This study of popular political thought focuses on urbanites between the ages of eighteen and thirty-five (especially students, teachers, professionals, and other educated people) because there are strong indications that they were the primary, although by no means the only, audience for popular political films.[3] But generalizations about the political thought of educated young urbanites are not necessarily valid for other groups.

Furthermore, by stressing the interest of young urbanites in the burst of serious political films that appeared in the early 1980s, I do not mean to suggest that they thought only of politics, that they were not inclined to watch anything else, or that their political thought can be entirely understood by examining the serious films they watched. We know that in the early 1980s educated urban youth thought about many subjects and that their film viewing included love stories, martial-arts adventures, and foreign thrillers. This chapter dwells on the *yansu* (serious) films because they were especially well liked by educated young city dwellers and because, compared to the other popular film genres, they afford us the most direct access to the political thought of this influential group. But the access gained through popular political films is by no means total. A full study of the thought of educated young urbanites (an undertaking far beyond the scope of this exploratory chapter) would have to account, among many other things, for the popularity of other film genres among these people. Similarly, a comprehensive analysis of their political thought would require an evaluation of many sources, not just the film materials discussed here.

The films of the late 1970s, the immediate post–Cultural Revolution period, are not very useful for our purposes because the Chinese film industry recovered very slowly from the political and artistic ravages of the ten-year Cultural Revolution. Large numbers of films were produced after Mao's death (129 features were made from 1977 to 1979, compared to only 109 features turned out in the Cultural Revolution decade) and box-office receipts soared to unprecedented heights, but the new films broke very little fresh political ground. One critic observed that the film audience was starved: "They flocked to the cinema to watch any film that was showing."[4] While significant numbers of literary intellectuals and reform activists were participating in the political protest movements of 1978 and 1979, filmmakers, according to Ding Qiao, deputy director of the Film Bureau in the early 1980s, were still making movies that "bore traces of the stereotypes" associated with filmmaking in the Cultural Revolution.[5]

This is not to suggest that the film industry was totally unaffected by the political protests of the late 1970s. But the impact became apparent only after the crackdown on Democracy Wall in late 1979 as films echoing and popularizing the concerns of the protesters finally began to surface. Many of these motion pictures were based on works of fiction published *before* the demise of Democracy Wall. The new political thrust of Chinese cinema became evident around 1980. True, filmmakers constituted a privileged elite, the film industry was still monopolized by the state and monitored by party censors, and the great majority of new works still contributed little to the popular political discourse or to the development of film art in China, but beginning in 1980 a small but potent cinema of social criticism, linked both in terms of form and content to the rich traditions of the 1930s and 1940s, began to emerge as the most popular genre of new films, especially among educated urban youth. Unprecedented numbers of works that clearly expressed unofficial political views slipped through state censorship organs.

In my estimation the most interesting group of popular political films was completed in the period from 1980 to early 1983, that is, the years between the fall of Democracy Wall and the launching of the campaign against spiritual pollution in 1983. Three of the most representative works that circulated in this unusual period are *The legend of Tianyun Mountain* (1980), directed by Xie Jin; *A corner forgotten by love* (1981), directed by Li Yalin and Zhang Ji; and *At middle age* (1982), directed by Wang Qimin and Sun Yu.[6] These films came closer than anything else produced after 1949 to an openly critical popular cinema. They were widely acclaimed by the film establishment, highly critical of the Communist party, extraordinarily popular among the film audience at a time when the film industry was beginning to get stiff competition from the television world, and subjected to tough criticism in the official press.

The legend of Tianyun Mountain, based on a short novel by Lu Yanzhou published in 1979, is the tragic story of a young intellectual, Luo Chun, who was attacked in the 1957 anti-Rightist movement and then cruelly victimized for more than twenty years.[7] The two women in Luo's life are studies in contrast. One woman, Song Wei, was engaged to Luo Chun in 1957, but, in order to avoid trouble and advance her political career, broke off the marriage plan and denounced her lover once he was identified as a rightist. The other woman, Feng Qinglan, who was Song Wei's best friend in 1957, fell in love with the pitiful Luo after he was denounced and then sacrificed her career and health to defend and comfort Luo during his long ordeal. More than twenty years later, in winter 1978, Song Wei, now a high-ranking local party official, is in charge of the department in the prefectural party office that decides who among those accused of rightism in 1957 will be rehabilitated. She wants justice to be done after so many years, but this would involve revealing the key role played by her present husband, the powerful secretary of the prefectural party committee, in the persecution of Luo in 1957.

Despite the fact that the novel had been criticized by party conservatives, the film version of *The legend of Tianyun Mountain,* produced at the Shanghai Film Studio, was received with great enthusiasm by the film audience and many film professionals. In early 1981 it was praised in *Wenyi bao;*[8] in June 1981 film periodicals announced that it had simply overwhelmed the competition (83 feature films were produced in 1980) by taking first place in five categories—including best feature, best director, and best screenplay—at the first annual Jinji Film Award ceremony, a high-profile event presided over by the film establishment. Even more startling, *The legend of Tianyun Mountain,* the first feature film made in China that focused on the anti-Rightist movement in 1957, shared first-place honors in the fourth annual Hundred Flowers film competition sponsored by *Popular cinema* magazine. It was named best picture on 861,831 of the 2,018,418 ballots cast by ordinary film fans.[9]

In spring 1981 and again in fall 1981, however, concerned film professionals were badly shaken by the assault launched by party conservatives on another critical film, *Bitter love* (1980), written by Bai Hua and directed by Peng Ning at the Changchun Film Studio. Characterized in the official press as a manifestation of bourgeois liberalization, *Bitter love* was never released nationwide, even though the screenplay had been published already, film previews had been held in late 1980, and advertisements were on display outside theaters and in popular film journals.[10] In a December 1981 address to 250 film artists, party general secretary Hu Yaobang, himself a victim of a campaign against bourgeois liberalization in 1987, tacitly acknowledged the existence of political factions among the privileged elite when he warned filmmakers about "attributing errors in party work" to the nature of the "socialist system" itself. Films that reach such a conclusion were said to convey "unhealthy political sentiments and bad taste."[11] In a matter of weeks the official press began to carry articles that assaulted the much heralded

Legend of Tianyun Mountain, now characterized as a film that "runs counter to reality" (*weifan zhenshi*).[12] Movie theaters and television stations were discouraged from screening it.

As a result of the controversy surrounding *Bitter love* in 1981, a second important film, *A corner forgotten by love*, was in serious political trouble even before it was released. A production of the small Emei Film Studio in Sichuan, this movie was based on an award-winning short story published in early 1980 by Zhang Xian, a victim of the anti-Rightist movement in 1957.[13] Completed in late 1981, *A corner forgotten by love* came extremely close to being "executed," that is, killed by cultural censors.[14] The film was finally released in early 1982, after the political dust of the first campaign against bourgeois liberalization had settled, but it was denied the usual publicity given to new productions.

Set in 1979, well after the death of Mao and the arrest of his leading proponents, the story is about an utterly destitute peasant household in a depressing and forgotten corner of a remote county. The head of the household, Shen Shanwang, had been a deputy co-op leader in the mid-1950s, prior to the collectivization of agriculture. During the Great Leap Forward in 1958, however, he was dismissed from his post and branded a rightist because he opposed the cutting down of valuable fruit trees to fuel backyard steel furnaces. Like the protagonist of *The legend of Tianyun Mountain*, Shen was treated as a social outcast for the next twenty years. In 1974, during the Cultural Revolution, his eldest daughter, Cunni, committed suicide after the local militia discovered that she was having a sexual relationship with a hardworking local lad.

A corner forgotten by love focuses on Shen's second daughter, Huangmei, who was born during the post–Great Leap famine. Haunted by the memory of her sister's awful fate, Huangmei must come to terms with the rumblings of her own sexual awakening in 1979. She is at once attracted to and frightened by a poor, but forward-looking, young cadre named Xu Rongshu, who insists that the grinding poverty the village has known since collectivization can be broken if the households are allowed to develop private cottage industries, sow cash crops, and sell their goods at the free market. Huangmei's mother suspects that the young man is about to make the sort of rightist errors that ruined her husband twenty years before and is terrified that another sexual scandal is on the horizon. Arrangements are soon made for Huangmei to marry a man in another village for 500 yuan, a sum that will get her family out of debt.

In mid-1982, within weeks of its release, *A corner forgotten by love* was attacked by hostile critics who disliked its graphic depiction of rural misery.[15] Still, *A corner forgotten by love*, like *The legend of Tianyun Mountain*, had many supporters in the press and film worlds. Zhang Xian's screenplay took first place at the second annual Jinji Film Award ceremony and He Xiaoshu, who portrayed the mother, Linghua, won the trophy for best supporting actress. Although this film was not among the top three vote-getters in the popular Hundred Flowers competition, it was on a very short list of works described at the award ceremony as the best-liked films of 1981. The ministry of culture also certified this film as one of the nine best features made in 1981.[16] Still, to this day, *A corner forgotten by love* is not permitted to be screened publicly outside China.

The last film I want to discuss, *At middle age*, a product of the Changchun Film Studio, was based on a novella published by Chen Rong in January 1980.[17] Like the other movies mentioned here, the filming of *At middle age* was interrupted time and again by the ongoing controversy surrounding the original work of fiction. Released in early 1983, the film took more than two years to shoot.[18]

Set in 1979, this film tells the sad story of a forty-two-year-old woman, Lu Wenting, whose physical and emotional health breaks down as she unsuccessfully attempts to play the conflicting roles of eye surgeon, wife, and mother of two. A promising medical graduate in 1961, Lu is completing her *eighteenth* year of residency at a Beijing hospital as the film opens. Despite her dedication and high level of skill, Lu, a nonparty intellectual, earns only 56 yuan a month (that is, less than a barber) in 1979 and her family of four lives in a 130-square-foot room. Her workload is oppressive, she feels guilty about neglecting her children, and her marriage is passionless. As she is recovering from a debilitating heart attack that weakens her still further, a major question is posed: Should she try once again to carry on with her work in hopes that the party's outrageous treatment of intellectuals will improve or, like her best friend and colleague Yafen, who has decided to emigrate to Canada, should she give up hope that life in China will someday change?

By the time *At middle age* appeared in early 1983, the political storm directed at the original work of fiction had subsided. It still had some powerful detractors, but, like *The legend of Tianyun Mountain* and *A corner forgotten by love*, *At middle age* did extremely well at the box office and was praised by many film professionals. Film viewers chose it as the best film of 1982 in the sixth annual Hundred Flowers competition and actress Pan Hong took top honors in the best actress category at the third annual Jinji Film Award ceremony sponsored by the film establishment.[19]

One way to begin to understand the popularity of political melodramas like these three films among many film professionals and among educated young city dwellers is to contrast the social views contained in such works to important, even pathbreaking, official pronouncements published at about the same time. Democracy Wall was gone by late 1979, but party ideologists were still under considerable pressure to explain the mistakes made by the party in the years after 1949. There was also a persistent call for a fundamental reevaluation of Maoism and the personal role of Mao Zedong following the establishment of the People's Republic. Reform-minded people inside and outside the party were demanding that the party send a clear signal that the nightmares of the past would not be repeated and that there was hope for political and economic reform. The spectacular trial of the Gang of Four, which opened in late November 1980, was welcomed by most urbanites, but even before the trial ended a flood of letters to *People's daily* and other publications, repeating the concerns of films like *The legend of Tianyun Mountain*, pointed out that the jailing of the defendants was only a partial solution to the political problems that plagued China.[20]

After much delay, the long-awaited official statement on the weighty issues mentioned above—a 30,000-character document entitled "Resolution on Certain Questions in the History of Our Party Since the Founding of the People's Republic of China"—was issued on July 1, 1981.[21] Those who hoped this Central Committee document would be as forceful as Nikita Khrushchev's famous denunciation of Stalin and Stalinism in February 1956 were undoubtedly disappointed. This unprecedented public statement received enormous attention in the domestic and foreign press, but, on balance, it amounted to a cautious and rather self-serving evaluation of the post-1949 period. Indeed, the resolution was considerably less critical than the highly popular films discussed here.

The 1981 resolution, published after the release of *The legend of Tianyun Mountain* and before the completion of *A corner forgotten by love* and *At middle age*, made headlines by admitting publicly what informed Chinese already knew: First, Mao Zedong "made mistakes in his later years" and, second, the Cultural Revolution was "initiated and led" by Mao. Though the resolution was the first major public attempt by the ruling elite to repudiate the cult of Mao and to reject the myth of his infallibility, it hardly constituted a denunciation of Mao and Maoism or raised fundamental questions about party rule. On the contrary, the tone was remarkably upbeat. There was virtually no criticism of Mao's role in the long period from the founding of the Communist party in 1921 to the establishment of the People's Republic in 1949, high marks were given to Mao and the party for their work in the 1949–1956 transitional period, and, even more astonishingly, the tumultuous years from 1956 to 1965 were characterized as a time when "the material and technical basis for modernizing our country was largely established." The resolution briefly acknowledged that there were "shortcomings" in the agricultural collectivization drive after 1955, that the "scope" of the 1957 anti-Rightist movement was "too broad," and that "left" errors had been committed during the Great Leap Forward, but no mention was made of the 20 million people who perished in the massive famine that followed the Great Leap.

The 1981 resolution treated in detail only the disastrous decade of the Cultural Revolution and left the clear impression that the social, political, and economic problems of the present day were attributable, in the main, to the upheavals of the Cultural Revolution, the diabolical machinations of Lin Biao and the Gang of Four, and the mistakes made by Mao in his later years. The resolution confidently asserted that the corner had been turned on the abuses and injustices associated with the Cultural Revolution when the Central Committee declared in December 1978 that socialist modernization was the main task of the party and people.

Finally, in case anyone had misunderstood the significance of the first assault on bourgeois liberalization waged in spring 1981, the July resolution stated in no uncertain terms that the Central Committee's criticisms of Mao and the Cultural Revolution reaffirmed, rather than questioned, the "four cardinal principles": the correctness of the socialist road, the proletarian dictatorship, the leadership of the Communist party, and the ideological hegemony of Marxism-Leninism and Mao Zedong Thought. In no case, the resolution warned, should the party's mistakes be used as a "pretext for weakening, breaking away from or even sabotaging its leadership. It is imperative," the Central Committee added, "to maintain a high level of vigilance and conduct effective struggle against all those who are hostile to socialism and try to sabotage it in the political, economic, ideological and cultural fields."

The basic social views expressed in the three films under review, it seems safe to say, were significantly more critical than the ones contained in this extraordinary benchmark resolution. The fact that these same films were highly acclaimed by many film professionals and young urban film fans tells us something about the gap between the official pronouncements of the party and popular political thought in the early 1980s. Of course, I do not mean to suggest that the interests and thought of elite filmmakers were identical to the thought of the ordinary people who frequent movie houses, or to deny that, in structural terms, films and filmmakers belonged to the official realm. It seems to me, however, that the popularity of these films can be explained, in part, by the audience's obvious approval of the basic social views espoused. The making of serious political melodramas in the early 1980s was not simply a matter of a few elite filmmakers suddenly and inexplicably embracing the unofficial and popular political views of urban youth. Nor was it a matter of renegade cultural elites patronizing and agitating among an apolitical and inarticulate urban mass. The process of political fertilization, I strongly suspect, was from both the top down and the bottom up. A central paradox of early 1980s Chinese filmmaking is that the serious political films were popular cultural artifacts produced by privileged film-makers who were able to work outside the mainstream of official ideology. Their state-funded work was unofficial in the sense that it represented minority or dissenting political positions held by influential elites, including party members. More importantly, at least for our purposes, their work was unofficial and popular in the sense that it actively sought to represent the political views of ordinary people who felt that party reform policies were inadequate. The fact that educated elites produced this work and that the state, in a sense, allowed this activity to take place does not mean that these films cannot be considered as expressions of popular political thought.

At the level of raw political analysis *The legend of Tianyun Mountain* was considerably more provocative than the July 1981 resolution, going far beyond the scope of the well-received "scar literature" (*shangheng wenxue*) produced immediately following the Cultural Revolution. Whereas most scar literature dwelled on the abuses people suffered during the Cultural Revolution and heaped blame on the Gang of Four for the sorry condition of China in the late 1970s, *The legend of Tianyun Mountain* said almost nothing about the Cultural Revolution. The underlying assumption of the film was that the difficulties that continued to plague China in the 1980s had their origins in the 1950s, especially during the time of the anti-Rightist movement of 1957, an enormously destructive period that was essentially whitewashed in the 1981 resolution. It was implied that not all the problems confronting the Chinese in the 1980s could be attributed to the odious Cultural Revolution leadership.

The film complained that those who stressed the destructiveness of the Gang of Four were missing the point. If there was moral justification for condemning the Cultural Revolution leadership after its fall from power (when such criticism was welcomed by the new leadership), should not the authorities acknowledge the contributions of those who had the courage to speak out during the Cultural Revolution (when such criticism was not welcomed) and those who protestsed obvious abuses before the Cultural Revolution?

The legend of Tianyun Mountain pointed out that many of the party faithful who were persecuted during the Cultural Revolution, cadres like Song Wei and her husband, Wu Yao, were precisely the ones responsible for victimizing party critics during the anti-Rightist campaign in 1957. Party veterans like Wu Yao were eager to have their names cleared and to be restored to positions of power after the Cultural Revolution, but they were extremely reluctant, once restored to power, to approve the rehabilitation of people like Luo Chun, who continued to suffer into the 1980s for speaking out in 1957. To rehabilitate such people would require admitting one's own complicity and conceding that the anti-Rightist movement was extremely unjust. That is why Wu Yao, even at the very end of the film, continued to regard Luo Chun as a rightist who deserved to be punished for life.

By refusing to review Luo Chun's case, Wu Yao demonstrated that he had learned the most elementary political lessons taught by the party in the 1950s: Never take the initiative; never question party policy; wait for directives to come down from above before acting. If one is required to exercise judgment, it is better to lean to the left (for example, refusing to hear the case of a victim of the anti-Rightist movement) than to lean to the right (being excessively lenient with those once accused of rightism). The party forgives leftist mistakes; it does not forgive rightist errors.

Perhaps the most astonishing feature of *The legend of Tianyun Mountain* is that it turned upside down many of the party's sacred moral categories. In the films produced in the 1950s and 1960s, mainstream party people, even those who waver momentarily, were ordinarily characterized as honest and virtuous, while rightists were characterized as morally deficient and evil. In *The legend of Tianyun Mountain* these stock roles were reversed. The film audience was told that rightists like Luo Chun were pure of heart, selfless, and respected by the people, while many party operatives who assumed power after the Cultural Revolution were vindictive and corrupt.

A corner forgotten by love, like *The legend of Tianyun Mountain*, looked well beyond the Cultural Revolution when it sought to identify the sources of problems that plagued China in the early 1980s. This work stated explicitly that grinding poverty became a characteristic of village life not in the Cultural Revolution, but with the advent of collectivization in 1956. The protagonist's father, Shen Shanwang, had been stripped of his leading position and ostracized because, like Luo Chun in *The legend of Tianyun Mountain*, he spoke out against the Great Leap Forward in 1958. And, like Luo Chun, he was not among those whose reputations were cleared in the years immediately following the Cultural Revolution. Three years had passed since the death of Mao, but this village was still dirt poor. Shen's family did not have enough to eat or enough to wear, and lived in a depressing hovel.

A corner forgotten by love, even more than *The legend of Tianyun Mountain*, argued that the party's failure to address political problems that pre-dated the Cultural Revolution made it extremely difficult for the rural economic reform policies adopted by the party center in 1978 to be implemented and for economic progress to take place. Xu Rongshu, the young cadre who returned from the navy in 1979, has heard that popular economic reforms, such as private household sidelines and private commerce, have been implemented elsewhere, but the veteran leaders of the village, like the cadre Wu Yao in *The legend of Tianyun Mountain*, are afraid of making rightist errors and refuse to consider reforms that will improve standards of living. They will wait until they receive the appropriate instructions from higher authorities.

The notion that China's economic development, especially in the rural sector, had stagnated for more than twenty years after 1956 was advanced in both films through the assertion that prosperity could be possible only by turning the clock back and adopting the plans set forth by those categorized as rightists and counterrevolutionaries in 1957. In the first film, rightist Luo Chun's elaborate plan for the development and modernization of the Tianyun Mountain region was dropped in 1957 and replaced by character-istically Maoist schemes, all of which failed miserably. Only in 1979 was Luo's plan rediscovered and adopted. In the second film, Shen Shanwang was victimized in 1958 for advocating the cultivation of cash crops. But in 1979 it was precisely the subject of cash crops that so excited young Xu Rongshu, who turned to the old rightist, Shen Shanwang, for advice.

Once again, the party regulars were the negative characters, while the rightists who had suffered for twenty years were presented as martyrs of the people. This tendency was especially apparent in the titillating and contro-versial scenes of youthful sexual awakening that lead to the suicide of Shen's eldest daughter. Official moral doctrine taught that premarital sexual activity is degenerate. Yet the audience could see that the two young lovers were not only sympathetic characters, but also that their union seemed to be the only source of joy and spontaneity in an otherwise loveless, colorless, and oppressive environment. Like the rightists, the sexual partners were presented as heroes and martyrs. She was driven to suicide and he began serving a long prison sentence. Critics of the movie, not surprisingly, accused the filmmakers of propagating bourgeois humanism. That is, instead of discussing the character of the young people within the framework of the various social classes, the film treated their behavior as a manifestation of universal human nature.

At middle age did not discuss the period before the Cultural Revolution in any detail. Instead, it focused on the sensitive topic of the party's poor treatment of nonparty intellectuals, especially middle-aged intellectuals, during and after the Cultural Revolution, an issue scarcely mentioned in the 1981 resolution. The film reached two sobering conclusions: First, the Maoist approach to intellectuals was an almost unqualified disaster and, second, very little was done in the immediate post-Mao era to correct the problem. Consequently, intellectuals like Lu Wenting, who believed they had sacrificed their youth for the noble cause of reconstructing China, were now full of self-pity, burned out professionally, and ambivalent about the party's latest modernization strategy. Lu Wenting was lonely, depressed, and indifferent toward life. Indeed, the ending failed to resolve the issue of her willingness and ability to carry on in her work.

As in the other films, the sharpest contrast was between the alienated hero and party bureaucrats who reassumed leading positions following a period of intense persecution during the Cultural Revolution. Vice Minister Jiao Chengsi, upon whom Lu Wenting performed successful cataract surgery, and his obnoxious wife, Qin Bo—openly ridiculed in the film as a typical "Marxist-Leninist old lady"—lived a life of extraordinary privilege and influence. Lu Wenting, on the other hand, did not even have the time to care for her children.

Qin Bo, a figure whose negative traits can in no way be traced to the Cultural Revolution or the Gang of Four, was the most interesting villain in the film. Lu Wenting's work was made much more difficult by this abusive party veteran who constantly expressed distrust of the middle-aged surgeon and questioned her professional competence because Lu was not a party member and because her official status was still that of a resident. The film suggested that even if people like Lu Wenting were able to summon up the energy to serve the party and state, it was by no means clear that powerholders like Qin Bo were prepared to give them a free hand to do their jobs. Lu Wenting made great sacrifices for the party, but the party did not appreciate or trust her.

The constant repetition of important political themes in these and other popular works produced in the early 1980s strongly suggests that the opinions of these privileged filmmakers resonated with the political thought of young and educated urban viewers. One of their most basic themes was the notion that the problems of the present were related to serious political failings of the party and state that were apparent before the onset of the Cultural Revolution and persisted after it ended. On this crucial point, the political concerns of the audience and the filmmakers discussed here contrasted quite sharply with the views contained in official ideological statements such as the July 1981 resolution.

It seems to me, however, that these films were appealing at other, less explicit, levels as well. Their popularity also had something to do with *how* the stories were told. In early 1984 a group of students from eight universities in Beijing was asked: What film subjects move you most? By a wide margin (51 percent) respondents stated a preference for films that treated "life's hardships and difficulties," a topic that is inextricably linked to political issues, but one that does not necessarily have to be treated, artistically speaking, in an explicit, heavy-handed fashion.[22] The films reviewed here were clearly full of political content, but, unlike the passionless treatment of Chinese life contained in official pronouncements like the 1981 resolution, the films humanized accounts of life's hardships and difficulties by converting them into melodramas that permitted, indeed encouraged, mass catharsis. Western viewers often find these works overly sentimental and unrealistic. But the Chinese audience, fond of such sentimentality, probably found it easy to identify with the victims of arbitrary force and injustice.[23] Skillful use and even manipulation of the weepy, melodramatic genre is precisely what links the popular political films produced in the 1980s by directors like Xie Jin to the rich tradition of Chinese cinema in the 1930s and 1940s.

The filmmakers' efforts to get the attention of the film audience and win their approval were facilitated by careful use of an important and time-honored Chinese storytelling device: The major characters are confronted by agonizing moral dilemmas that are familiar to the audience, especially dilemmas that involve complex love relationships, a subject that was virtually banned from Chinese screens during the Cultural Revolution. The films were appealing, in part, because the audience was not offered easy solutions to complex social problems. On the contrary, the audience was forced to witness and, in a vicarious sense, feel the intense suffering of the protagonists.

The dilemma that confronted Song Wei, the woman who abandoned Luo Chun in *The legend of Tianyun Mountain,* is related to the important issue of life strategies. In 1957, during the anti-Rightist campaign, she had to make a difficult choice. She could remain loyal to Luo Chun, her true love; the film made it clear that this was the morally responsible thing to do. But to do so would have meant the destruction of her career, social isolation, scorn (young children are shown throwing rocks at rightists), and material deprivation. Or, she could do the politically expedient thing by closely following the advice of party insiders, but only at the cost of denouncing the man she loved and entering into an essentially loveless union with the doctrinaire Wu Yao, whose political star was rising. The audience undoubtedly knew that, in moral terms, the choice was clear, but they were probably not surprised when Song Wei reluctantly followed the practical path.

Shen Huangmei, the central protagonist in *A corner forgotten by love,* faced a similar choice that also involved a triangular love relationship. She could demonstrate filial respect for her poor mother, erase the family debt, and have a more comfortable future in a prosperous village elsewhere by agreeing to a traditional arranged marriage (to a man she had never met). The other option was to take her chances with the local lad, Rongshu, the first person to make her conscious of her sexuality. The problem with this choice was that she had not yet completely abandoned the notion, shaped by the tragedy of her sister's permarital love affair, that her emotions could not be trusted and that her natural instincts were somehow immoral. Furthermore, it was by no means clear that the young man had a promising political future. The ideas he espoused were ones that had been identified with rightism time and again after the 1950s.

Once again, the choice was not as obvious as it might appear, especially if the audience dismissed the artificial happy ending tacked on to satisfy the censors. The popularity of *A corner forgotten by love* among young people who wanted more freedom of choice in marriage does not mean that viewers, faced with the same problem in their own lives, would automatically defy their parents. Many young viewers who would not run the risk of choosing someone like Rongshu in real life are perfectly sincere when they applaud Huangmei's daring decision to do so onscreen.

Lu Wenting, the heroine of *At middle age*, had no way to leave China. But the youthful urban film audience was undoubtedly interested in her reaction to the dramatic news that her alter ego, Yafen, had decided to emigrate to Canada, a rich capitalist country. The most poignant sequence in the film is a sad farewell dinner which Wenting and her husband share with Yafen and her bitter husband. A guilt-ridden Yafen confesses that she agonized over the decision to give up on China. Her husband, Xueyao, says that he is an "unworthy son of the Chinese people." He agrees that the bad times are behind the Chinese people, but he can no longer wait for the good times to come to his house.

Lu Wenting, like the film audience, was forced to choose. She could approve of Yafen's decision to leave the motherland and undergo a spiritual rebirth in another land, but to do so would be tantamount to conceding that the logic employed by the parting couple was correct. She could disapprove of Yafen's decision, but this would imply that she accepted the upbeat official view that the future is bright and require her once again to muster the energy to serve the noble cause of nation building. If Yafen was wrong, there was every reason to continue to work hard and sacrifice; if Yafen, a good person, was right, then it would be enough to go through the motions at work. Again, the choice was not obvious. It is likely that many in the audience had high hopes for the future, while many others were skeptical of the party's latest promises.

After *At middle age* was released in early 1983 many filmmakers and ordinary film fans were eager to see more serious films produced, films that dealt with life's hardships and difficulties. But the architects of the official campaign against spiritual pollution, initiated in autumn 1983, disapproved of films like *The legend of Tianyun Mountain, A corner forgotten by love,* and *At middle age* because these works challenged the notion that the primary purpose of the film industry is to communicate the official word of the party to the audience. But Xie Jin and the other defiant directors of serious political melodramas who worked in the official sector continued to promote a cinema that gave greater expression to the unofficial political views of both privileged elites and ordinary people, even though the unofficial often clashed with the official.

The tension between these two tendencies was reflected in public remarks made by Shao Mujun, a senior researcher affiliated with the China Film Association, in October 1984, after the storm of the campaign against spiritual pollution had subsided. "Some people here," Shao insisted, "are quite loath to admit that there is a problem of freedom of expression in filmmaking. To talk about it is even considered a reactionary tendency of bourgeois liberalization." Shao boldly asserted that "a main target of the Chinese film industry on its road to reform is to fight for full freedom of creative expression, stand against 'crude interference,' and break away from the agitprop task of illustrating current policies."[24]

Despite the brutal suppression of alienated students and disaffected young workers that commenced in June 1989, and the subsequent launching of a nationwide cultural crackdown, none of the issues raised in this chapter have been settled. The struggle between directors who want to give expression to unofficial and popular political criticisms of the state and party and cultural bureaucrats who demand that filmmakers engage in political agitprop work will continue for some time. Furthermore, the popular political complaints conveyed in the serious films of the early 1980s are still heard in urban China. The street demonstrations of disgruntled students in late 1986 and the massive protests in Tiananmen Square and elsewhere in spring 1989 were, in some respects, foreshadowed in the sometimes bitter speeches and remarks of characters in the films discussed here. Economic reforms were welcomed, these film voices seemed to be saying, but a political renovation of the system should be undertaken as well. It is too early to evaluate the long-term impact of the crushing political and cultural repression carried out in summer 1989. But we do know that the short-lived official campaign against bourgeois liberalization launched in early 1987 did little to discourage filmmakers like Xie Jin or to dampen popular enthusiasm for political reform. Indeed, the spectacular success of Xie Jin's *Hibiscus town* in 1987, when international film critics were focusing their attention on the imaginative but relatively unpopular "new wave" of Fifth Generation filmmakers in China, underscores the profound popular appeal of political melodramas.[25]

But how should the political thought of young and educated urbanites be characterized? The evidence provided by the popular film material highlighted here is far from conclusive, but it suggests answers that would have been doubted by both the most uncritical supporters and the most vehement detractors of the Chinese Communist party in the early 1980s. If these amazingly popular works offer any hints about the political thought of young urbanites in the early post-Mao years, it is that despite their self-pity and alienation they basically accepted the system and recognized, however grudgingly, the authority of the party and state. The main audience for Xie Jin's films of the early 1980s were people like himself who thought primarily in terms of the reform of the party and state rather than their elimination. The films reflect both a widespread popular disillusionment with the party and a sincere hope that the party will be able to reform itself. These works identified retrogressive forces that had to be eliminated from the party and state, but had little in common with the views advanced by daring anti-Marxist dissident intellectuals who fundamentally opposed the party (and who, before June 1989, enjoyed relatively little support among ordinary urbanites). Films like *The legend of Tianyun Mountain* were depressing, but they usually included depictions of honest and loyal cadres who were dedicated to the reform of the system.

This tentative conclusion supports the notion that while the official and the unofficial are not identical, they should not be thought of as being opposite. On the one hand, elements of popular political thought, filtered through films and many other media, helped fuel the political reform movement at the elite level by exerting a measure of political pressure. On the other hand, it seems clear that the contours of mainstream popular political discourse in the years immediately following the death of Mao were still being shaped to a significant degree by the political categories and even the language set forward by the party in the early 1950s. Ordinary urbanites (who had very few options in the realm of politics) in all likelihood did not think much about alternatives to the socialist system when they demanded justice and accountability in the early 1980s. The enormously popular serious films of this period reveal the glaring gap between official political thought and the political thought of educated young urbanites, but they also suggest that the bitter complaints of many such urbanites had little in common with outright dissidence or the barely audible calls for organized opposition to the single-party state.

NOTES

1. For a solid study of cinema and elite politics after 1949 see Paul Clark, *Chinese Cinema* (Cambridge: Cambridge University Press, 1988).

2. Margaret Pearson, "Film in China: The Domestic System and Foreign Imports," U.S. Department of State Cultural Background Series, U.S. Embassy, Beijing, January 21, 1982, pp. 1–2.

3. In a 1983 survey of young Shanghainese, "serious films that reflect social issues" were preferred by more respondents than any other type of film, including foreign films. Among those surveyed, it was university students (93 percent), Youth League cadres (94.3 percent), and young industrial workers (83.2 percent) who showed the greatest degree of interest in serious films.

Type of film	Percentage who acknowledged liking this type of film
Serious	77
Foreign	75.8
Adventure	41.5
Light comedy	33.8
Revolutionary history	32.6
Adaptations of great fiction	30.4
Hong Kong films	27.7
Ancient history costume dramas	13.1

Military stories 8.1
Operas 5.9

See Xu Miaoting, "Shanghai shiqu qingnian dianying quwei qianxi," *Qingnian yanjiu*, no. 1, 1983, pp. 40–46. There is also evidence that working-class youth had a strong interest in political melodramas in the early 1980s (see *Dangdai Zhongguo qingnian gongren de xianzhuang* [Beijing: Gongren chuban she, 1984], pp. 37–39). I want to thank Stanley Rosen for bringing these publications to my attention.

4. Shao Mujun, "Chinese Film Amidst the Tide of Reform," *East-West Film Journal*, vol. 1, no. 1 (December 1986), p. 63.

5. Ding Qiao, "Chinese Cinema Today," *China Reconstructs*, August 1982, p. 62.

6. *Tianyun shan chuanqi*, Xie Jin, dir., Shanghai: Shanghai Film Studio, 1980; *Bei aiqing yiwang de jaioluo*, Li Yalin and Zhang Ji, dirs., Chengdu: Emei Film Studio, 1981; *Ren dao zhong nian*, Wang Qimin and Sun Yu, dirs., Changchun: Changchun Film Studio, 1982.

7. Lu Yanzhou's *Tianyun shan chuanqi* was published in the inaugural issue of Qingming, no. 1 (July 1979).

8. "Tan yingpian *Tianyun shan chuanqi*," *Wenyi bao*, no. 2, 1981. Also see Cai Chuan and Lin Guang, "Dui yi bu hao yingpian de piping," *Zuopin yu zhengming*, May 1981, pp. 49–51, for a friendly view.

9. *Dazhong dianying*, June 1981, pp. 2–5.

10. See *Dazhong dianying*, September 1980, for an example of prerelease publicity.

11. Pearson, "Film in China," pp. 1, 4.

12. Yuan Kang and Xiao Chuanwen, "Yi bu weifan zhenshi de yingpian: ping *Tianyun shan chuanqi*," *Wenyi bao*, no. 4, 1982.

13. Zhang Xian, "Bei aiqing yiwang de jiaoluo," *Shanghai wenxue*, January 1980.

14. Paul Fonoroff, "Perhaps the Beginning of a Vital Film Culture," *Far Eastern Economic Review*, May 3, 1984, p. 54.

15. See Liu Nan, "Yingpian *Bei aiqing yiwang de jiaoluo* de zheng lun," *Zuopin yu zhengming*, June 1982, pp. 60–61, for a summary of the March 1982 debate.

16. *Zhongguo dianying nianjian, 1983* (Beijing: Zhongguo dianying chuban she, 1984), pp. 159–166.

17. Chen Rong, "Ren dao zhong nian," *Shouhou*, no. 1, 1980.

18. Qi Ming, "Intellectuals' Problems Spotlighted by New Film," *China Daily*, March 9, 1983.

19. *Dazhong dianying*, June 1983, pp. 2, 8.

20. *Asia Week*, January 16, 1981, p. 32.

21. "Resolution on Certain Questions in the History of Our Party Since the Founding of the People's Republic of China," *Beijing Review*, no. 27 (July 6, 1981).

22. Zhou Yongping, "Da xuesheng yu dianying," *Dangdai wenyi sichao*, no. 3, 1984, pp. 22–32.

23. Commenting on the ability of films like *A corner forgotten by love* to "arouse emotions of sorrow and joy" (*bei xi qinggan ciji*), a young respondent surveyed in Shanghai in 1983 said, "I felt as though my heart had been dealt a heavy blow and I too opened the gates and let my tears flow freely, feeling grief and indignation about the way feudalism, backwardness and poverty doomed these characters to a tragic fate." See Xu, "Shanghai shiqu qingnian dianying quwei qianxi," p. 44.

24. See Shao, "The Tide of Reform," pp. 65, 67.

25. *Furong zhen*, Xie Jin, dir., Shanghai: Shanghai Film Studio, 1987. *Hibiscus town* was voted best picture of 1987 in both the Hundred Flowers and Jinji Film Award competitions.

PART TWO

Marriage and the Family

4

"How Come You Aren't Divorced Yet?"

ZHANG XINXIN

Writer Zhang Xinxin, a Chinese Studs Terkel, once explained her passion for interviewing ordinary people about everyday life by saying that a few hours of talk "gives you a story, a whole human life, a sculpture that needs no reworking." Her discussion of divorce in post-Mao China demolishes the picture of marital harmony that has pervaded the pages of official publications since 1949. Marital unhappiness, separation, and divorce are now epidemic among young, well-educated urbanites. The problem is especially acute among those between the ages of thirty and forty, Zhang's own generation. The older generation, those between forty and fifty, generally put up with unhappy marriages rather than file for divorce, while the younger generation, those between twenty and thirty, too young to have experienced the exhilarations and disillusionments of the Cultural Revolution, are more casual and experimental in their approaches to sex and marriage. Zhang's generation is caught in the middle. The men she interviews are eager to dissolve their unhappy marriages, but they are not casual about love. Although men and women of her generation engage in extramarital sex, many do so as part of a quest to find the ideal mate and the perfect modern marriage. To the bewilderment of the court, many of those who file suit cite Western-style "incompatibility" as the grounds for divorce.

—Eds.

"How come you aren't divorced yet?" I laughed aloud when I heard these words, and so did the friend who relayed them to me. They had been

---

Translated by Perry Link and Richard Madsen.

spoken by a college classmate of ours, and they represented him perfectly: shallow and cocky, yet somehow charming. He hadn't changed a bit! He was in Beijing now, doing a film about a soccer match that allegedly took place between foreigners and Chinese around the end of the Qing dynasty. He had invited some classmates to dinner, and naturally took the occasion to boast about his recent achievements as a film director. He also referred casually, and with great self-satisfaction, to his divorce "war." He went on to praise the beauty of his new wife, and then, with childlike sincerity, sprang that laughable question.

Unhappily, but unknown to him, each of the other three classmates at the table was secretly facing the problem of divorce.

Before the 1980s, divorce in China was a rarity—indeed, a scandal. In those days I had a childhood friend who decided to break off with her fiancé after getting a marriage license but before the wedding. Since the two sides agreed, they did not need a court; they just went to the office of the neighborhood committee and asked for a "divorce certificate." The people in the office warned the girl with brutal honesty: "When you got your marriage license it was as good as hopping into bed; who's going to want you now?" And sure enough, people in the neighborhood and at her workplace began pointing and gossiping. Nobody could understand. Why would an honest-looking girl, with everything going her way—a good job, a fiancé in international relations at prestigious Beijing University—ruin it all by getting a divorce? People jumped to the conclusion that she must have some hidden flaw that the boy had discovered only after their marriage license allowed them to become sex partners.

The girl was forced to bow her head under the burden of the rumors in the neighborhood and at work. She was surrounded by a prison of evil tongues until she was finally able to marry someone else, a young man who also happened to be a childhood friend of mine. His home had been ruined during the Cultural Revolution when his parents were held in solitary confinement for "political investigation." He had taken to the streets and become a hooligan, and was himself arrested in a knifing incident. After the Cultural Revolution, in acknowledgment of the unfair political treatment his family had received, the government reduced his sentence by ten years and released him. Out of prison, he, too, was beset by rumors, and found a companion in misery in my "divorced" classmate.

After the marriage, I asked my friend why she had left her first fiancé.

> Because we had nothing to say to each other. It may sound strange, but when I was in the construction corps in Inner Mongolia, I couldn't wait to get back to the city. I thought life in Mongolia was living hell. It took me eight years of struggling—begging all the influential people I knew—to get transferred back to the city. But then when I got back, I suddenly felt, "So what?" Soon I began to miss my life in the countryside. I remembered what it was like when I first volunteered and was sent out to Yan'an. We were so enthusiastic then . . . whenever we got Chairman Mao's latest instructions over the radio, we'd begin—even if it was midnight—to celebrate and bang on our

washbasins. The peasants didn't respond as we did. Their caves stayed entirely dark and quiet. We used to wonder how they could live in the cradle of the revolution and still be so "backward." Although a few in our group were already plotting how to return to the city, most of us decided to volunteer for Inner Mongolia. Eventually we got some sense knocked into us, of course.

But for whatever reason, I kept thinking about those days. I couldn't help telling my boyfriend about them. He was completely bored, however. He said I talked about nothing but trifles. He had never gone to the countryside. He had gotten a factory job in the city, and eventually made it to college. All he talked about were his ideas about various books, which excited him but left me cold.

Our problem was that we already had the marriage license. He was firmly against the idea of getting a "divorce," even though we weren't formally married and I was still a virgin. He knew as well as I that we had nothing in common, but was concerned about his reputation. He got so mad he would bang his head against the wall. I felt sorry for him, and more than once thought about just sticking it out for the sake of form. But it really was true we had nothing to say to each other. . . .

In the late 1970s having nothing to say to each other would never be sufficient grounds for divorce. But by the late 1980s it had become a possibility. So had many other reasons. My girlfriend got divorced again in the 1980s, and then remarried again. She is no feminist activist, or even an intellectual in the habit of reflecting upon the course of life. She is just a busy clerk in the labor union office of a small factory.

According to statistics from China's Department of Civil Administration, 17.8 Chinese per thousand were married in 1987, and only 1.1 per thousand were divorced. But these are average rates, which obviously vary a great deal across different sectors of China's populace. For example, I have twenty college classmates, and fully half of them were facing either divorce or remarriage in early 1988. Among Beijing people in my age group (thirty to forty years), including both my acquaintances and the people I interviewed for my book *Chinese profiles (Beijing ren)*, virtually everyone seemed to have encountered the divorce question.

These facts are, I have to say, intriguing to me. I can't help noticing how often it happens that, in conversations about people of my generation, someone casually says, "By the way, they're getting divorced." What's even more intriguing is the response of people in other generations—as young as twenty-five and as old as sixty—when I ask their views on this divorce trend. I get such strong and personal reactions! Nearly everyone admits that they, too, have had problems of this sort. People of other generations seem to differ only in the kinds of solutions they seek. Still, for the purposes of this chapter, I will concentrate on the group I know best: urban intellectuals aged thirty to forty.

A new player who has been responsible for many a broken home has appeared on the Chinese marriage scene. Divorce courts have begun to refer to "a third party stepping in," and the term *third party* (*disanzhe*) has become common in the language of daily life. According to government pronouncements, the third party problem has resulted from the opening to the West and the influx of the sexual revolution into China. Some provinces and cities, in order to protect the stability of the family institution, have suggested that the work units of offending third parties punish them by placing administrative warnings into their personnel files. Third parties have also become key characters in the social commentary of Chinese writers and artists. They have appeared abundantly, and by no means always negatively, in fiction, film, and television soap operas. It has even been suggested that the outsider in certain triangular relationships is rightly viewed as one of the married couple—for example, in the provocative film title *Who is the third party?* In any case, most of the people who have discussed their divorces with me have had a third party involved.

Guo Yanjun, male, thirty-five years old, had gone to a May Seventh Cadre School with his father. Later he joined the army and was subjected to the hostility that soldiers from the country direct against those from the city. After that he worked in a prosecutor's office, where he handled some fairly important political, economic, and criminal cases. When I interviewed him he was a political columnist for a major journal that dealt with legal affairs. Along the way he had helped many people win their divorce cases. The most famous and mysterious of these was the divorce of a certain vice minister, who afterward married a well-known writer. The vice minister's attorney, a woman named Zhou Naxin, had been virtually unknown before the case, and afterward was already famous enough to be head of the Beijing Legal Affairs Institute.

Guo filed his own divorce case in 1986. Three years earlier it would have been impossible for him to do so, because of the pervasive public view that women need to be protected. Even when men *could* file for divorce in the late 1980s, it remained difficult. He said to me in the interview,

> God, am I miserable! What would I do without my motorcycle? First I have to take my girlfriend home from her office, then I have to deliver my son from nursery school to my wife's place, then I have to come back to my office—
> which doubles as my bedroom. My wife gets hysterical every time she sees me. This isn't my imagination—she herself says it. She says everything's fine until I show up. And my office gives me the creeps. It's in a building that also houses a top-security factory, so the whole building is locked and guarded from 8 P.M. to 8 A.M. All night there's nobody in there except me and the rats.

I asked why he didn't live with his girlfriend, since she had a place of her own.

> Impossible. She'd love it, but I work with the law and know what the consequences would be. My wife still doesn't know a thing about my girlfriend, and has no idea how she could win this lawsuit against me. But if I use my connections in court, I can win it in no time. I can even make use of the woman judge's lover. . . . But I couldn't bring myself to be that unfair to my wife. So you see, sometimes I can help others win lawsuits, but can't help myself.

In this big city, where human relationships have grown ever more cold and businesslike, where the pressure for survival grows with the population density, and where dust storms and monotonous gray buildings continue to spring up, Guo can be counted a modern hero. I got to know him, ironically, through a number of cases in which third party involvement was being used as a basis for divorce. Many people have asked me about divorce strategy, including how to play the third party card. I in turn have consulted Guo, who asks his friends in the district courts. Until Guo cleared them up, certain questions always puzzled me: How could all these people, who have good educations and plenty of life experience, be so ignorant of divorce procedures? And why don't they bring their questions to a court or a lawyer's office, instead of relying on hearsay and the back door? "Every lawyer has an endless pile of cases," Guo explained. "And the courts don't even have time for the formal lawsuits. Consultations? Out of the question!"

One incident, however, made me realize that extraordinary psychological pressures can impinge when a person tries to handle a marriage crisis through private channels. Zhu Weiguo, male, thirty-two years of age, was the son of a peasant from the hills of Fujian. After graduating from college with a major in literature, he went to work as a literary editor for a major press. In 1987 he edited a book called *Stories of Chinese women in love and marriage.* Since I have been described by some literary critics as a writer who represents the thinking of young women intellectuals, Zhu sought me out and we began to exchange letters on the topic of modern women's literature. In one of these letters he writes:

> To return from fiction to real life, let me recount some observations I have made of my wife. I have always said she is a model of traditional feminine virtues. Rice, vegetables, oil, and firewood have dominated her life. Whenever we run short on something, she is out the door with her basket to re-stock us. Recently I tried to do the shopping myself—running here for oil, there for rice, getting in one line after another—and came to appreciate the burden that she has quietly been carrying. I realized that I myself would not be able to deal with this tiresome daily cycle. While sincerely praising her virtues on the one hand, I was living off them on the other. After all, she has a college degree, too, and can hardly be unaware of the condition she's in. Now I have a new appreciation for the idea of two people handling daily life together. . . .

Not long thereafter, he was standing before me explaining what happened next.

> My leader at work called me in. My wife was besieging him with telephone calls—as many as six or seven a day—asking where I was living. My leader didn't know the answer, and was baffled by the incessant questioning. I didn't feel like explaining to him—or to any leader. The most I felt like saying was that she had a boyfriend, and that it was only after her affair that I got myself a new girlfriend. The problem is that she doesn't want to break up any more. I can't see why, though, because her new man's a good catch. He's a Chinese American working in Beijing, and he could get her out of the country. . . .

At this point he betrayed a smile that made me begin to suspect his story. I told him that I wondered whether all of the praise for his wife in his earlier letters had not been just a coverup for his own guilt feelings, and whether he now wasn't just trying to cover real problems with a pretty story. He admitted as much. Then I smiled, teasing him that his readers would never guess the true motivations for his editing a book on women in love and marriage. When he, too, smiled, I went farther and told him straightforwardly that I doubted the depiction he had given of his wife's new boyfriend.

He confessed to beautifying the facts. The description of the man upon second telling was this: merely a lonely businessman residing in Beijing, ready to spend a little money and seeking the spice of a casual affair. He was also such a coward that a single strange phone call—which he assumed to be from the husband of his paramour—had frightened him into moving his office from one hotel to another. Until this happened, my friend the husband had, ironically, been wanting to meet the businessman so that the two could discuss and provide jointly for the future of the wife.

Our conversation then turned to the question of whether the third party problem, and the troubling stories it generated, could be attributed ultimately to undue pressures in the lives of Chinese intellectuals.

Actually, my wife and I have *always* fought. It's never been over money, though we're hardly rich. She's a very caring person, really. Last fall, at the mid-autumn festival, she prepared a little banquet for me. I had been out to see some writers and just packed off some manuscripts to press, and I came home exhausted. All I wanted was to lie down. This made her angry. She said I didn't care a whit for her feelings, that I hadn't even glanced at her banquet table. It was true that I hadn't noticed it until she flew into a rage. Still, I told her I *had* seen it, and I *was* grateful, but I was just too tired. So why are we constantly fighting? I have to admit she's right. If men and women are equal, women shouldn't have to tolerate things like this.

She later told me she had pursued her affair purely for revenge. When she said she was going on a business trip, actually she was going on a vacation with him. At the height of some of our arguments, she would even describe what went on between them. Then she would say that, of course, *spiritually* I was superior to that fellow, and that she still basically loved me, not him. Now, I admit that I am only the son of a peasant. But I couldn't forget the things she described to me, so I asked for a divorce.

Our child was not an issue. We both loved her, and custody with either parent was fine. We decided to have her stay with me, for fear that she might become an obstacle to remarriage for my wife. We were always careful not to fight in front of her. Whenever she appeared, we would stop fighting and put on smiles, so that there would be no harm done to her psychologically.

But deep down, my heart was bleeding, as if being ripped apart. Our situation was nothing like the one in that story of yours,[1] where the couple manage to develop new feelings for each other as divorce draws near. Even as they are finishing the paperwork, they go out for lunch together. Not us! We were still yelling and screaming at each other right in front of the clerk who was doing our papers. Neither of us would give in. But deep inside I was almost paralyzed. Part of me wanted to beg her to come home and never mention the word "divorce" again. We had been classmates ever since junior high school, and it had all been quite natural that we should get together and eventually marry. All these years we had shared a kind of closeness that I didn't fully appreciate until I was in the divorce office. I was fighting with her and wanting her to stay at the same time.

A hitch in our paperwork suddenly seemed to bring reprieve. We were both supposed to hand in our marriage certificates, but mine was unacceptable because our little daughter had torn it badly. The office would not accept the shreds and insisted on a replacement certificate from my work unit before they would give their approval.

But my reprieve was short-lived, because I had to move out the next day anyway. My wife said that if I didn't move out, she would. She spent that very night in a crummy little hotel across the street, so the next day I just had to leave. I went to stay with a friend.

I couldn't go home to visit her, because when I did she would hold me and start weeping, asking for forgiveness. What could I do? My mind was changing every minute—no, a thousand times a minute! If I were to marry my new girlfriend, I knew that my wife, like the female characters in *Rebecca* and *Wuthering Heights*, would still not let go of me.

All this chaos and confusion brought me a pervasive sense of defeat. I thought of myself as a peasant boy fresh from college who had suddenly been thrown into the baffling fast-lane life of the big city. . . .

This last remark struck me as particularly significant. It reminded me of another account of divorce I had listened to.

I think my failure in marriage was due to several factors. First, we didn't have our own place when we got married. We had to share an apartment with her brother's family. Eventually we wangled our way into a place she had borrowed, but I was never able to give her the sense of security she needed. Second, I was just out of college and had gone to work for a drama troupe, but right then we didn't have a play to work on. To her I must have seemed idle and somewhat weak. Third, I was taking care of every detail of her life. I even packed her things when she traveled to other cities. When she asked for a divorce, she said, "I've always let you manage everything. Why don't you listen to me just this once?" Fourth . . .

We had both paused to chuckle at the point-by-point logic of his self-analysis.

Wu Xiaojiang, male, thirty-five years old, was my college classmate. In college he was never much of an actor (people would laugh when he got up onstage, even before he opened his mouth), but later he became an outstanding theater director. In 1987 he was working on Eugene O'Neill's *Long Day's Journey into Night;* he also likes Tennessee Williams and Edward Albee. He is talented and highly civilized. In college I always had the impression he was low-key and level-headed.

He married the year we graduated, and I met his wife at the wedding. She seemed to me a mild woman—the kind who knows when to stop, and who can keep emotional surges under control. They seemed to be a couple made in heaven. Yet she asked for a divorce after only two years. His account:

> I moved to the theater house, into a little room without heat. I begged her to postpone the divorce until I could get a housing assignment from the theater troupe. But she thought I was saying this just to hold onto her, and to keep her from marrying her new boyfriend. Actually I felt fine being alone. All I had to do was learn how to light a stove. What's so hard about that?
>
> Later I came to realize that those two years of marriage had been the most exhausting and irritating years of my life—even in comparison to the years I had spent laboring in the Heilongjiang countryside. I wondered if I was just more suited to bachelorhood. Maybe my past had molded me to be this way. During nine years in the countryside, one year working in the city, and five years of college, I had always lived in a dorm. Whatever the environment, or the kinds of people in it, I would always find a little nest for myself, a nest that gave me my own psychological space. When I had to share the nest with somebody, maybe it just got too close and I couldn't adjust.

His self-analysis was calm and sincere. It seemed a pity that all the caring he gave to his friends could not be given to a woman who lived even closer to him.

All the people in these examples are from the generation that went through the Cultural Revolution and spent time in the countryside. All their marriages followed a period during which they had been at loose ends—fending for themselves as they labored in the countryside, returned to the cities, and then looked for work or sought entry to college. No matter how calm they were as they told their stories or did their self-analyses, they all felt uneasy inside. They felt strong desires to settle down—but in life had found this goal elusive. Their problems with third parties and fourth parties were clearly connected with their psychological longings for security and for order in their lives. As they told me their stories, they sometimes would hide some of the truth, or fail to face reality. Yet their introspection was sincere, and it covered the period not only of their broken marriages, but of all that had happened to them.

Even though I believe we must try to clarify the dramatic phenomenon of the third party by analyzing growth, change, and questions about one's own behavior, I also believe we should discuss sex when we discuss divorce.

Hu Zhongming's story surprised me. In 1987, he told me about his dating experience. I discovered that this thirty-four-year-old man, who happens to be very handsome and, as an outstanding sound engineer, is always working with celebrities, was totally ignorant about sex. A year later, when he came to talk again, he told me he had taken out a marriage certificate. He and his girlfriend had worked hard and had made 10,000 yuan. They renovated their whole apartment and bought all the furniture. In spite of all this, he still felt he had failed because of his ignorance about sex.

This woman he is with now is doubtless very experienced sexually. This time in our conversation, he confessed that he was too shy to tell me last time "something I realized is very important. I have to talk about it. I took

a plane to see my woman friend because she had rented a small room in a
boat, which I thought was sort of like a cheap brothel out of a novel—the
time, the scene. I can't really tell you anything more of what I said. Do
you understand me?" I said I thought I did.

> I told her right away, "I'm scared." That's exactly what I said; that was the
> first time I had ever seen a woman like that. Afterwards she said, "I hate you."
> All she said was, "I hate you." After that, in the one year of our contact,
> sometimes she would suddenly say, "I hate you." I remember it very well. I
> would write to her, call her, but she seldom wrote back. Maybe it wouldn't
> have had to be like that if we could have exchanged some thoughts. The
> problem was our different cultural backgrounds. She was a star, with everybody
> waiting on her. The time that I flew to see her, I only stayed for one day. I
> couldn't stand it. I felt that that room in the boat had nothing to do with me.
> Before I left, I wrote down in detail in which drawers she could find her
> socks, her underwear, and her dresses. At that time I was still cleaning up after
> her. I also saw some very passionate letters she wrote to others. She used to
> say that I was the most dependable man she had ever met. For the past year, I
> have read a lot, especially books about sexual hygiene, which we had bought
> together in preparation for marriage. I think she's patiently waiting for me,
> trying to open me up. .... I dare not tell my male friends about this. They
> would definitely laugh at me. What did I do wrong? Should I have jumped at
> the opportunity? I have many opportunities to become involved now that I live
> in hotels very often. There are always hotel attendants who come to chat with
> me. I don't know if they are giving me hints when they start telling me how
> bad their boyfriends are, but I feel I'm getting on that track. Am I being too
> conservative? Am I supposed to go for it now?

I especially noted one sentence he uttered, that he "read a lot," including
bestsellers in pop psychology such as Dale Carnegie's *How to Win Friends
and Influence People,* millions of which were printed in both original and
abridged forms. All my interviewees read newly translated if not new books.
The reporter, Guo, in the course of his divorce, read Niccolo Machiavelli's
The Prince over and over again, and he thinks it changed his whole outlook
on life. Zhu, the one who edited the love and marriage novels, is reading
Nietzsche and Milan Kundera. I find this interesting.

The life path of our generation is continually defined and suggested by
such books and theories. However, we cannot accept Nietzsche's philosophy
without reservation. Instead, we are like Nietzsche himself, constantly longing
to love and to be loved. Our generation, the one born in the 1950s, received
an orthodox education in the 1960s and was raised to be idealistic. From
the 1960s to the 1980s, our idealism went through a tremendous and
fundamental shock and is challenged today by reality. Nevertheless, our
generation is still idealistic, although conservative.

When Hu was analyzing his attitude toward sex, he couldn't get anything
straight, but he accurately used the word *conservative,* a word widely used
to define our generation's attitude toward sex. Although practically everyone
I talked with had either a girlfriend or new opportunities to have one, their
choice of a sex partner was always in direct conflict with their moral standards.

Guo once frankly and painfully analyzed his relationship with his girlfriend. He felt that she was asking too much from him and didn't understand him at all. He couldn't get rid of her, because they were trapped in a vicious circle: The more emotional turmoil the relationship caused, the prouder they were of persevering in it. People between forty and fifty are faced with the same crisis in marriage and the number of actual divorces for this age group is much larger than the official statistics. Yet, there is an obvious distinction between the two groups. Members of the older generation, in their idealism, choose to put up with the pain of a bad relationship. On the other hand, the age group between twenty and thirty, it seems to our generation, mostly demands uncommitted, casual sex.

To further understand such relationships, we must realize that people like Hu, who find out about sex through books but have no real experience, are neither rare nor abnormal. This is a common example of the consequences of a "good" childhood education. Guo comes from a soldier's family and went to boarding school when he was small. Although allegedly 90 percent of young boys know how to masturbate, Guo says he knew nothing about it. "It may sound stupid, but I was taught by my girlfriend who's younger than me." A confining education makes one beautify or simply ignore bad situations. Although things are improving, the hangups of this generation still persist. Could this be a kind of virtue? When Hu was in the countryside, he once saw a man copulating with an animal. Yet, he still frowns at the sexual revolution of the younger generation.

To get an accurate picture of why marriages end up in divorce, we must also know how women feel. Although it is easier for me to talk to women than to men, I have, unfortunately, not yet talked to any of the above men's wives. While I was listening to the men, I thought to myself, if I could talk to the women, I might be able to clear up some of the misunderstandings between them. This was probably naive. In fact, my relationship with the men has eliminated any possible relationship with the women. The more I tried to invite the women over, the more they shrank away from me. Maybe the positive comments of their husbands about me made them think that I'm the men's ally.

The only one who did want to talk to me was Zhu, the editor's wife. She works in the marriage consultation group in the Chinese Women's Association, which has contact with millions of bitter women every day. According to her husband,

> If you see how patient, kind, systematic, and efficient she can be when she's with those miserable women, you'd never imagine she'd get hysterical with me. The funny part is that her rich boyfriend is giving her the money to set up a few hotlines for a women's crisis intervention center in Beijing—it's very difficult to install a telephone line here, you know. Women in distress will be able to use these hotlines to get psychological advice.

She asked her husband to tell me that she wanted to talk with me about contemporary women's problems in marriage. Her husband told her that I was very busy. Thus, the line between us was cut off even before it was established.

Still, there are a lot of women who knock on my door. Besides helping some of them with the technical problems of divorce, I also counsel many divorced women who belong to my age group and now are raising their children on their own. I listen to all of their similar yet different stories.

One woman gets up at 6:00 every morning. She has to wash up and cook for herself and her daughter before her daughter gets up at 6:15. At 6:30 they leave the house together. The woman puts her daughter on the back of her bicycle and takes her to the bus stop, through side streets so the traffic police will not catch her carrying her daughter on the bicycle. Then, after helping her daughter elbow her way onto the bus, the woman pedals alongside the bus to make sure the girl safely reaches school. Only then does she go off to work. The daughter attends an important primary school very far from her home. In order for the mother to enroll her in this school, she had to pull a lot of strings to use her *guanxi* (connections). The problem of attending this school, however, is more complicated than just seeing that the child gets there safely.

Since the school does not cook lunch for the first-graders (because little children get sick easily and the school cannot take the responsibility), the mother, during her own lunch break, has to take her daughter's lunch to school. First she goes to a friend's house nearby to warm the food she prepared the night before and dropped off that morning. Then she has to take the food to school. Luckily, a few parents have started taking turns cooking and delivering the lunches.

In the afternoon the mother naps at her desk for a while, then returns to school to pick up her daughter. Again, she goes through the same routine: elbows her daughter onto the bus, follows the bus on her bicycle, and carries her daughter on the bicycle back home. In the evening, she reads while her daughter practices the piano. After her daughter goes to bed at 8:30, she writes letters under the desk lamp. Each Sunday, she takes her daughter to the piano teacher's place, paying 20 yuan every month for the lessons. Occasionally they go to a movie, a fair, or the amusement park together.

At her divorce, the court decided that her ex-husband must pay 15 yuan a month for child support, but the average expenses for a child like hers in Beijing are about 60 yuan per month. Because she works for the government, she cannot get any kind of premium or subsidy and her monthly salary is merely 120 yuan. Her ex-husband has remarried; once in a while he takes their daughter to his place to spend some time with him. But every time she comes back, the girl asks her mother, "How come I don't have a dad like everybody else?"

This woman's name is Wang Jiu and she's thirty-nine. She used to be a top student at an important girls' high school before the Cultural Revolution.

How should I explain all this to my child? Should I say, "Your dad is bad, he is irresponsible"? I'm the one who brought her up, but one visit with her father ruins everything I have tried to cultivate. Perhaps I should explain to her that her father's already got a new home and a new kid. . . . I don't know what a child thinks of the parent's divorce. Sometimes I try to imagine how my daughter feels. But I can't do it, because I didn't have this kind of experience when I was small.

I thought about my contribution to our marriage (which he ruined), my mistakes within it, and the reasons for its failure. I thought that maybe I had neglected my husband after our daughter was born. He needed a lot of love, but when we had our daughter, most of my love and care shifted to her. His temper grew worse and worse. In retrospect, I see it was a demonstration of his discontent. I let him go and, of course, he left. Sex may also have been a reason for the divorce. At first, everything was ok in the marriage. But later I always found myself too tired after a day's work to engage in sex. Also, the idea of having an abortion if I became pregnant scared me to death. He was horny all the time and he didn't like condoms. So I finally just said the hell with it and gave him whatever he wanted, yet he still left me. I know he felt that life was boring. He complained about everything. Actually, he is both intelligent and talented, but he was too bored to do anything. This is where I differ from him. But I can still understand him.

Everyone examines himself or herself at the time of divorce, but few share their reflections with others.

Let's hear what Guo Yanjun had to say after he returned from the courtroom.

I racked my brains all night last night. I was trying to picture what the judge would look like, the judge who would handle my case and confront me face to face. I tried to imagine what kind of a person he'd be. Maybe the judge would be a woman and, if so, how would she react to a divorce case filed by a man? Actually, I only had to tell the judge the problems between the two of us, because my wife didn't know a thing about the third party. As a matter of fact, it was only a problem between the two of us. The problem was that there didn't seem to be a problem. The two families had compatible social status. We got to know each other through a mutual friend. She was the first girl I had ever kissed and it was also her first time, so I felt I should be responsible for her the rest of my life. Even now, I'm still the only man she's ever had. What if we had more experience in this kind of thing? Not political experiences or general life experiences—we've had enough of those. But, if we'd had more experience in sex, we wouldn't have had this ridiculous tacit agreement. I can't live with my wife any more. But she doesn't even want anything from me. She won't even ask me to buy a box of matches for her, let alone ask for sex. She only asks me to be her husband. That's what life should be, to her. As for where I go, what I do day after day, she doesn't want to know. At first she did ask, but now she doesn't give a damn. She's not even aware of the existence of my girlfriend, doesn't notice that I'm spending most of my time with my girlfriend. She never tries to control me. She might not be aware of this, but the only thing she ever asks me is that I accept things as they are. We kissed, so we married; we married, so we had a baby. Everything happened just as it should have.

It was during my wife's confinement at childbirth that I realized something was wrong. She had asked me to get some soy sauce. I went out and bought it and when I brought it back, at the doorway, I knocked the bottle against the wall. All of a sudden, I felt that our apartment was too crowded, although we had three rooms. I shut myself in the bathroom, slapped my face, then opened the door and started doing everything I was supposed to do: washing diapers, disinfecting the feeding bottle. As time went on, I found that there was less and less discontentment in life, but more and more boredom. So I felt like destroying something.

The way I'm talking to you is just how I was talking to the imaginary judge that night. I was the plaintiff, so I had to explain everything clearly; not only clearly, but also persuasively and touchingly. Can such a plain story touch the listener? Can he or she understand? Perhaps I should sneak in the anecdote about my girlfriend? If the judge was a man, he might sympathize with me. But now I can't even stand my girlfriend, although our sex life is wonderful. She needs me to be with her all the time. She can't understand why I'd want to spend some time with my son or bring him to kindergarten. She suspects that I'm having another affair. She always regards her having sex with me as a sacrifice. Actually, I'm pampering her. If she wants sex, I'll go along with it, if she doesn't, I won't ask her. Even if I forced myself to devote all my time to her, after a few days she would find me boring. Then, at the dinner table or during a conversation, she'd fix her eyes passionately on those socially established and charming forty- to fifty-year-old men. I've told her that I have to establish myself, and she has said she'll wait. But then she will laugh at me and say, "What the hell have you accomplished?" She's right. What can all this amount to: running around interviewing people? I've said, "Let's drop the whole thing. You don't really need a vulgar guy like me." But she won't let go. If a female judge heard all this, I'm sure she'd be disgusted and reject my appeal at once.

Who can really understand that something's gone wrong with my life? While I was waiting in the hallway of the court, I was still wondering what was the matter with me.

Everyone really should go to court once. It's quite an experience, a very funny place. You find all kinds of people there, even strangers, exchanging advice about divorce. There was this woman yelling at the top of her voice in front of everybody, "I'm trying to get into the party. But he, he is an economic criminal! How could I enter the party with such a person!" By my side, a couple was discussing how to divide their property. While I was busy imagining what the judge would look like, their words hit my ear: the "liquified," the "liquified." I couldn't make out what that was, so I strained to hear. The woman said, "How could I have boiled the baby's milk without it? I have to have the liquified." I realized that the liquified was the bottled-gas stove. The man said, "OK, I'll have the color TV then." Again the woman: "Then I'll have the fridge." Now the man's turn: "I want the high-fi." The woman started yelling at him, "How come we're ending up with nothing to look at or listen to? If you have all these pleasant things around you, how could you ever be unhappy!"

Then I went into the courtroom and sat by my wife. Three couples getting a divorce were sitting together. The place was very small. We were all crammed into a corner. My wife and I couldn't help smiling when we looked at each other. As a plaintiff, I had prepared a six-page speech to support my point. She had also filled out seven pages to defend herself. In front of us sat a young boy of about twenty. He started seriously, "I represent the law . . ."

You can't even represent yourself, I said silently to myself. I didn't even have
the desire to open my mouth. Then the young boy came to talk to each of us
again. He acted cool and tried to give me some tips: "In your case, you'd
better revoke the court action, because they'll reject your appeal the first time
anyway. You can refile a case right after the revocation. You save yourself a
month this way." I said, "No, I can take it easy." He looked at me, stupefied.
I know all the tricks, you know. Law is also my profession. I looked at his
young, inexperienced face and realized all of a sudden that I was letting things
follow the conventional way.

The above narrators have all reached the halfway point of their lives. They
feel there is a social reason for their broken marriages. But none of them
choose to lead a single life. Instead, all of them long to settle down and
are searching very hard for a way to do just that. I listened carefully to
everyone and became surprised to find out that their standards kept becoming
lower and lower. Of course, there were some stories of passionate love, but
these affairs usually lasted for only a year. Then the fire burned out and
new complaints popped up.

There was also a returned overseas student, who has a master's degree
in economics. He is a very generous person. He complained to me that he
wanted to break up the materially modernized family he had established.
He said, "Now I want an equal, peaceful, and mediocre partner." In the
courageous action of breaking up his old marriage to set up a new one,
there is an implied contradiction:

> When we were still young, we traveled to various places, tasted all kinds of
> bitterness, went through ups and downs of political campaigns, and saw all
> kinds of ugliness and cruelty. But we were never so lonely as now. When the
> future was full of uncertainties, we clung harder to our other half. It was no
> longer a struggle with the world, nor a confrontation in ideology. It was just a
> peaceful stroll of two people, hand in hand.

Zhu's description of his future partner is full of warm feelings.

> She works as a medical doctor and lives in the suburbs. She comes home by
> the night bus and has to go through a field all by herself. She is older than I
> and not as pretty as my wife. She was married once but her husband walked
> out on her, so she knows how to value a relationship. She is caring, extremely
> caring. She's my wife's girlfriend. When she first came over to visit my wife, I
> scarcely noticed her. I started talking to her when my wife and I began to
> have problems. It all came to me so naturally one day when we were having a
> conversation. I didn't need a woman with a very strong personality. I needed a
> wife like her.

Wu's summary of his search for a wife is very concise and mirrors an
old Chinese saying: "Warm, kind, respectful, frugal, and modest." Guo's
words are very interesting: "If I'm going to marry again, I'll marry a woman
just like the one I married before."

The women's situation is much more complicated than the men's. Equality between men and women has put us into the same lot for survival as men politically, economically, and even physically. Where can women find strong, reliable sexual partners who can protect them? Disappointment among women is common.

As Wang Jiu calmly put it,

It's funny. We meet each other every ten years. I even saw him when he got married. And last time I went abroad for a short visit, the only time I have ever gone abroad, we met again. Ten years had passed by then. I came back but he stayed. I feel it will be quite some time before what he learned can be applied here. His way of thinking is way out of place now. He won't be at home here. We only write to each other. Just like that. The other day I heard a pop song over the radio. Very simple words, very, very simple: "Although we are apart/You are always in my heart."

This generation is still full of idealism. Their longing to settle down and their faith in higher aspirations are hovering in the air side by side, up and down, up and down . . .

NOTES

1. Zhang Xinxin, "Zai tong yi dipingxianshang" [On the same horizon], *Shouhuo* [Harvest], no. 6, 1981.

5

Love and Marriage in North Chinese Peasant Operas

R. DAVID ARKUSH[1]

"I'll wear red at your funeral, you old dog!" Is this the way Chinese daughters talk to their fathers? University of Iowa historian David Arkush was surprised to find that many of the colorful characters who appeared in popular north China peasant operas in the 1920s behaved in ways that contradicted Confucian ethical norms, especially when matters of love and marriage were involved. The emotional relationship between husbands and wives was often portrayed as warmer and closer than relationships between parents and offspring; the separation of lovers or spouses was frequently presented as the source of great personal anxiety; and women often appeared in these operas as competent and resourceful exemplars who were morally superior to men in many respects. Professor Arkush's research suggests that the quality of relations between spouses may be different from the standard picture that stresses the dominant parent-child relationship and affectless marriages. He cautions, however, that it would be wrong to assume that all viewers of these popular operas actually behaved like the characters onstage. Rather, the popularity of the operas reveals an underlying dissatisfaction with conventional codes of behavior and a desire to fantasize about (if not act out) titillating alternatives.

—Eds.

It is striking how much romance, sex, and conjugal love are to be found in the north Chinese village operas available to us. Though romantic themes appear in the high literature and popular culture of various societies at various times, love, particularly that between husband and wife, is not everywhere an important concept. In the medieval European troubadour tradition, for instance, love occurred only outside of marriage, and medieval theologians tended to disapprove of marital love, quoting Saint Jerome: "A man who is too passionately in love with his wife is an adulterer."[2] Lawrence Stone, in his study of the family in early modern England, called love "a product . . . of learned cultural expectations," which he found "became fashionable in the late eighteenth century thanks largely to the spread of novel-reading."[3] The sociologist William Goode, surveying the histories of a number of societies around the world, found that on the whole the "conjugal family," with its "emphasis on emotionality, especially in the relationship of husband and wife," was a product of industrialization.[4]

In particular, we would not expect marital or premarital love to be a prominent notion in a society like that of north China in the early twentieth century. Virtually without exception, marriages were arranged. As late as the late 1930s, a survey of 360 rural marriages in north China, Fujian, and Jiangsu found only one case in which the parents had asked the consent of the young man (and he was not a peasant but a college student). Chinese arranged marriages, in which not even a pretense was made of obtaining the couple's consent, have been deemed unusually authoritarian in comparison to Roman, early English, Russian, Muslim, and Japanese customs.[5] In Chinese villages, marriage was regarded not as an individual but as a family matter, much too important to be left to the whims and emotions of adolescents. Where survival depends on family cooperation, desires like sexual gratification and the thrill of romance may be expected to be subordinated to family goals.

Fei Xiaotong thought there was little warmth between husband and wife in the Chinese peasant family. Some couples hardly spoke to each other, in his observation, nor did the character of their joint economic and social functions require them to do so. The Western "madness" of romantic love, he said, was a luxury that could not be afforded where marriage was too weighty a business to be decided on the basis of emotion. The horizontal relationship between spouses was weaker than the vertical one between parent and child.[6] Others, too, have thought closeness between spouses was discouraged in China because it would threaten the more important parent-child, and especially father-son, ties. From a different perspective, Margery Wolf's theory of the "uterine family," the family bonds important for women, also stresses the importance of the vertical ties of mother and children over horizontal ones between spouses.[7] In short, Chinese marriages were not entered into for love, there was no premarital romance, the conjugal relationship was not particularly valued, and, as one scholar put it long ago, "Romantic love was no part of what husband and wife expected in a marriage."[8]

With this in mind let us look at rural opera. In 1929–1930 in Ding county, Hebei, a large number of local operas (confusingly known in Chinese as *yangge* or rice-planting songs) were written down from oral informants by researchers working under the direction of the sociologists Li Jinghan and Zhang Shiwen of Y. C. James Yen's Mass Education movement. This collection, published soon afterward,[9] has certain advantages for our purposes. The texts are relatively unedited, unlike most other published folk plays, which is clear from the dialect expressions and the scandalous sexual joking and immodest behavior; and they were gathered by modern-minded scholars who wanted to preserve them for study before they died out: "Because we were worried about taking too long, we did a minimum of arranging, but simply recorded them, trying as much as possible to preserve them as they really were and present them naked and unadorned for specialists in folk literature to study."[10] We also know much more about just where the Dingxian plays came from than is the case with most Chinese folklore. We can be sure that these really are rural and not urban works, performed mostly by and for ordinary peasants in villages or rural market towns.[11] Finally, this is a large collection, forty-eight operas (of widely varying length) in over a thousand pages, at least half a million words. It must be a significant part of the operas people heard, which makes it more suitable for analysis than other more haphazard and spotty collections.[12] Examining folk opera may also be particularly appropriate at this time when it is apparently being revived in villages all over China.

The assumption that we can learn something about ordinary people's shared ideas from such operas rests partly on the fact that the operas seem to have been shaped to a considerable extent by ordinary people. Few were written down, we are told. They were performed by troupes of amateurs or semi-professionals, mostly illiterate villagers who learned them orally and performed them during the agricultural slack season when there was relatively little farmwork. Though literary versions can be found for some operas, these are only a small minority and the literary analogues are often quite different from the oral versions.[13] For the most part the operas seem not the creations of individual, literate authors, but rather to have been molded over the years by actors who were basically ordinary villagers responding to what their audiences seemed to like.[14] Qu Junong's judgment does not appear unwarranted—that these operas are "peasant literature" (*nongmin wenxue*), a product of peasant mentality, feelings, imagination, way of life, and so on.[15]

Apart from the matter of authorship, it also seems reasonable to think that operas must have influenced the ideas of ordinary people. There is ample anecdotal testimony to the avidity with which performances were watched—by both men and women—and how important they were in shaping people's ideas.[16] That influence, presumably, is why Chinese officials had been trying to suppress or control them at least since the Song dynasty.[17] In Dingxian, *yangge* operas were put on in most villages and were the favorite entertainment of peasants, male and female, young and old. They provided a rare opportunity for women to leave the home; female relatives from other villages were often invited to come for several days to view performances. People would miss no opportunity to watch operas at New Year's, other festivals, and temple fairs; at other times peasants sang songs from the works. In sum, "their ideas, concepts, and behavior were all influenced by *yangge.*"[18]

LOVE AND MARRIAGE

What do these operas say about love and marriage? In the opera *Lanqiao hui* (The meeting at the blue bridge), a handsome and wealthy student encounters a beautiful eighteen-year-old woman who is married to an ugly fifty-three-old man (ages are Chinese-style *sui*—one is considered one year old at birth and two years old when the next lunar new year arrives). They are mutually attracted, but she is already married. She quotes the proverb, "A good horse does not carry two saddles, and a good woman does not marry two husbands," to which he replies with the saying, "A flower only blooms for a hundred days," meaning she will not be in her prime for long.[19] In an isolated spot they kneel and vow to meet in the middle of the night, then part after exchanging tokens. *Da niao* (Shooting a bird) portrays a young exiled prince who sees a beautiful girl in a garden, which he enters on the pretext of retrieving a bird he shot. They converse, fall in love, and carry out their own wedding ceremony in the garden. He then leaves, promising to return, and she promises not to tell her parents. In *Guanwang miao* (The temple to Lord Guan), a man who had come to Beijing and squandered 3,000 taels in a brothel out of love for a prostitute is reduced to living in a temple in poverty and illness. The prostitute, who returns his love, smuggles him money with which he will take her back home and study for the civil service examinations.

There is a rather free spirit toward conventional sexual morality here, which is much of the reason authorities have tried to suppress folk opera so frequently over the centuries. Not all sexual licentiousness in operas involves romantic love; some of it is just risqué banter or play.[20] Three plays involve the attempted seduction of a future emperor as a way for a woman to get ahead.[21] But even without affection, free love concerns the idea of two people coming together of their own accord, and much of the time affection is involved. As a modern Chinese scholar said of another opera about a young couple in this collection (*Yang Ershe hua yuan*), their love is "frank and daring, a mockery of feudal ethics; the play shows the resistance of laboring people to the feudal marriage system."[22]

This spirit is evident in the involved and amusing plot of *Shuang suo gui* (The two locked chests). Because a girl's fiancé has become impoverished, her father breaks the engagement (by the ruse of announcing that she is dead and staging a mock funeral for her) and quickly has her engaged to another. She still wants to marry the original fiancé, however, and while her parents are out invites him into her bedroom. But the parents return unexpectedly and she hides him in her chest. Then, before he can get away, she and the chest (which contains her dowry) are carried off to the house of the new fiancé for the wedding. There that man's sister opens the chest, discovers the original fiancé inside, recognizes him as someone she had previously been attracted to, and takes him off to *her* bedroom where he ends up in *her* chest. The two girls decide that they both want to marry him, and the three of them run away. They are apprehended and taken to court, where—note the values being encouraged here—the magistrate fines the father for breaking the engagement and the second fiancé for marrying an engaged woman and turns the fines over to the two women, who go off as wives to the first man, presumably to live happily ever after as a ménage à trois.

What is undoubtedly significant is the frequency with which the audiences for these operas saw, and clearly were expected to sympathize with, a couple matching themselves up—whether for marriage or sex—without participation by others and, indeed, often against the will of the older generation. In one play, a woman tells her son how she and her husband had come together: "On Qingming your father visited his family's graves, saw me sitting on a boat, and came on board. He and I felt a desire to marry each other."[23] In fact, in spite of the occasional statement that "marriage is impossible without a go-between,"[24] we find young people not infrequently carrying out their own ritual. The scene from *Da niao* mentioned above, of the young couple in a garden, includes the following passage:

She: I would like to marry you, but fear you will not go along.
He: I am willing, but we lack a go-between.
She: If you are willing and I am willing, what need is there for a go-between?
. . . I break off three flower branches to use as incense.
He: Instead of paper money we burn leaves and flowers.
She: Instead of a food offering, we offer gold dust.
He: I kneel on the ground.
She: Let us compare ages. I am 16.
He: I am 18, two years older. . . .[25]

Note that the initiative in this marriage is hers, as was the case in *Shuang suo gui*, about the man and two women. There the cerermony involved a sort of wedding banquet in the first woman's room; then, when they decided to become a threesome, they went together to a family temple where they knelt to "worship Heaven and Earth" (*bai tiandi*).[26] The significance of this as a wedding or betrothal ritual is explicit in *Cui Guangrui dachai* (Cui Guangrui gathers firewood), in which a wood cutter encounters a fairy, the fourth daughter of the Jade Emperor, who is fated to marry him. He fears she is an evil spirit but she tricks him into saluting, bowing, kneeling, and kowtowing together with her and then announces that they have worshiped Heaven and Earth and are thus now married.[27] In another play, worshiping Heaven and Earth seems to constitute a betrothal ceremony.[28]

Again, these rituals are carried out by the couple themselves, on their own initiative, without the participation or approval of their families. It is, furthermore, a ritual in which man and woman are equal partners; nothing in it symbolizes the subordination of one to the other. This image of free marriage is consistent with a more or less uniformly negative depiction of arranged marriages in the plays. Audiences heard, for instance, about deceitful and greedy matchmakers pairing young girls with old men,[29] being bribed to make an inappropriate match for an ugly girl,[30] or being the cause of a young wife's misery.[31] Or they would hear of a father making a bad match because he was drunk.[32]

Such dramas of free love and do-it-yourself marriages are, of course, fantasies and not portrayals of actual social practice. But fantasies are indicative of people's feelings and attitudes, conscious or unconscious, toward social practices.

SEPARATION ANXIETY

One of the commonest plots in the Dingxian operas centers on an unwelcome and distressing separation, a separation that many times is overcome as the resolution of the opera. In the overwhelming majority the separation is between spouses or between an engaged couple.

The operas about engaged couples are simpler and more apt to be straightforwardly romantic. We have already discussed *Shuang suo gui* in which the girl's father breaks the engagement but in the end the couple marry themselves. In *Xiao huayuan* (A small garden), a girl is literally sick with longing for the return of her fiancé, who had been brought up partly in her family. She counts the days, weeps, says he should marry her now when she is eighteen or nineteen, and has erotic fantasies. He finally arrives, says to himself on seeing her that he has "fallen in love with her" (*aishang ta*), and after he has tested her by pretending to have failed the examinations and become a beggar, they joyfully go upstairs to her bedroom. In *Liu Yulan shang miao* (Liu Yulan visits the temple), an avaricious matchmaker wants to break a girl's engagement in order to arrange a marriage between the girl and a rich old man. The girl remains true to her young and handsome fiancé, however, and runs off to live with him in poverty.

Yang Fulu tou qin (Yang Fulu visits his fiancée's family) and *Yang Ershe hua yuan* (Yang Ershe reduced to begging) are similar operas about impoverished young men who have been robbed by a groom while on a journey. Among other things, the groom takes the young man's betrothal tokens (*ding qin bao*) and uses them to gain acceptance by the fiancée's family, such that when the true fiancé presents himself he is not recognized but beaten and thrown out. He is on the verge of suicide, but eventually all is solved by means of a face-to-face meeting with the fiancée, who is true to him and lends him money with which one way or another he will be able to get things straightened out. In both operas the man and woman swear fidelity to each other; in one she declares she has been yearning for him and bitterly curses her father for breaking the engagement, saying, "I'll wear red at your funeral, you old dog"[33] (so much for the vertical relationship).

More complex than those about threatened engagements are the many operas concerned with the separation of spouses. Some dwell directly on

love between husband and wife, and even those that do not still convey a
sense of the value placed on husband-wife relations. In *Shuang hong da
shangfen* (Two lovers [?] visit a cemetery), the husband had left three months
after his wedding to take the civil service examinations and then taken up
a post as an official. An evil kinsman deceives the wife into thinking him
dead. Going to his family's cemetery on Qingming festival to express her
wifely love (*fuqi enaiqing*), she tells of her loneliness, addressing herself to
him:

> Because you are not at home I use no powder or rouge, nor wear good
> clothes. I dare not live with my natal family for fear people may take advantage
> of me. Daytime is bearable, but the nights are a disaster. The empty bedroom
> seems like a dark cave. There is no one to light the lamp; I light it myself and
> spread out the bedding. Against my warm body the *kang* [brick bed] is as cold
> as a mountain of ice. If I stretch out my legs my "golden lotuses" [bound
> feet] are cold; if I curl them up my feet hurt. There is no one to rub them for
> me. "Happy couples," the proverb says, "find the days too long and the nights
> too short," but for widows one night feels like half a year. Only half asleep I
> dream of my husband returning home; seeing you I reach out—but it is only
> the cold bricks on the edge of the bed. I weep for my husband all the time,
> but there is not a word of encouragement from anyone. I tell myself not to
> cry.[34]

Then he appears and she does not recognize him—it has been twelve years
after all. But after tokens and proofs she finally allows herself to believe
and, needless to say, the reunion is joyful.

Similarly, *Gao Wenju zuo huating* (Gao Wenju sits in the courtyard) is
about a husband who, after taking top honors in the examinations, had been
forced to marry the daughter of a high official, who forged a letter of divorce
to the man's original wife. She falls into poverty, sells herself as a servant,
and is bought by the official's family, who mistreat her. Eventually the couple
reunite (he doesn't recognize her at first), happily confident they will be
able to get the emperor to rectify the situation.[35]

Divorce, which comes up in this last play, occurs not infrequently in the
operas, though it was extremely rare in the rural society that produced
them—the 1929 Dingxian survey found only two cases in 515 families.[36]
A means of dramatizing the pathos of husband-wife separation, divorce in
the operas is generally forced on a husband who is reluctant but too weak
to resist. Usually it is demanded by his mother, and the ethic of filial piety
requires obedience to a parent over all else—a demonstration that the vertical
parent-child relationship is *morally* more compelling than the horizontal tie
between spouses. But all the same, the dramatic thrust of the operas suggests
that *emotionally* the bond between husband and wife is stronger. In *Xiaogu
xian* (The good sister-in-law), for instance, a cruel mother, acting out of
groundless hatred, orders her son to divorce his wife; he is tearful but feels
he must comply. In the end the mother relents after her own daughter, who
is good and sides with the wife, threatens suicide.[37] In *Jiang Shichuang
xiuqi* (Jiang Shichuang divorces his wife), the wife is falsely accused of

stealing goods and putting curses on her mother-in-law, who consequently demands that she be divorced. The husband is reluctant and tries to get relatives to persuade his mother to relent, but in the end has no choice. The wife, rejecting suicide, takes refuge in a Buddhist nunnery.

The demands of vertical relations predominate ethically over the horizontal also in the need to have an heir to carry on the family line, as can be seen in *Wang Mingyue xiuqi* (Wang Mingyue divorces his wife), about a husband who decides he must divorce his childless wife to remarry, in hopes of having children. But here, too, the dramatic emphasis on the tragedy of divorce and the joy at not having to go through with it suggest a different message. After the wife tearfully reminds him how devoted and helpful she has been for so many years, the husband relents; in the end the gods reward him with children, for he has long been a virtuous man. *Erhuan ji* (The story of the earrings) tells of a ne'er-do-well husband who has gambled away his fortune and is forced to sell his wife during a famine (he must keep his son to have an heir). After spending three years with her new, rich husband, though he has treated her well, she believes he has had his money's worth. Getting him and his servant drunk, she escapes back home to a happy reunion with her children and her original husband, who, in spite of having sold and pawned everything else, has kept the earring she left with him as a token.

Separation of husband and wife also comes up in other operas. In two (*Miaojin gui* and *Daoting men*), the man has been killed and the wife abducted by the murderers; resolution occurs when she is able to avenge her husband. *Bai she zhuan* (The white snake) is a version of a widespread folk legend about the love and marriage between a man and a female deity who is allowed to stay on earth only until she has given him a child. The drama centers on their coming together, parting, reunion, and then final, fated separation.

In a few family separation operas, the interest is more in the children than the husband and wife. *Luo qun* (The gauze skirt) shows a wife turned out by her husband after his concubine falsely charges her with adultery (the concubine had hidden a monk's clothes in the wife's room). The husband soon decides he has made an error and tries to get her back, but the separation is not overcome and most of the opera is about the suffering of the children. *An'er song mi* (An'er brings rice) involves a wife who has been driven out by her oppressive mother-in-law and taken refuge in a nunnery, where she is visited by her seven-year-old son. She asks about her husband, explaining her concern with the proverb, "One day as husband and wife [creates] emotional bonds for a hundred" (*Yi ri fuqi, bai ri en*).[38] But the husband's attitude is unclear, and the focus is on the woman's relationship with her son. In *Dinglang xun fu* (Dinglang seeks his father), a man has been framed by an evil official and forced to flee, leaving behind his pregnant wife. He has remarried in the south, where now, twelve years later, the son he has never known comes to find him and be accepted by him. But even the operas focusing on parent-child relationships also involve marital separations, and it is worth noting, too, that such works are much less numerous than those directly suggesting the emotional importance of the husband-wife tie.[39]

The prominence of such stories of separation, which usually include reunion, suggests that this theme vibrated with meaning and dramatic intensity for the audiences who watched the Dingxian operas. The bond between husband and wife must have been emotionally important to them.

THE GOOD WOMEN OF DINGXIAN

A final question that might be asked in considering romance and marital affection is how women were depicted in the operas. Do women seem generally contemptible or are they admirable; are they people for whom men could feel love and respect?

Women are, without any question, in an inferior position in these plays, as in real life. They refer to themselves with a term, *nu jia*, that has overtones of *servant* or *slave*.[40] Women are frequently victimized: beaten, cursed, maltreated, and dominated by men, and also by other women. In many of the operas about husband-wife separation, the woman is an innocent victim, often divorced or driven out, or almost so.[41] Other operas involve a daughter-in-law's abuse at the hands of her mother-in-law.[42]

Women are also victimized outside the family, sometimes violently. *Daoting men* and *Miaojin gui* are about women who are taken captive by their husbands' killers, forced to live for years as the wives of villains. In two others, women tell of having been abducted by robbers while on a journey and then released by a sympathetic robber's mother.[43] We see a widow murdered by an evil monk after he fails to seduce her in *Longbao si jiangxiang*, and a girl robbed while traveling in *Luo qun ji*. Elsewhere, we hear of a slave girl being murdered by an evil official to frame an innocent man.[44] Suicide is committed or attempted or contemplated by a woman in at least eleven of the forty-eight operas, but only twice by a male.[45] This—quite consistent with the actual pattern of suicide by young females in China— is another way in which women are thought of as victims.

Most of these victimized women are not in the least contemptible. They are rather models of virtue worthy of sympathy and admiration. The wife who was driven to a monastery by her cruel mother-in-law refuses to speak ill of her, and instead virtuously asks about her mother-in-law and her husband (*An'er song mi*). The two women whose husbands were killed are praised for not taking the easy way out and immediately committing suicide, but working to see their husbands avenged (*Daoting men; Miaojin gui*). Widows avenge their wronged husbands in *Sha xu* and *Longbao si jiangxiang*, too. The wife whose in-laws had convinced her that her husband was dead nevertheless remains faithful and refuses to remarry (*Shuang hong da shangfen*). Not only victims, but other women as well are frequently moral paragons: the good sister-in-law who gets her mother to abandon an unjust campaign against her brother's wife (*Xiaogu xian*); the second wife who, to the disadvantage of her own child, generously persuades her husband to recognize his son by an earlier marriage (*Dinglang xun fu*); or another second wife who does not follow the natural inclination to favor her own son over her stepson (*Fan tang*). Of course, there are also evil women and good men in the operas, but the image of the woman as moral exemplar is strong and persistent.

Virtuous or evil, the women in these operas are strikingly often stronger than the men. This is particularly true in operas about domestic conflict. In several of the divorce operas the villain is a woman and the husband a nonentity. In *Jiang Shichuang xiuqi*, the husband's mother has been turned against her daughter-in-law by an evil god-daughter (*gannü*); the son weakly protests his mother's order to divorce his wife but soon gives in. In *Xiaogu xian*, the mother orders the divorce but is deterred by her daughter; the husband seems to count for little. The husband seems hardly a factor in *An'er song mi*, which focuses on the wife's uterine family. In *Luo qun ji*, it is a concubine who makes accusations against the wife that lead a weak husband (he soon changes his mind) to expel his wife. Apart from comedies about henpecked husbands (*Ding deng; Ding zhuan*), there are also strong wives and passive husbands in *Liu Xiu zou guo, Yang Wen taofan*, and *Dinglang xun fu*.

Women often seem more competent and resourceful than men, and we see not a few stories in which they bail out bungling men. In *Jie dang* (To borrow and pawn), a young man runs up gambling debts with his schoolmates that must be satisfied without his father finding out. He goes first to a female cousin and then to his fiancée, who lends him her savings and also some of her clothes, which he pawns. He is then arrested on suspicion of having stolen the clothes, and she must rescue him again, coming to court to testify (from behind a screen, out of modesty) and, Cinderella-like, to put on one of the tiny shoes to prove it is hers. She is capable, he a bungler. In *Erhuan ji*, likewise, the husband's uncontrollable weakness for gambling causes the family to be broken up; the wife's enterprise eventually restores it.

We twice see husbands, one an official, consult their wives in *Miaojin gui;* and in *Fan tang* a magistrate, unable to decide a murder case involving his own sons, turns the judge's seat over to his wife, for, as a prime minister's daughter educated in the Five Classics, she is intelligent and perceptive. In *Gao Wenju zuo huating*, we learn that Gao's success in the highest examinations was due to his wife, who had taught him seal characters as well as the Four Books and the Five Classics of Confucian doctrine. The boy in *Luo qun ji* asks his sister for help in reading a note that their mother had written, and in six other operas we find literate women reading or writing; in only one is there an indication of female illiteracy.[46] Two operas show women warriors: in *Yu Taijun guan xing* a woman goes to rescue a brother besieged in battle; *Xue Jinlian ma cheng* is about two female generals (one of whom leaves her ugly husband, indeed, kills him, to marry a handsome enemy for love). Three plays are essentially dialogues between women employers and a male donkey boy or hired hand or repairman.[47]

Perhaps it is part of this vision of women as worthy of respect that the wife or fiancée often comes from a wealthier or socially higher family. She is the daughter of a prime minister or some such lofty person in several operas.[48] Three operas involve engagements where the husband-to-be has become impoverished, and in a fourth he pretends to have become poor.[49] In four cases we see men borrowing money from their fiancées.[50] Three operas depict a different sort of hypergamy: the marriage of an ordinary man with a divine woman.[51] Complementing competent and admirable women are men who are weak and morally inferior. The most frequent example of this is the gambler who has squandered a comfortable family fortune, a pattern that comes up again and again.[52] In a couple of other operas similar kinds of male pleasure-seeking have frittered away the man's or his family's fortune.[53]

Women in these plays, then, are not depicted on an equal level with men. There is no question of their inferior social position and their vulnerability to abuse and victimization. But in spite of that, it would seem, women are consistently shown as more virtuous, more resourceful, and in important ways superior to men. Women may have thus been regarded as worthy of admiration and affection, an idea consonant with love between the sexes. As two of the operas put it in concluding with almost identical final exchanges between husband and wife: "*Wo fu ni, hao laopo,*" "*Wo yi fu le ni le, da hanzi,*" which might be translated, "You have my respect, wife," "You have my respect, too, my man."[54]

*   *   *

What, then, can we conclude from these operas? We must not, of course, assume that people actually behaved like the characters in the dramas. Fiction is fiction, after all, and people do not go to plays to see their own everyday lives. They want rather to escape everyday life in pleasurable fantasies, fantasies that may tell us of their inner yearnings and desires. Regarded as fantasy, these plays reveal a desire for a kind of romantic love and sexual gratification that people's real lives lacked, a desire for free-choice marriage, and a desire for escape from family domination. Perhaps such indulgence in vicarious romance, rather than weakening hierarchical familism, really made it bearable by providing a safe outlet for purely imagined escape. Still, there is evidence here of considerable chafing and resentment—maybe unconscious—against arranged marriages and family authority. Such underlying dissatisfaction would seem consonant with the surprisingly speedy acceptance of marriage reform in twentieth-century China.

In addition these plays suggest the possibility that the quality of relations between spouses in the north Chinese countryside may have been different from what is implied by the picture of dominant parent-child relations and loveless marriages. This possibility is raised partly by the work of a recent French historian, Martine Segalen, who, with sensitivity and wide learning, has offered the view that among nineteenth-century French peasants marriage may not have been, as has commonly been maintained, a relationship of absolute authority of the husband over the wife, but rather a cooperative relationship in which the woman had considerable autonomy and control over the household, and in which there may well have been love, tenderness, and affection between spouses. Segalen's argument rests partly on folklore, which suggests that love and sexuality were present in peasant life ("Peasant society was imbued with a permanent sexuality"), and partly on the nature of farmwork then, which was a joint effort involving a high degree of cooperation between husband and wife.[55] Closer to the time and place we are concerned with, Martin Yang had the impression from his childhood in rural Shandong, during the 1920s and 1930s, that a young wife would "respond with great warmth" to her husband and he would be apt to "express his romantic ideals and reveal his love" to her, and that a couple "often achieve a genuine affection for each other after a brief period of living together" and "usually become much attached to one another."[56]

Folklore cannot definitely tell us the emotional content of marriages in the peasant household. But it can tell us about mentality, and whether the vocabulary and the concepts for marital love, tenderness, and affection existed. The Dingxian plays indicate that although villagers may not have married for love, nevertheless the ideas of romantic love and conjugal affection were part of the consciousness of those who watched such operas, and part of the vocabulary of concepts with which they thought about family relationships and relations between the sexes.

NOTES

1. I am grateful for helpful comments—some, I fear, raised thornier problems than I have been able to solve—from Paul Pickowicz and other participants in the Conference on Popular Thought in Contemporary China, and from Susan Nelson, Margery Wolf, Andrew Nathan, and Edward Friedman. An abbreviated version of this chapter was presented at the Fairbank Center at Harvard University, and I also received constructive criticism from a number of scholars there.

2. Jean-Louis Flandrin, "Sex in Married Life in the Early Middle Ages: The Church's Teaching and Behavioural Reality," in *Western Sexuality*, ed. P. Ariès and A. Béjin (Oxford: Blackwell, 1985), p. 122.

3. Lawrence Stone, *The Family, Sex and Marriage in England 1500–1800*, abr. ed. (New York: Harper Torchbooks, 1979), p. 191.

4. William J. Goode, *World Revolution and Family Patterns* (New York: Free Press, 1963), p. 14ff. Angela K. Leung, in a recent article on love in Yuan dynasty drama, found half of the dramas to be licentious, "glorifying physical and premarital love," which she says shows that Confucian morality had not yet thoroughly penetrated the common people ("L'amour en China: Relations et pratiques sociales aux XIIIe et XIVe siècles," *Archives de sciences sociales des religions*, no. 56, 1983, pp. 59–76).

5. Olga Lang, *Chinese Family and Society* (New Haven: Yale University Press, 1946), p. 123, nn. 35, 36.

6. Fei Xiaoton, *Shengyu zhidu* [The institution for reproduction] (Shanghai: Shangwu, 1947), pp. 55–65; Fei Xiaotong, *Xiangtu Zhongguo* [Rural China] (Shanghai: Guancha, 1948), pp. 42–50.

7. Margery Wolf, *Women and the Family in Rural Taiwan* (Stanford: Stanford University Press, 1972).

8. Marion Levy, *Family Revolution in Modern China* (Cambridge: Harvard University Press, 1949), p. 177.

9. Li Jinghan and Zhang Shiwen, *Dingxian yangge xuan* [A selection of operas from Dingxian] (Mass Education Movement, 1933; reprint, 4 vols., Minzu congshu #38–41, Taibei: Orient Cultural Service, 1971).

10. Ibid., p. iii.

11. The ways in which these works differ from city operas are discussed in Chao Wei-pang, "Yang-ko: The Rural Theatre in Ting-hsien, Hopei," *Folklore Studies*, vol. 3, no. 1 (1944), pp. 17–38. See also Li Jinghan, *Dingxian shehui gaikuang diaocha* [Survey of social conditions in Dingxian] (Beiping: Mass Education Movement, 1933), pp. 336–340; and Sidney D. Gamble, *Ting Hsien: A North China Rural Community* (Stanford: Stanford University Press, 1954), pp. 329–335.

12. The availability of English translations in Sidney D. Gamble, ed., *Chinese Village Plays from the Ting Hsien Region* (Amsterdam: Philo Press, 1970) is also a convenience, though the translations, done by a number of different hands, are unfortunately too uneven to be relied on. The Dingxian operas have been surprisingly little studied, apart from one Ph.D. dissertation (Judith Johns Johnson, "A Critical Study of the 'Ting-hsien Yang-ko Hsuan,'" Florida State University, 1978).

13. *Guo Ju mai zi* is a story from the Song *Ershisi xiao*, twenty-four exemplars of filial piety; *Zuo lou sha xi* is after chapter 20 (in the 70-chapter version) of *Shui hu zhuan;* there are high opera (*daxi*) versions of *Xue Jinlian ma cheng, Guanwang miao, Zuo lou sha xi, Zhuang Zhou shan fen,* and *Bai she zhuan.* A much larger number have other folk versions; variations of *Jie didi, Xiaogu xian,* and *Wang Xiao'er ganjiao,* among others, can be found spread over several provinces. To give one example of the folk character of even those with literary sources, the Dingxian *Guo Ju* opera, rather than stressing the sacrifice of the child to save the grandmother, emphasizes the attempt to borrow from a better-off kinsman and this kinsman's reprehensible attitude of contempt for the poor.

14. The notion of local shaping is supported by Eberhard's finding in Taiwan concerning the "great difference between . . . two performances [of the same play] by the same troupe on two consecutive days" (Wolfram Eberhard, "Thoughts About Chinese Folk Theatre Performances," *Oriens Extremus*, vol. 28, no. 1 [1981], p. 2).

15. Li and Zhang, *Dingxian yangge xuan*, foreword.

16. Of Shandong around the turn of the century, an English official on the spot wrote, "The drama (such as it is) provides the most popular of all forms of amusement among the agricultural class" (Reginald F. Johnston, *Lion and Dragon in Northern China* [New York: Dutton, 1910], p. 130). An American missionary reported, also from Shandong at around the same time, "When a village gives a theatrical representation, it must count on being visited, during the continuance of the same, by every man, woman and child, who is related to any inhabitant of the village and who can possibly be present" (Arthur H. Smith, *Village Life in China* [reprint, Boston: Little, Brown, 1970], p. 44). Barbara Ward, speaking of Hong Kong, considered that "what the Chinese theatre disseminated was the major part of what ordinary people . . . knew about the vast complex of Chinese culture and values—both orthodox and heterodox" ("Regional Operas and Their Audiences: Evidence from Hong Kong," in *Popular Culture in Late Imperial China*, ed. Andrew Nathan, David Johnson, and Evelyn Rawski [Berkeley and Los Angeles: University of California Press, 1985], p. 187). In Taiwan, Wolfram Eberhard's finding that temple oracle slips contained references to theater showed the influence of theater and the familiarity of the common folk with some 750 dramas ("Orakel und Theater in China," *Asiatische Studien*, no. 18/19, 1965, pp. 11–30). More recently, Edward Friedman has written,

on the basis of fieldwork in Hebei, "Villagers often describe [opera fairs] as the happiest moments in their lives ("Maoism and the Liberation of the Poor: Review Article," *World Politics*, no. 39, 1987, pp. 408–428).

17. Tan Daxian, *Zhongguo minjian xiju yanjiu* [A study of Chinese folk theater] (Hong Kong: Shangwu, 1981), pp. 17–22.

18. Li and Zhang, *Dingxian yangge xuan*, pp. ii–iii.

19. This proverb is also used in two other operas by an eighteen- or nineteen-year-old girl wishing her fiancé would marry her soon (*Xiao huayuan*, p. 181; *Jie dang*, p. 120), and in another by a mother urging a match on her daughter (*Liu Yulan shang miao*, p. 413). The Dingxian survey found in 1929 that the most popular ages for marriage for women were sixteen, seventeen, and eighteen (Li, *Dingxian shehui gaikuang diaocha*, p. 144). All ages here are Chinese *sui*; Western equivalents would be about a year less.

20. See, for example, *Wang Xiao'er ganjiao; Ju gang; Zhao Meirong diaoxiao;* and *Jin zhuan ji*. Even at its least romantic, though, the depiction of sex in these plays is nothing like that in the thirteenth-century French tales described by White, in which vulgar language and grotesque imagery depict sex as a tool for dominance, revenge, defiance, and humiliation in a cynical world of scarcity, social struggle, and male-female competitiveness (Sarah Melhado White, "Sexual Language and Human Conflict in Old French Fabliaux," *Comparative Studies in Society and History*, no. 24, 1982, pp. 185–210).

21. *Zhu Hongwu fangniu; Liu Xiu zou guo; Bai cao po*.

22. Li Yuenan, *Minjian xiqu geyao sanlun* [Essays on folk opera and songs] (Shanghai: Shanghai chuban gongsi, 1954), pp. 64–65.

23. *Bai she zhuan*, p. 1048.

24. *Liu Yulan shang miao*, p. 372; *Shuang hong da shangfen*, p. 459.

25. *Da niao*, p. 39.

26. *Shuang suo gui*, pp. 75, 95.

27. *Cui Guangrui dachai*, pp. 859–860.

28. *Bai she zhuan*, p. 977. In Dingxian in the late 1920s, wedding ceremonies included the groom twice "kowtowing three times to the tablet of the god of Heaven and Earth" and the bride also worshiping *tiandi shen* (Li, *Dingxian shehui gaikuang diaocha*, p. 381). For more detailed descriptions of the ritual from the 1940s, see *Chūgoko nōson kankō chōsa* [Survey of rural Chinese customs] (Tokyo: Iwanami, 1953–1958), 5, pp. 127–128 (northeastern Hebei); and Paul Serruys, "Les Ceremonies du mariage: Usages populaires et textes dialectaux du sud de la préfecture de Ta-t'oung (Chansi)," *Folklore Studies*, vol. 3, no. 1 (1944), pp. 136–140.

29. *Liu Yulan shang miao; Shuang suo gui*, p. 72; and perhaps *Lan qiao hui*.

30. *Jie nü diaoxiao*.

31. *Si quan*.

32. *Jinniu si; Ding deng*.

33. *Yang Ershe hua yuan*, pp. 32–33.

34. *Shang hong da shangfen*, pp. 461–462.

35. The basic plot here is an old one in Chinese drama, but versions differ significantly. The Peking opera *Zha mei an*, for instance, lacks the theme of marital love that is so strong in the peasant *Gao Wenju zuo huating*. In the former, the husband willingly marries into a high family (the emperor's sister) after winning top honors in the examination, and then refuses to recognize his first wife when she shows up, instead hiring someone to kill her.

36. Gamble, *Ting Hsien*, pp. 38–39.

37. This is quite different from the "new" *yangge* of the same name translated in Ellen Judd, "New Yangee: The Case of *A Worthy Sister-in-Law*," *CHINOPERL Papers*, no. 10, 1981, pp. 167–186.

38. *An'er song mi*, p. 261. This significant expression is also used in *Bai she zhuan*, p. 1033.

39. *Zhuang Zhou shan fen* (Zhuang Zhou and fanning the grave), rather atypical of the Dingxian operas, involves a different kind of marital separation. The Daoist philosopher discovers a woman (the goddess Guanyin in disguise) fanning a grave, who explains that she had promised her late husband not to remarry before his grave was dry. Zhuang decides to test his own wife, who has sworn she would never remarry were he to die; three days after he pretends to die she is ready to jump into bed with a handsome young man. Widows not remarrying was a Confucian value not much observed in rural Dingxian (Gamble, *Ting Hsien*, p. 37). Possibly we can also see an indication of the importance of the marital bond in the emphasis on a wife's love and fidelity here.

40. This is the kind of term that was regularly edited out of folklore published after 1949.

41. *Xiaogu xian; Jiang Shichuang xiuqi; Luo qun ji; An'er song mi; Shuang hong da shangfen; Gao Wenju zuo huating; Wang Mingyue xiuqi;* and *Erhuan ji.* In most of these, the villain is the mother-in-law or another family woman.

42. *Si quan; Banbudao qingke;* in *Liu Yulan shang miao* it is the stepmother; in *Bian lü*, a comedy, this situation is reversed and the daughter-in-law beats the mother-in-law.

43. *Bai cao po* and *Gao Wenju zuo huating.*

44. *Dinglang xun fu.* In *Zuo lou sha xi*, a woman is beaten and killed by the man she lives with, but in this opera the woman is depicted as scheming and unsympathetic, not an innocent victim. *Zuo lou sha xi* is an episode from the *Shui hu zhuan* and is in various ways quite uncharacteristic of the Dingxian plays. Even here, though, the focus is on the (pseudo-) husband-wife relationship.

45. Women commit or contemplate suicide in *Miaojin gui; Zhao Meirong diaoxiao; Longbao si jiangxiang; Shuang suo gui; Si quan; Jiang Shichuang xiuqi; Xiaogu xian; Liu Yulan shang miao; Jie dang; Daoting men;* and *Zuo lou sha xi*—though the attempt in this last seems humorous. Men attempt suicide in *Yang Ershe hua yuan* and *Yang fulu tou qin.* Suicide predominantly by women, and in particular young women, is quite consistent with the impressive statistics analyzed in Margery Wolf, "Women and Suicide in China," in *Women and Chinese Society*, ed. M. Wolf and R. Witke (Stanford: Stanford University Press, 1975), as well as with the findings in Andrew C. K. Hsieh and Jonathan D. Spence, "Suicide and the Family in Pre-Modern Chinese Society," in *Normal and Abnormal Behavior in Chinese Culture*, ed. Arthur Kleinman and Tsung-yi Lin (Dordrecht: D. Reidel, 1980); and Wolfram Eberhard, *Guilt and Sin in Traditional China* (Berkeley and Los Angeles: University of California Press, 1967).

46. Literate women are found in *Yang Ershe hua yuan; Longbao si jiangxiang; Xiaogu xian; Daoting men; Erhuan ji;* and *Jin zhuan ji*—this last is a fragment of the famous Liang Shanbo-Zhu Yingtai story about a girl who, disguised as a boy, goes to school. A woman is depicted as unable to read in *Miaojin gui.* In *Shuang hong da shangfen* a woman says she must bring a legal accusation orally as there is no one to write it for her, but presumably she is to be understood only as unversed in legal forms, for later in the play she is able to read the four characters on a jade belt.

47. *Wang Xiao'er ganjiao; Wu Dasa zuohuo; Wu Dasa zuohuo;* and *Ju gang. Daoting men* puts a magistrate's wife together with a *yamen* underling.

48. *Daoting men; Fan tang; Gao Wenju zuo huating;* and *Dinglang xun fu*—the second wife in these last two.

49. *Shuang suo gui; Yang fulu tou qin;* and *Yang Ershe hua yuan.* The husband pretends in *Xiao hua yuan.*

50. *Jie dang; Yang fulu tou qin; Yang Ershe hua yuan;* and *Guanwang miao.*

51. *Bai she zhuan; Cui Guangrui dachai;* and *Fan tang.*

52. *Erhuan ji; Jie dang; Ding deng; Wang Xiao'er ganjiao;* and *Yang fulu tou qin.*

53. *Guanwang miao,* the story of a scholar and a prostitute; *Yang Wen taofan,* in which the man says he wasted his inheritance on food, drink, and pleasure.

54. *Ding deng; Yang Wen taofan.*

55. Martine Segalen, *Love and Power in the Peasant Family: Rural France in the Nineteenth Century* (Chicago: University of Chicago Press, 1983). The quoted passage is from p. 131.

56. Martin C. Yang, *Chinese Village: Taitou, Shantung Province* (New York: Columbia University Press, 1945), pp. 54–55.

6

My Mother's House

DEBORAH DAVIS

*While conducting interviews with middle-aged women in their
Shanghai homes, Yale sociologist Deborah Davis paid special attention to
the ways in which the homes were furnished and decorated. She began to
think about the use of interior space as a manifestation of the way people
identify the boundaries between private and public domains in post-Mao
society. Not only were political paintings not displayed, homes (including
those of party members) were normally devoid of all connections to state,
party, and workplace. The failures of Maoist mobilization spawned mass
disillusionment with state orthodoxy and encouraged a flourish of
popular culture that explicitly rejects state intervention in private space.
Household members may not be able to articulate the social and political
meaning of family decisions about the use of space, but Professor Davis
argues that these decisions reflect moral priorities that define private
values and preferences. The new vocabulary of private interest, she finds,
is the traditional one of family loyalties, especially female-centered
loyalties, that animate popular resistance to state power. The kinship-
centered morality and female voices that determine the use of interior
space deny party ideology the power to define the context of private lives.*

—Eds.

It was unseasonably hot, and a steady drizzle increased everyone's dis-
comfort as the bus crept through the outer boulevards of Zhabei district.
Acres of rubble stretched out along the rail lines; a billboard promised a
future vista of modern cement estates set along tree-lined streets, but the
immediate reality was a horizon crowded with two-storied timber and plaster
cottages, crumbling in a morass of mud. Turning toward the central city,
we gazed out at the sooty, streaked balconies of a newly completed highrise

that mutely testified to the meagerness of even the best new housing. Suddenly my companion became animated. "Here," she pointed, "Here is my mother's house (*wo muqin de jia*). See that stall? See that alley, that is where I lived until I was married. My primary school was just around that corner. There's the place where we got our rice. Next time, I'll take you to visit. Next time, I want you to see my mother's house."

*   *   *

In June 1987, I had no time to accept the invitation, but I did not forget it. In fact, I found the phrase "my mother's house" (*wo muqin de jia*) had particular resonance. This woman of thirty had been born and raised in Shanghai, had been married nearly five years, and held a position of some authority in her work unit. Yet she spoke with such emotional intensity about her *mother's* house that I wondered if perhaps her father had died when she was very young, or if her mother was a recent widow in need of special attention from her children. Later I learned that her father was alive and had always been an active member of the family. The phrase "my mother's house," however, continued to fascinate me. I had noticed other Shanghai men and women use it and, as I was leaving for the airport, I finally asked two of my hosts—a woman of sixty with two unmarried sons and a woman of thirty-eight who lived with her husband and daughter— whether it was common for young adults whose fathers were alive to refer to their natal homes as "my mother's house." In particular I wanted to know whether the phrase was just a modern version of *liang jia*, a traditional phrase women used to refer to their natal homes after marriage. The older woman replied that the phrase was widely used, and that although it might sometimes function as a modern form of *liang jia* it also meant more, and had different meanings. For example, both unmarried and married children would use it, men as well as women. Her younger colleague agreed, and offered as proof the custom among her friends to designate Sunday as the conventional time to visit their mother's house.

European and U.S. researchers have often observed housing arrangements and home interiors as a key locus for creation and expression of popular culture. In particular, homes offer a venue for exploring subjective but potent loyalties that never enter the published record but nevertheless directly shape how people think and behave.[1] In general, anthropologists examine housing and home interiors to trace connections between the home and the symbolic structure of the resident's larger community, while sociologists and historians have been more apt to look at domestic space as an expression of status aspirations or a response to cultural subordination and domination. In this chapter the latter tradition guides my inquiry. Like Mihaly Csikszentmihalyi and Eugene Rochberg-Halton, who observed living-room furnishings in Chicago, I have assumed that the material objects within a home identify not just individual tastes but also primary loyalties that connect the people in that household to one another and to others outside that home. Purchase, display, and discussion of household objects therefore can reveal much about the content and power of social ties.[2]

In addition, because domestic space shows outsiders ways in which people value social relationships that may be invisible in the workplace or in commercial transactions, home interiors may articulate differences between public and private responsibilities more vividly than self-conscious questioning that requires the respondent to verbalize distinctions for which he or she has no words. It is commonplace to talk about how subordinate groups resist the dominant culture by turning the language or status symbols of their superiors to their own use; in the case of Shanghai homes, we have some of the most direct and tangible evidence of resistance to state intervention.

Like Lizbeth Cohen, who studied home interiors of immigrant workers in New England towns at the turn of the century, I believe studies of domestic space may be particularly important to understanding the cultural repertoire of people whose housing choices are especially restricted. When families must accept whatever housing is tolerable and they have no choices regarding the exteriors, the neighbors, or the physical structure, interior displays and purchases for use exclusively in the home are very likely to highlight the values that define where the obligations and restrictions of the workplace end and those of the individual and the family begin.[3]

The connection between the cultural values embodied in a home and the practice of modern Shanghai residents who name their natal home "my mother's house" is also well established in the literature on popular culture.[4] In the case of contemporary urban China, the female bias has particular significance because traditionally China has had a consistent patriarchal organization of kinship rituals and household arrangements. Marriage did not signal the creation of a new household, but the expansion of the male-defined family. A woman was married into the family to provide sons and grandsons. She kept her own father's name, and if she failed to have sons she was replaced by someone who could. If she was widowed and later remarried, her children stayed with their father's kin and she had no ritual or legal tie to them. Every home had an ancestral altar devoted to worship of patrilineal kin; females at best could be venerated as someone's mother.

But after four decades of collectivization, industrialization, and active assault on patrilineal ancestor worship, the Chinese Communist party (CCP) leaders have radically altered the physical and ritual ground on which urban families maintain a household. As early as the mid-1950s the CCP had succeeded in popularizing the economic and social conditions that redefined the modal household as the self-contained residence of a nuclear family in which females and their children were the majority of members. With production moved entirely outside of the living quarters and the networks of male kin that sustained peasant men and their agnates no longer central to either work or leisure, urban family life revolved around the world of a married couple and their children rather than the ritual needs of an extended patrilineal family. Thus the seemingly simple phrase, "my mother's house" captures a primary strand of contemporary urban culture that distinguishes it from that of the rural areas and also from its own precommunist past. A more detailed description of the layouts and furnishings of the homes I visited in June and July 1987 will illustrate concretely how the interior of the mother's house sheds light on one dimension of urban popular culture.[5]

THE SETTING

The Shanghai homes I visited in 1987 were all in an administratively created neighborhood on the western boundary of the city proper. Before 1949, the district was home to a few textile mills and scattered clusters of artisan workshops but most of the land was used by truck farmers. After the liberation in 1949, the municipal government aggressively developed the area, building many large factories and creating new "villages" (*xin cun*) to house the expanded workforce. Nevertheless, as late as 1980 the area continued to be seen as a distant, fringe neighborhood and only the frenzy of post–Cultural Revolution construction created a physical continuity with the city to the north of Suzhou Creek.[6]

The exact location of my survey was 12 six-story blocks that flank the main traffic artery leading out to the suburbs. Because of the placement of a police station, a pre-existing pumping station, and a bend in the road, the buildings do not completely conform to the usual residential grid. Nevertheless, the initial impression is one of uniformity and utilitarian design. Each block is exactly the same height and has the same dimensions; the only variation is that some first-floor units are used for offices or warehouses rather than living quarters. Every floor of every building reserved as residential space has 12 apartments. Each apartment has two rooms, but not every apartment is the same size. Half are large flats with 27 square meters, and half smaller ones of 24 square meters. In comparison to national averages, these homes are small and crowded,[7] but when compared to the general situation in Shanghai—where the housing shortage is especially intense—they are average in size, and above average in quality of construction.[8] Housing estates of this design fill the outskirts of every Chinese city from Guiyang in the south to Harbin in the north. The exterior provides no clue to the region of the country or the social class or status of the residents. Yet to the women in my Shanghai survey, these blocks represented a major improvement over their previous housing, and they have invested heavily in making the sterile, uniform rooms into their very personal homes.

CROSSING A THRESHOLD

In this Shanghai "village" each building has three entrances; each entryway is on the north side so that every family gets a balcony with southern exposure. Immediately inside the entrance a broad cement staircase leads to the second floor, hugging the north wall. During my visits, most hallways had been swept clean of household refuse and personal possessions, and the overall impression was of a neat institution. However, if the respondent lived on the top floor or my visit departed from the prearranged schedule, the halls more closely resembled those I had seen on more informal occasions in other Chinese cities: Bicycles were chained to the railings, dusty bamboo couches hung from nails high on the wall, scraps of building materials were thrown into corners, and, as usual, the overhead lamp sockets were empty. However, once beyond the securely bolted doors and over the threshold, I entered a tidy, private refuge. If I had gone at night the distinction would have been even more striking, as entry would have brought me from the nearly pitch black of the stairwell into the warm lights of the home.

Although each block has two differently sized apartments, the layout of interior space is virtually identical. From the outside hallway one steps into a narrow corridor. At one end of this corridor is a poured-cement sink around which a gas burner, cooking utensils, and pantry cupboard create a kitchen; at the other is an enclosed toilet. Leading off this interior hall— one door slightly to the left, the other toward the right—are two inner rooms. In ground-floor apartments one can enter a small backyard through a door in one of the inner rooms. The yard is walled, and most residents had jerry-built a third room or storage shed to take advantage of the extra space. On the upper stories, a door from one inner room leads onto a balcony that either provides space for plants and laundry or, in some cases, functions as a sleeping porch. Unlike traditional Chinese apartments, where inner space was subdivided by movable wooden partitions that allowed for frequent expansion and rearrangements (in response to changes in household membership), rooms in these new Shanghai apartments are permanently defined by thick walls of concrete, and families must arrange themselves and their possessions to accommodate designs dictated by the city architects and construction teams.

The uniform floor plan was echoed by similarity of furnishings. In almost every house a large double bed occupied the corner of each room, a mirrored wardrobe and a chest of drawers (usually a matching set) were against the wall opposite the entryway, and a couch faced the wardrobe. A small square table with four chairs was pushed up under the window. In addition, many of these families owned the three most highly sought-after home appliances of the post-Mao consumer revolution: washing machines, televisions, and refrigerators. The washers, small portable models that agitate and spin-dry four kilos of wet wash, usually stood near the kitchen sink or outside the lavatory door. Refrigerators were often in the larger of the two inner rooms, but if the refrigerator belonged to a married child it was kept near his or her bed, even when not set aside for that couple's exclusive use. Virtually every home had a television, and in apartments with a young married child there were often two sets; in one case there were three.

In commenting on the similar arrangement of the furniture in the apartments, several respondents noted that the layout of the rooms eliminated any alternate placement. Yet despite the severe restrictions of rigid cement walls and limited floor space, there was one uniformity so impractical that it requires interpretation. In every home I visited, a large double bed occupied one-third to one-quarter of the "living room." In most homes the bed was pushed into a corner, but in several it was positioned in the middle of the room, as if in an advertisement for a bedroom suite. A heavy velour or satiny bedspread clearly prevented the bed from being used as a work area or couch, and forced a great deal of family activity to the periphery of the room. My tentative reading of this impractical arrangement, which is absent in Hong Kong—where bunk beds prevail—and Japan—where beds are hidden away except at night—parallels that offered by Cohen in her discussion of featherbeds and flounces in the homes of New England immigrant factory workers.[9] For these Shanghai families, like the Slavic and Italian peasants who emigrated to the United States, the large double bed is a central symbolic expression of economic success and adult status, and for women it symbolizes their primary loyalties as wives and mothers. Thus, the large bed is a nonverbal statement about the roles that women fill through marriage and childbirth, which also define exclusive (and sexual) obligations distinct from those of the workplace and politics.

DECORATIONS AND SMALL DISPLAYS

In contrast to the uniform exteriors and the similar placement of basic furnishings, the decorations and small displays of the Shanghai apartments were varied, and often unique. In the rooms of couples who had been married in the past three years, wedding presents still tied with red bows and red slipcovers and bedspreads suffused the room with a pinkish glow. Whenever possible, the wedding gifts—tea sets, wine cups, cosmetic creams, wine, and instant coffee—were placed on or in front of a mirrored surface to magnify the bounty and brightness. Rooms of older couples had more worn furniture and less color, but they were not bare. Pictures crowded the bureaus, lamps had decorated shades, and a small rock garden or bonsai tree stood on a table or shelf. By contrast, the rooms of young adults who had not yet married were extremely spartan.

One particular room made a lasting impression. It was in the home of a widow who was still practicing as a senior doctor in a district hospital. She lived with two sons aged eighteen and twenty-two, the younger a cook, the elder a plumber. The interview took place in the young men's bedroom. Two old, metal hospital beds were arranged in a right angle. To accommodate this arrangement the bed against the outer wall had been raised on scraps of wood, so that the head of one bed could fit over the foot of the other. Both beds were covered with worn army blankets. To decorate the room, the younger brother had pasted magazine photos of planes, flowers, and cats on the wall over his pillow; the older brother had used a post card of a jet, a photo of a larger plane, and a small plastic model of a motorcycle. On a rickety wicker bookcase there was a collection of old high school textbooks, a plastic model plane, and a tiny metal crane, its painted surface scratched and dull.

INTERSECTION OF PRIVATE AND
PUBLIC OBLIGATIONS

In the current era of intellectual ferment, religious revival, and economic decentralization, the national leadership, which in the past arrogantly denounced and cruelly excised any view of society that did not accord with that of the party-state, finds itself groping for a new logic and ideology, as well as for new institutional arrangements that will grant private interests a modicum of legitimacy but still permit the state to control society. To date, they have settled for a compromise that grants limited autonomy to certain spheres of life on the condition that they don't threaten the primacy of the party-state. Religious belief seems to be treated in this way; fashion and art have also benefited from these efforts to reduce government censorship.

In the area of family life, however, there is a profound contradiction. Under the Deng Xiaoping leadership, the CCP has relaxed efforts to control family rituals such as those connected with betrothal, marriage, and death. They also have increased the supply and choice of home furnishings, thereby giving urban residents new opportunities to invest their time and energy into the private realms of consumption and leisure. Simultaneously, however, the government has implemented—and enforced—the most extreme family planning program in history, thus inserting state surveillance more deeply into the center of family life than at any time since 1949. This chapter cannot adequately deal with this vast subject, but it needs to be at least briefly noted because it bears directly on the meaning Shanghai residents—especially women, as mothers—give to their homes and bedrooms.

State efforts to dictate the universal one-child family have created enormous tensions in Chinese society, dramatically pitting the desires of individual families against the officially defined needs of the state. In the countryside, families actively resist; in the cities, and particularly in Shanghai where the campaign has been successful, the population generally supports the limitation because they personally have paid a high price for the pro-fertility policies of the 1950s, in terms of job and housing shortages. Nevertheless, the requirement that only a few exceptional families be permitted a second child arouses deep ambivalence among individuals, who feel that their own family life has been severely curtailed. Perhaps, in the extreme care with which young couples prepare their bridal suites and the heavy wedding expenditures by the parental generation, we are witnessing efforts to compensate for the inability to have large families through massive outlays on the establishment of each new family.[10]

Domestic efforts to commemorate the past reflect another intersection of public and private priorities. In the 1950s, and in the early years of the Cultural Revolution, the CCP leadership denounced most of China's traditional cultural practices as feudal and reactionary. After 1949, Chinese leaders used the exigencies of military mobilizations or metaphors of military combat to justify a public morality of self-sacrifice and denigrate particularistic, or familistic, codes of honor. In the 1950s, the immediate threat to national integrity imposed by the Korean War and the bravery and honesty of the new government inspired the vast majority of urban residents to voluntarily (even enthusiastically) comply with government attacks on Confucian or familistic morality as feudal and antisocialist. With fresh memories of the corruption and cruelty of the Guomindang (Nationalist party) and the heroism and honesty of the People's Liberation Army (PLA), many urban residents sincerely supported the new government's censorship of old traditions and its emphasis on a militaristic culture and ideology. Citizens chose simple wedding ceremonies and rejected elaborate funerals. The government denounced arranged marriages, which made marriage a familial, parental investment, and the young urban residents—the respondents in my 1987 survey—seem to have fully supported greater independence and a more secularized family life. For many, the superiority of a proletarian culture forged in the civil war was unimpeachable.

By the 1980s, however, many had grown disillusioned with the state's rather limited cultural repertoire. The political and economic decentralization sponsored by the post-Mao reforms permitted thousands of communities and millions of families the physical and moral space in which to express and preserve memories not of the state's design. Within this context of rediscovering a personal past and redefining private interests, *my mother's house* serves as a template for articulating one dimension of contemporary urban culture. In a mother's home the vocabulary of private interest is the traditional one of family loyalty and obligation. It is also fundamentally a female voice. The furnishings reflect the primacy of marriage as the threshold to adulthood, and the birth of children (now only one child) marks the boundaries around a new family. This family, in which both parents and child are bound by multiple ties of interdependence, may often be patrilocal in form, but matrifocal in content.[11]

Home interiors also indicate how one segment of Shanghai's population defines the boundaries of their private past. It is first and foremost the past of a nuclear family, often as clearly traced out through female as through male lines of kinship. With the exception of one rather bizarre silk painting that depicted Stalin greeting Lenin as the latter stepped off a small skiff onto an empty marshland, none of the apartments had any decorations with explicit political content. A few respondents had hung their certificate of glorious retirement, a mass-produced document, whose upper border includes the national flag, that can be purchased in most bookstores. But in general the homes were devoid of all connection to the state, the party, or the workplace, and the most common decorations were pictures of parents and children displayed in the respondent's bedroom/parlor. These were glossy color photos from the recent past, usually a group photo at a wedding, birthday, or a Chinese New Year's feast. Everyone wore their finest clothes and the women often had elaborate hair styles and wore make-up. There were almost no black-and-white photos from the 1950s or 1960s; indeed, there seemed to be almost no evidence of the family's existence before they had moved to this apartment. There was, however, one important exception, an exception that again reveals the strong maternal influence over domestic space in urban China.

In several apartments the only framed pictures were large black-and-white portraits of gaunt, elderly men and women. Some were photographs of the husband's parents, but just as often they were a picture of the respondent's mother taken soon before her death.[12] In the apartments of the best educated there were scrolls of calligraphy, usually done by the husband, and in those of the better traveled there were pictures of Chinese landscapes. But the primary decorations were family photos and furniture the couple had brought with them from their parents' homes or their own bridal chambers. Thus the past that shaped these rooms was the past of a nuclear family, which by its inward gaze and kinship-centered morality denies government and party ideology the power to define the content of private lives.

ALLOCATION OF SPACE

Before 1949, the Chinese government did not systematically control migrations from rural to urban areas or between cities. As a result, my respondents had moved in and out of Shanghai according to economic incentives and individual preference. Most had spent at least a portion of their youth outside Shanghai in the villages and small towns of either Jiangsu or Zhejiang province. Jobs in textile mills or marriage to a clerk or small peddler brought them to the city; afterward, they became permanent residents. In the first four or five years after Liberation, they changed addresses easily. Some built new houses, others rented rooms or doubled up with family members who had extra space in an attic or storeroom, and a minority moved into new municipal housing estates.

The introduction of a nationwide system of household registration (*hu kou*) in 1955, which distinguished between rural citizens who were required to grow their own grain and urban citizens who were entitled to purchase state grain rations, abruptly reduced mobility. Changes of address required prior approval of Public Security cadres, and all changes in household composition, even for temporary visitors, had to be reported to the local police. After 1979, grain rationing became less restrictive, and millions of rural residents were permitted to move temporarily to work in large and small cities. Yet the household registration system and bureaucratic controls still dictate the size and composition of most Shanghai households.

For example, most new housing is allocated through work units, not as a result of individual purchases and sales. There are city and district plans for building and assigning new housing, and families who wish to move must register, qualify—and wait—before they can relocate. Frequently two years elapse between the time the family receives permission to move and the actual moving day. To guarantee that no family will use this time to gain two homes, housing authorities use the household registration system to make sure that the people to whom they have allocated a new apartment remain as one not two households. To accomplish this they immobilize household membership by "freezing" every member's *hu kou* as soon as the family has been promised space in a new building. During this interval, even if alternate space is found, individuals legally cannot move because their *hu kou* has been frozen. In one instance, a respondent described the situation of a colleague and his wife, who had been forced to move back in with his parents, married brother, sister-in-law, and niece after the rent on two rooms he leased from a suburban peasant trebled. Unable to meet this expense, the couple was forced to sell all their wedding furniture in order to squeeze back into the house of the husband's parents, with whom they and their son were still legally registered. Even when his work unit was willing to allocate them an apartment on the basis of hardship, they were unable to move because "his *hu kou* was frozen at the home of his parents."

In another case, a middle-aged daughter-in-law waxed eloquent over the goodness of her mother-in-law, whose primary concern throughout a painful terminal illness had been to survive long enough to bequeath her family an additional 5 or 6 square meters of living space. Their home had been slated for demolition and they were waiting for a new apartment. If the mother-in-law was a member of the household when the new apartment was allocated, they would be a family of seven rather than six, and therefore entitled to two large rooms with a separate kitchen and toilet. As a family of six they would qualify for a smaller apartment and be required to share a toilet. As the elderly woman began to fail, she often lapsed into semiconsciousness. But each time she rallied her first question was, "Have we gotten our new apartment?" According to her daughter-in-law, she died several hours after they had received official notification of the relocation to this housing project.[13]

In terms of overt criticism of the household registration system, or explanations of how *hu kou* determines job and marriage strategies, respondents were articulate and self-aware. However, there were other aspects that respondents did not articulate but that I found relevant to understanding the gendered quality of domestic space.

First, because marriage rather than a job assignment grants a young adult a new *hu kou*, the system reaffirms the centrality of parent-child ties among both female and male young adults. Most young people remain registered as the dependents of their parents until they qualify for separate housing. University students and PLA soldiers are temporarily removed from the registry of their parents, but if upon graduation or demobilization they return to live in their parents' home they are reregistered in that household, and their housing situation is dealt with as a family rather than an individual matter.[14]

Second, a child's *hu kou* follows the female line. Thus, when young couples who have no housing of their own live apart, their child is registered with the mother, who uses her natal family's address to arrange schooling or daycare facilities. Overall, the practice of housing assignments places parents in a dominant position in shaping the housing of both males and females in the younger generation. The registration system also creates a tendency for urban residents to see their home as their mother's house, and thus perhaps intensifies identification of the home as female- rather than male-centered space.

REPRESENTATIVENESS
OF THESE SHANGHAI HOMES

In terms of occupational status and party membership, the families in my survey were above average, but were not members of the elite. Sixty percent of the husbands were employed as either production workers or low-level staff; 25 percent were factory managers or held equivalent posts in administrative or commercial units; the remainder were engineers or doctors. Thirty-six percent were members of the Communist party.[15] Therefore, as a sample of the total Shanghai population these families represent a selection drawn from a range between the upper levels of the working class to the lower echelons of the professional classes. They thus do not reflect the situation of the lowest 25 percent of the Shanghai labor force, who work in collective enterprises and often live in privately owned homes, nor do they represent the top 10–15 percent, who live in the privileged compounds of military or party elite. In general these families are typical of the solid middle class of Shanghai, who, before 1979, were poorly housed and as a result view their new homes as a significant material gain of the post-Mao era.[16]

Even more important than these limitations of social class, however, is the potential bias of my respondents' particular generational position. Families were selected for this study on the basis that the household included a woman born between 1925 and 1935. For this reason the home interiors I observed primarily represented the tastes of women raised before 1949, who set up their own households in the first decade after Liberation. As a result, the cultural significance of their home interiors may be restricted to one birth cohort whose tastes and ideals are likely to differ both from those of women fifteen or twenty years their senior, who established their homes before 1949, and from those of women fifteen or twenty years their junior, who came of age after the Cultural Revolution. Nevertheless, to the extent that these limitations are made explicit, observations of these homes offer a legitimate—and still somewhat unique—entry into the private realms where contemporary popular culture is nurtured and displayed, from which students of contemporary China have too long been excluded.

NOTES

1. Several recent discussions that focus explicitly on the home and have influenced the interpretations in this chapter are: Pierre Bourdieu, *Distinctions* (Cambridge: Harvard University Press, 1987); Lizbeth A. Cohen, "Embellishing a Life of Labor," *Journal of American Culture*, no. 3 (Winter 1980), pp. 752–775; Mihaly Csikszentmihalyi and Eugene Rochberg-Halton, *The Meaning of Things* (Cambridge: Cambridge University Press, 1981); Herbert Gans, *The Levittowners* (London: Allen Lane, 1967);

Edward O. Lauman and James S. House, "Living Room Styles and Social Attributes," in *The Logic of Social Hierarchies*, ed. E. Lauman, Paul Siegel, and Robert W. Hodge (Chicago: Markham, 1970), pp. 189–204.

2. Csikszentmihalyi and Rochberg-Halton, *Meaning of Things*, p. 6.

3. Cohen, "Life of Labor," p. 761.

4. In the work of both Bourdieu and Cohen (cited in note 1), the assumption is that domestic space in urban settings will be predominantly female.

5. Since 1979, I have interviewed more than 300 urban women in Beijing, Nanjing, Shanghai, Wuhan, Changzhou, and Shijiazhuang about their work lives. Approximately one-third of the interviews have been conducted in people's homes. One of the most recent investigations was a study in the summer of 1987, when I interviewed 100 Shanghai women randomly selected from a neighborhood registry of women born between 1925 and 1935; observations made during visits to the homes of these women provide the illustrative material for this discussion of female-centered domestic culture.

6. Between 1950 and 1980, Shanghai added 23.13 million square meters of new housing. Between 1980 and 1986, an additional 25.16 million were added (*Beijing Review*, no. 9 [February 29, 1988], p. 21).

7. Average household size among interviewees was 4.6 people. In terms of floor space, those in the larger apartments averaged 5.8 square meters per person, those in the smaller apartments 4.8 square meters. In 1986, the average urban household had 3.82 residents and averaged 6.36 square meters per person (*Renmin ribao*, December 3, 1986, p. 21; *Zhongguo tongji zhaiyao 1987* [Beijing: Zhongguo tongji chubanshe, 1987], p. 102).

8. In 1985, Shanghai households averaged 5.5 square meters per person (Hu Renxi, "Shiqu gaoling laoren zhuzhu qingkuang chouyang diaocha" [Survey of housing situation of very old in urban districts], in *Gaoling laoren wenti yenjiou*, ed. Research group of Shanghai municipal committee on problems of elderly [Shanghai: Shanghai shi laonianxue xuehui mishuzu, 1987], pp. 71–80). In terms of amenities, however, these apartments were superior. They all had running water, individual kitchens, private indoor toilets, and city gas. In 1986, only 82 percent of urban homes had running water, 61 percent had private kitchens, 30 percent had private indoor toilets, and 12 percent had gas (*Beijing Review*, February 16, 1987, pp. 22–23).

9. Cohen, "Life of Labor," p. 767.

10. In 1987, a typical wedding in Shanghai cost 4,000 yuan; two young workers usually saved no more than 40 yuan per month, and only with large contributions from both sets of parents could they furnish their homes. In the early 1980s the practice was for the bride and her family to buy everything that was soft, as well as the dishes, and for the groom and his family to provide all that was hard. On the day the couple moved to their new home, or room, all the items were displayed, and as guests walked through they would know what each family had contributed. In 1987 I was told engaged couples would pool their savings and gifts to purchase items together. However, in my interviews parents who were saving for their children's marriages were observing the old distinctions, buying hard items—such as furniture—for sons, and soft things—such as clothing and cooking items—for daughters.

11. Eighty-four of the 100 women in the survey had at least one married child, and in 65 percent of these families one or more married children lived with the respondent. However, in 80 percent of these joint households the married child was a son, only 10 percent less than the percentage of patrilocal joint residence when the respondents themselves had first married in the 1940s and early 1950s.

12. It is of course possible that a whole range of other pictures were removed in honor of my visit. However, even if this was the case, it remains a telling statement

that portraits of elderly parents were considered the most appropriate decoration to remain.

13. Although I have no means to verify the veracity of these two anecdotes, I personally observed that others who heard the stories found them credible and worthy of empathy, and thus I have included them as legitimate artifacts of Shanghai popular culture.

14. For example, in Shanghai priority in 1987 was given to families in hardship (*kunnan hu*). Depending on one's work unit, hardship was defined as per capita space of under 2.8 to 3.5 square meters, which meant less than two rooms for couples with children over twelve or an elderly parent with two children of opposite sex over the age of sixteen. Thus, if a young worker planning marriage was living with parents whose housing conditions would not deteriorate to hardship level upon entry of the child's spouse, the new couple was rarely eligible for a separate apartment.

15. Wives had considerably lower status. Sixty-five percent were production workers, 25 percent were low-level staff, and only 10 percent were professionals or factory-level cadres. Party membership was also lower among wives than husbands, 19 percent as opposed to 36 percent. These percentages are based on all 100 families in the survey, not merely the 50 I visited in their homes.

16. During the interviews it became apparent that particularly when the blocks were first available many families perceived the housing as mediocre. The area was not well served by city buses, there were few amenities, shopping was difficult, and the neighborhood lacked a key-point middle school. However, only one of the youngest (and highest status) respondents explicitly expressed ambitions to move. She hoped that the family could trade on the husband's professional seniority to get the three-room apartment she felt was more appropriate to their social position. It is also noteworthy that this was one of the least well decorated homes, clear evidence that this family had not made the same emotional investment as other respondents.

PART THREE

Religion, Ethnicity, and Propriety

7

The Catholic Church in China

Cultural Contradictions, Institutional Survival, and Religious Renewal

RICHARD MADSEN

There were as many Chinese Catholics in 1979, after the ravages of the Cultural Revolution, as there were in 1949, when the atheist Communist party came to power. Richard Madsen, sociology professor at the University of California–San Diego, explains how this small religious community survived in the face of total isolation from foreign support and thirty years of government suppression. Self-interest theorists are confounded by the behavior of those who ignore material and political disincentives and join the Church today. Professor Madsen suggests that the answer lies in the long history of the Chinese church. At the grassroots level, the meaning of being a Chinese Catholic has come to be defined in terms of fidelity to the bonds that link one to kin and ancestors. Upholding the faith has become intertwined with obligations to honor one's Catholic ancestors and the religion they bequeathed to their descendants. As the state began to penetrate and control family life after 1949, Catholics viewed the Church as a defender of traditional community values. The party's decision to cut the Church off from international support had the unintended effect of rooting it more deeply in Chinese society and thereby legitimizing it. Similarly, discrimination against Catholics tended to reinforce rather than destroy their identity.

—Eds.

Neither the title nor subtitle of Carma Hinton's film, *To Taste a Hundred Herbs: Gods, Ancestors, and Medicine in a Chinese Village,*[1] prepares us for the revelations of the opening scene: Shen Fasheng, the documentary's main character, sits under a brightly colored picture of a blue-eyed Jesus, Mary, and Joseph and devoutly sings the "Christmas Song," a Chinese-language version of "O Come, All Ye Faithful." As portrayed in the movie, Mr. Shen's life is indeed defined by his intertwined devotion to gods, ancestors, and medicine, but his gods are different from what one would suspect. He is a Catholic, as are, the film tells us, about 20 percent of his native Long Bow village.[2] To those who know Long Bow through *Fanshen,* William Hinton's classic saga of land reform and collectivization in that rural community, it is surprising that there are any practicing Catholics left in the village.

Fanshen describes a violent persecution, led by the village's Communist cadres during land reform, of the Catholic community, which is portrayed as a detested outgroup hostile to the revolution.[3] The book leaves the impression that this Catholic community was utterly (and deservedly) crushed by the revolutionary juggernaut.

This impression is corrected somewhat by Hinton's subsequent book *Shen Fan.*

> By the time the Communist Party held its Twelfth Congress in 1982 Party and government leaders had convinced most people that they would again allow freedom of religion. Catholics who had for years been meeting secretly for worship, or who had dared not meet at all, began to hang pictures of the Virgin Mary on their walls, quite often on the wall opposite a portrait of the still-revered Chairman Mao, and dared attend Sunday services in the open. Horse Square [Long Bow's neighboring village] today is as solidly Catholic as it was at the time of liberation in 1945, while the Catholics of Long Bow can still claim about one-third of the population as believers.[4]

Yet nothing that Hinton says about Catholicism throughout his book prepares us to assimilate this observation. The villagers, whom he interviewed in 1971 to gather the stories that provide most of the book's substance, admit that Catholicism survived the persecutions of the land reform period but claim that it was virtually wiped out by the late 1960s. Hinton's observation about the persistence of Catholicism in the 1980s is tacked onto a long account of an interview with Wang Tingmo, one-time party secretary of the local county, who describes a great "Catholic uprising" in 1966 during which "tens of thousands" of believers converged on a mountain near Taiyuan in the expectation of an apparition by the Virgin Mary. According to Wang, the party exposed the miracle of the mountain near Taiyuan as a hoax and broke up the Catholics' organization, after which "most of the Catholics repudiated their imperialist religion" and "production began to rise."[5]

Thus, even if one has read *Shen Fan*, it comes as a surprise that someone like Shen Fasheng, portrayed in *To Taste a Hundred Herbs* as a revered village doctor, practices his Catholic faith so openly, comfortably, and confidently. And little in the social sciences literature about the People's Republic of China (PRC) from the 1950s through the 1970s prepares us for the fact that *To Taste a Hundred Herbs* seems to reflect accurately the condition of Catholicism throughout China. There were about 3 million Catholics in China in 1949, who belonged to a Church heavily dependent on foreign support. Only 30 out of about 140 Catholic dioceses were headed by Chinese bishops—and most of those bishops had been consecrated only after 1945. Since the 1930s, the Vatican had taken a firm stand against communism and indeed had proscribed Catholics from identifying themselves even with moderate socialists.[6] Seeing the Catholic church as an important political threat, the Communist party expelled foreign missionaries and imprisoned—and sometimes killed—many native priests and bishops. In 1956, the government formed the Chinese Catholic Patriotic Association, and allowed open practice of the faith only to Catholics who renounced their ties to the Vatican and joined this association. Out of twenty-eight Chinese bishops, five joined the Catholic Patriotic Association. For refusing to join, many of the other bishops, together with priests and lay leaders associated with them, were sent to prison. During the Cultural Revolution, all churches were closed and many church buildings were destroyed; even members of the Catholic Patriotic Association were persecuted because of their beliefs.[7] In view of the harsh political power that was marshaled against this small Church, so dependent throughout its history on foreign support, it comes as a great surprise that by conservative estimates there are still at least 3 million practising Catholics in China—at least as many as there were on the eve of the communist takeover in 1949. Approximately 600 churches and more than 1,000 chapels have been reopened since 1978, and there are about 30,000 baptisms annually. There are about 1,000 priests and about 50 bishops (most of these bishops consecrated after 1956, without Vatican approval, by bishops associated with the Catholic Patriotic Association). The average age of these clergymen is about seventy, but new seminaries hve been opened to prepare young men for the priesthood. These institutions are filled to their present capacity with about 600 seminarians, and there are reportedly large waiting lists of candidates seeking admission. A number of novitiates for nuns have been opened, each housing about 140 novices.[8]

How can we explain the survival of such a small, apparently weak Church in the face of isolation from all foreign support and thirty years of government suppression? How can we account for the apparent renewed vitality of this Church under a political regime in which religious practice, although once again officially tolerated, is systematically discouraged—where the profession of religious faith seemingly can bring few if any material rewards and always has the potential of causing much trouble to the believer?

Such questions confound the most prevalent Western economic, political, and sociological theories, which tend to explain social phenomena as results of the rational pursuit of self-interests by individuals. Such self-interests are usually described in terms of some combination of interests in wealth, power, and status. On the face of it, however, it would appear that most "rational actors" seeking to maximize their wealth, power, and status would not have found reason to remain loyal to the Catholic church in the hostile political climate of the first thirty years of the People's Republic; and they would not risk acquiring a share of the benefits possible under the new economic reforms by joining the Church. To explain the survival and resurgence of Chinese Catholicism—and for that matter, I would suggest, to explain the re-emergence of many other forms of religious expression in China—one has to find a way to understand the meanings—the faith—embedded in the religious institutions. In the case of Chinese Catholicism, one has to understand how the Church has shaped a certain identity among its adherents that causes them to perceive their self-interests in distinct ways. We would have to understand the factors that either reinforce that identity or break it down. We have to account for changes and continuities in that identity over time.

I do not mean to suggest that Catholics in China, or for that matter anywhere else, all believe the same things or understand participation in the Church in the same ways. In sociological terms, the Catholic church is indeed a *church* as opposed to a *sect*. In the famous distinction made by Ernst Troeltsch, a church differs from a sect in its inclusivity and diversity. A sect is a relatively small, homogeneous religious group whose members stay together because they all believe the same doctrines and maintain the same standards of conduct. A church is a large heterogeneous group, whose members share common rituals but interpret the rituals in a variety of ways and adhere to the church's moral teachings with differing degrees of commitment. A sect expels members who do not match its particular definitions of sanctity. A church consists of sinners as well as saints; it takes people where they are and tries to educate them in whatever degree of religious commitment they are capable of.[9]

The individuals who belong to a church, then, differ widely in both fervor and religious understanding. This is generally true of the Catholic church around the world, and China is no exception. Yet insofar as individuals have not irrevocably broken with the Church, they come under the sway of common ritual practices, a common history, a common array of formative influences. To understand the life of a church at a particular time, we have to understand how the meanings implicit in the structure of the institution intersect with the particular interests and life experiences of various member groups and individuals.

In this chapter I will primarily focus on the meanings carried by the Chinese Catholic church as an institution. These meanings are not static. Although there is a basic continuity of ritual, doctrine, and authority structure within the Church, there is also constant change in the exact ways in which the Church performs its rituals, preaches its doctrines, and exerts its authority. To appreciate the meanings now carried by the Chinese Catholic church, we have to understand them in the light of that Church's history. I will try to show how the particular history of that Church, the history of its relations with the worldwide Catholic church, on the one hand, and with Chinese society, on the other, has helped to shape the identity of Chinese Catholics.

Secondarily, I will try to show how various groups and individuals within the Chinese Catholic church have responded to the common meanings implicit in the institution. This is secondary not because it is less important than the institutional analysis, but because it is very difficult to do with the data at our disposal. In a recent newsletter, the Weixin group, five Hong Kong-based Jesuits who are well trained in the social sciences and publish the well-informed *China News Analysis*, writes that "the present situation of the Catholic Church in China is so complex and multifaceted that to write about it is a very hazardous venture. Visitors may not stay long enough to appreciate the diversity of situation according to places and to see through many deceptive appearances."[10] By focusing on the institutional level of analysis, which is relatively easy to do now—although, as we shall see, not without its own considerable difficulties—we can at least prepare the way for a more subtle understanding of the meanings particular Chinese Catholic individuals and groups give to their common heritage, as better information becomes available.

CONSCIOUSNESS, CONTRADICTIONS, AND HISTORICITY

The common institutional legacy now confronted by Chinese Catholics is ambiguous and fraught with tensions. The specific tensions, indeed, the contradictions, that characterize the Catholic church in China today differ from the tensions that characterized it in the past and they will undoubtedly change in the future. There is a perennial structure to these tensions, however. It is the tension between a faith perceived as universal—coming from God, valid for everyone, everywhere, at all times—and an expression of that faith conceived as particular—incarnated in the particular circumstances of a particular time and place. This structure of belief forces Catholics to question how their experience of belonging to a particular community of Catholics, situated within a particular social and political context at a particular time, is related to the universal meaning carried by the whole Church throughout its history.

These are not simply questions for professional theologians. If an ordinary Catholic cannot believe that the way he or she lives the faith is consistent in some fundamental fashion with what Catholicism has always and everywhere meant, it is difficult to identify oneself as a Catholic. (A Protestant, on the other hand, might be able to say that his or her reading of the Bible has led to a personal faith that is more authentic than that of other professed Christians at other times.) Realistically, there is never any unequivocal answer to how to relate one's particular Catholic experience with that of the universal Church. For example, many members of the U.S. Catholic church believe that the practice of artificial birth control is consistent with the fundamental meaning of the universal Catholic traditions concerning the sanctity of sexuality and the nature of the family. Many other Catholics, including the present pope, do not think contraception is permissible. But persons on either side of this controversy have to make some effort to relate their stance to the totality of the Catholic tradition; otherwise, there is no point in calling oneself a Catholic. To understand the experience of a local Church, then, one must start with an examination of common challenges faced by members of that Church—ordinary members as well as professional theologians—in reconciling their claims to be true to themselves, faithful to the requirements of their own particular situation, and loyal to the common faith of a universal Church. We must then examine how the sociological structures of the Church as an institution push its members, at specific periods in the Church's history, to resolve these challenges in particular ways.

The main axis of the tension between universality and particularity varies for different Catholic communities in different historical contexts. To explore the axis of a particular time, we must try to develop constructs—intellectual models of interrelated symbols—that can plausibly encompass as many diverse expressions of this tension as possible. An indispensable aid to doing this is an understanding of how the main axis of tension has developed over the course of history. One must be careful not to assume that the specific axis of tension characteristic of a previous era is also characteristic of the present. In the seventeenth and eighteenth centuries, the tension between the Chineseness and the Catholicity of the Chinese Catholic church revolved around the issues that constituted the Rites Controversy. To understand the tensions that define the experience of the Chinese Catholic church in the present, we have to understand both how they proceed out of a history that began with the Rites Controversy, but have now moved beyond the issues of that time.[11]

THE RITES CONTROVERSY:
UNIVERSAL DOCTRINE AND PARTICULARISTIC CHINESE ETHICAL PRACTICE

During the Rites Controversy the tension between Chineseness and Catholicity was expressed through the opposition of Catholic orthodoxy and Chinese orthopraxis. Could the normative practices that constituted a Chinese way of life—fidelity to the familial obligations of sons to fathers, wives to husbands, and youth to their elders—be reconciled with Catholic doctrines? At the crux of this issue were the Chinese rituals that celebrated the solidarity of their extended families through veneration of their ancestors. Were these rites a kind of ancestor worship? If so, in the Catholic view they constituted idolatry. Or were the rites merely an expression of filial piety, a Chinese way of fulling the comandment, "Honor thy father and mother"? In the seventeenth century, the Jesuit missionaries led by Matteo Ricci claimed that the rites were merely a legitimate expression of filial piety. Dominican and Fransciscan missionaries, however, claimed the rites were idolatrous. The issue was finally settled in the early eighteenth century by a papal decree that agreed with the Dominicans and Franciscans. Obsessed with doctrinal purity, the post-Reformation Vatican was in the end unwilling to allow the practice of Chinese familial rituals that might be inconsistent with a strict interpretation of its doctrine, even though most Chinese considered their familial responsiblities the very essence of a right relationship to society. The Vatican decision was a devastating blow to the hopes of creating an indigenous Chinese Catholic church, making it extremely difficult to remain culturally Chinese while becoming a Catholic.

The basic problem expressed in the Rites Controversy, that of relating a particular Chinese experience to the universal Catholic tradition, remains. Yet a key to understanding the extraordinary resilience of the Chinese Catholic church in contemporary China lies in the recognition that with the passage of time the specific issues of the seventeenth-century Rites Controversy have been resolved in favor of traditional Chineseness, that is, in favor of those lived practices of familiality that have historically constituted a Chinese way of life. Rather than being defined in terms of assent to abstract doctrines, the meaning of being a Chinese Catholic is now popularly defined precisely in terms of fidelity to those particularistic bonds that link one to family members and kin in the present and obligate one to honor one's common ancestors in the past.

In *To Taste a Hundred Herbs,* a local cadre criticizes Long Bow's Catholics for adhering to a foreign belief. "The main problem with Catholicism," he says, "is that it came from abroad. It is not a native belief." The Catholic Shen Fasheng retorts, "This complaint that Catholicism is a foreign belief has nothing to do with us. All we know is that our ancestors passed it down." Shen, indeed, is portrayed as being unusually devoted to the rituals of ancestor veneration and unusually committed to traditional familial bonds. To renounce his Catholicism would be to dishonor his ancestors and, perhaps more important, to cut himself off from all of those familial relations that situate him in his segment of the Long Bow community. The Long Bow Catholics only marry other Catholics. Most of their brides seem to come from a neighboring village (probably the place William Hinton, in *Shen Fan,* calls Horse Square village) that is exclusively Catholic. The principles that bind Shen to his Catholic community are then the same principles that bind Chinese in general to their lineages and segments of lineages. Membership in the Church is not so much a matter of a voluntary commitment as of an ascriptive status. Even if one wanted to leave the Church one's nonbelieving neighbors would not allow it. They might be suspicious of anyone who claimed to be free of the ties that connected him or her to kin and ancestors. They would not let such a person truly become one of them. Under such circumstances, social and political discrimination, and even persecution, may well have reinforced rather than destroyed Catholic identity (in somewhat the same fashion as discrimination against Subei people in Shanghai intensifies their identity rather than leading them to renounce it).[12]

The pattern of ascriptive, particularistic, familistic solidarities that is suggested in *To Taste a Hundred Herbs* seems to be common throughout rural China. Catholics generally live in totally Catholic villages or occupy segments of villages that are organized along the same principles as are lineages within all ordinary Chinese communities. The largest and most active concentrations seem to be in areas where large numbers of such Catholic communities are linked together in ascriptive patterns of association defined by practice of a specialized, inherited occupation. For instance, according to Jin Luxian, a newly consecrated auxiliary bishop of Shanghai, most Shanghai Catholics live in rural areas; in fact, most of them are boat people.

> As a group [these boat people] are fervent and pious, faithful to the traditional practices of their religion. At dawn and dusk, it is not uncommon to hear the chanting of morning and evening prayers rising from the boats moored along the water's edge. Parents are concerned about the Catholic education of their children, who from infancy are taught the rudiments of the catechism and their prayers. The boat people live in a world apart, somewhat isolated from the influences of the larger society. They hold firm to their traditions and their faith.[13]

The liveliest Catholic community rituals are often those that express the solidarities traditionally associated with such rural communities, in forms that place a Catholic veneer on common Chinese practices. Thus one of the most popular Catholic pilgrimage sites in China is the Church of Our Lady of Sheshan, near Shanghai, to which fisherfolk flock in patterns similar to pilgrimages to shrines of Mazu.[14] (Images of the Blessed Virgin are often drawn in a manner very similar to images of Mazu.) And in a fashion reminiscent of the way in which whole villages once turned out in honor of traditional deities, 3,000 of the 4,000 residents of the all-Catholic village of Ma Chang, in Shanxi Province, joined in a procession and Solemn High Mass on June 6, 1986, the feast day of the Sacred Heart, who is the patron of the village.[15]

In the need to affirm the dignity of the inescapable Catholic heritage that has constituted ties to a native community, even as it has brought that community so much recent trouble, Catholics may even outdo ordinary Chinese in carrying out the rituals of piety toward their ancestors. In March of 1986, Bishop John Wu, the bishop of Hong Kong, was allowed to return to Guangdong Province and visit, among other places, his native village. Because of the revolution, he had been separated from his family there for forty years. When he finally arrived, he went first to the village cemetery, where he prayed at the tombs of his grandparents and his father. Only after this did he proceed to his family home, where his mother and her sons with their families were waiting to greet him.[16]

In urban areas, too, the strength of attachments to Catholicism seems to depend on the degree to which Catholicism has been embedded in extended kinship networks. The "old Catholics" of Shanghai, for example, a network of intermarried families who trace their faith all the way back to Matteo Ricci's conversion of Xu Guangqi, have produced many of the most prominent, indominable "martyrs" against communist efforts to control and suppress the Church.[17] One could build an important research agenda around the hypothesis that it is precisely in areas where Catholic community ties have been most thoroughly intertwined with the ascriptive (mostly familial) bonds that have traditionally constituted Chinese community—in Catholic communities where Chinese rites of familial piety are still most powerfully alive—that the Church has most successfully retained its members, and that it has lost members under the pressure of persecution in areas where Catholic community ties have not been so intertwined.

Thus, although the Rites Controversy illustrated the perennial challenge of relating the experience of the particular Chinese church to an understanding of the fundamental claims of a universal Catholic tradition, its primary concerns no longer provide the axis of tension along which this challenge is experienced.[18] Spokespersons for the Catholic Patriotic Association—the government-sponsored unit of the Chinese Catholic church—are wont to say that the main line of tension today is that created by the legacy of nineteenth- and early twentieth-century colonialism. I will argue, however, that this tension, too, has been superseded by the course of history.

CATHOLICISM AND IMPERIALISM: EUROPEAN VERSUS CHINESE NATIONAL CULTURES

In the nineteenth and early twentieth centuries, the main tension that defined the contradiction within the Chinese Catholic consciousness was indeed the tension between the Catholic cultures of imperialistic European nations and the culture of an emerging Chinese nation.

I use *culture* here in the totalistic sense in which the nineteenth-century forerunners of modern anthropology used the term. They defined culture as the "total way of life" of a people, including beliefs, moral practices, styles of artistic representation, social conventions, and so forth. Such a definition tended to view all of these dimensions of life as tied together in a unified whole that defined the destiny of particular nations. The strength of powerful nations derived from their cultures, which legitimated the imperialist drive to impose their cultures on weaker nations.

Thus the French missionaries, who dominated Chinese Catholic mission work in the late nineteenth century, saw themselves as propagating a faith that was intimately linked with what they considered the essence of French life. They built Gothic cathedrals that were named after French saints and adorned with French-style iconography. Depending for their work on French military protection, the often saw their mission as an intimate extension of

French economic and political interests. In 1901, Bishop Reynaud of Ningpo referred to his territory as "France in Chekiang."[19] One consequence of this identification of missionary work with the propagation of a national European culture was the missionaries' insistence on keeping total control of the Chinese church in their own hands and their consequent refusal to consider the appointment of Chinese bishops.

In the early twentieth century, the Vatican came to deplore control of the Chinese missions by national European churches. Such control was in effect a threat to Vatican autonomy. In 1919, Pope Benedict XV issued the encyclical *Maximum Illud*, which, as Eric O. Hanson describes it, "deplored the effects of European nationalism on the Catholic Church in China and called for eventual Church administration by Chinese clergy. The missionary clergy in China gave the letter a lukewarm response."[20] For its own political reasons, the Vatican therefore took the side of an emerging Chinese nationalism against the nationalistic Catholic cultures of the European imperialistic powers. It acted slowly and tentatively, however. Pope Pius XI appointed six Chinese priests as bishops in 1926; Pope Pius XII officially ended the Rites Controversy in 1939 by declaring that the rites honoring ancestors were civil and not religious ceremonies. A large group of Chinese priests were made bishops between 1945 and 1949, but on the eve of the founding of the People's Republic, the Church remained dominated by foreign clergy; to be a Chinese Catholic was to be oriented to a foreign-dominated Church.

CATHOLICISM AND LENINIST POLITICS: UNIVERSAL CHURCH AND STATE POWER

The Chinese Communist attacks against the Catholic church were carried out in the name of resistance to foreign imperialist control. The campaign succeeded in purging the Church of the legacy of foreign imperialism, although with consequences that may not have been anticipated: It made the Church truly Chinese—nationalistically Chinese—by giving it its own martyrs. The most celebrated of these was Bishop Ignatius Gong Pinmei, of Shanghai. Appointed by the Vatican in 1949, Bishop Gong refused to cooperate with the party's attempt to set up the Catholic Patriotic Association. For this he was arrested on a charge of espionage in 1955 and tried and sentenced to life in prison in 1956. By this time, however, it was implausible that ordinary Catholics would consider clergymen like Bishop Gong tools of foreign imperialism. Gong belonged to that segment of the clergy who had elected to stay on the mainland and face a very uncertain future rather than flee to Hong Kong or Taiwan—a gesture of loyalty to the Catholics of their local communities. These clergy were staking out a claim to be thoroughly Chinese, but in a way different from that prescribed by the communists.

By the time Bishop Gong and many of his colleagues were imprisoned, the issue was not whether the local Church would continue to receive foreign aid—that was now completely cut off—but whether it would be able to manage its own affairs. The Catholic Patriotic Association was one of those mass organizations that the party was establishing in all areas of life to be channels of party social control. In resisting this, people like Bishop Gong were resisting control of the Church by the atheistic party. Bishop Gong made a sacrificial gesture for the sake of the integrity of the Church, as against the claims of the Chinese state. And he was doing this as the state was rapidly losing its legitimacy, at least among urban intellectuals, by ruthlessly trying to crush all dissident opinion during the anti-Rightist campaign.

One basis for the claim of European churches that they needed to exercise tutelage over the Chinese church was that they were more mature than the Chinese church, being the heirs of a long succession of saints and martyrs. Now the Chinese church could claim equality in that regard. And at the same time it had the basis for claiming a kind of solidarity with fellow Chinese of all persuasions who were feeling the arbitrary pressure of the Chinese state.

Yet, even though the persecution of leaders like Bishop Gong enhanced the Chinese Catholic church's claim to spiritual equality with other branches of the worldwide Church, it also helped deprive it of another important dimension of its life—the sacraments. One of the most fundamental aspects of Catholic belief is faith in the spiritual efficacy of the sacraments. With the exception of the sacrament of baptism, these rituals—the Eucharist, penance, confirmation, matrimony, holy orders, and the anointing of the sick—require an ordained priest to be validly performed. Priests like Bishop Gong who refused to cooperate with the government were put in prison or, at the very least, prohibited from performing these rituals. The only priests available were those who had joined the Catholic Patriotic Association; Chinese Catholics faced the hard choice of either accepting the consolation of the sacraments from the hands of these priests or affirming their spiritual solidarity with martyrs like Bishop Gong. There have been great variations in the ways Chinese Catholics have reconciled this dilemma.

It seems that, between the two extremes of total acceptance of any priest who has joined the Catholic Patriotic Association and acceptance only of those priests who have refused to have anything to do with the association, there is a large and constantly shifting middle ground. There are Catholics, for instance, who refuse to receive the sacraments from priests who have collaborated fully with the Catholic Patriotic Association, but will receive the sacraments from those who have shown some signs of resistance to the association even though they now work under its aegis.

One important sign of resistance involves celibacy. During the Cultural Revolution, to demonstrate rejection of Vatican authority, the Catholic Patriotic Association pressured priests to reject celibacy. Many priests did so, although in some cases they seem to have entered simply into marriages of convenience, often with Catholic nuns, in which the couples never lived together and never had children. Anecdotal evidence gathered by foreign Catholic priests who have visited China in recent years suggests that Chinese

Catholics widely reject priests who gave in to the association's encouragement to marry. For example, according to one such foreign priest,[21] whom I interviewed, there is a married priest in northern China whom many local Catholics call the Thirty Pieces of Silver priest (after the price paid to Judas Iscariot for betraying Jesus). He was recently assigned by the Catholic Patriotic Association to work in a parish of a newly opened church, but most local Catholics will have nothing at all to do with him. My informant observed another example of the reaction of Chinese Catholics to priests who renounced celibacy when he attended the official reopening of a church in south China. The priest who had been pastor there had entered into what appeared to be a marriage of convenience. Although he and his wife seem never to have lived together, the local Catholics made it very clear when the church was reopened that he was not to say Mass. He was present when the church was officially reopened, but sat inconspicuously off to one side. The publicness of the marriage may also make some difference. It is widely rumored that Bishop Fu Tieshan, the bishop of Beijing and one of the leaders of the Catholic Patriotic Association, is married. If this is so, however, he does not publicly admit it. The rumors undoubtedly detract from his acceptability to some Chinese Catholics—he would be more acceptable if he could plausibly deny them—but he seems to be more acceptable than if he had publicly married.

Another factor in enhancing acceptability of priests associated with the Catholic Patriotic Association is whether they suffered any form of persecution for their faith. During the Cultural Revolution, even participation in the Catholic Patriotic Association was not enough to prevent priests from being harassed, humiliated, or imprisoned. Such experiences help confer legitimacy.

On the other hand, when overseas Chinese Catholic priests have managed to return to their native places in the past decade and celebrate Mass in their communities, they have often been greeted by unusually large and enthusiastic crowds. One could interpret this enthusiasm as a desire to receive the sacraments from priests other than those associated in any way with the Catholic Patriotic Association; the government's reaction to this enthusiasm suggests that it suspects this interpretation to be correct. In 1986, the Chinese Catholic Bishops Conference (under the aegis of the Catholic Patriotic Association) and the Chinese Catholic Church Administrative Commission together issued "Regulations concerning the clergy's faculties to administer the sacraments." These regulations stipulate that "In accordance with China's Constitution and the Chinese Catholic Church's principle of the independent administration of the church, clerics from foreign countries, Hong Kong, Macao and Taiwan, who come to China to travel or to visit relatives, do not have faculties to administer the sacraments." The document also stipulates that "A cleric who has been punished and stripped of his political rights due to violating the law, immediately and automatically loses his authority to administer the sacraments."[22] The Catholic Church Administrative Commission is the conduit from the government's Religious Affairs Bureau and the party's United Front Work Department to the Church. The above regulations seem to reflect the party's real concern that politically incorrect priests would attract a significant following.

If such regulations (which reiterate similar regulations published in 1981) are successfully implemented, of course, we will have no hard evidence for determining whether Catholics would prefer to receive the sacraments from priests who are not connected with the Catholic Patriotic Association. But neither could we determine whether compliance with the regulations is simply the result of effective government surveillance and coercion or the result of a change of heart by members of the Catholic community. To get evidence bearing on this issue, we might look to those occasions when visting clergy manage to accomplish something that the government probably dearly wishes to avoid—a direct confrontation with party regulations.

The return, in 1986, of Bishop Wu of Hong Kong to his native region in Guangzhou occasioned such a confrontation. Fr. John Tong, one of the Hong Kong priests who accompanied the bishop on his historic trip, provides a description.

While the Bishop had been invited to say Mass in Beidouzhai by the local pastor, who was his former teacher in the seminary, and although he had accepted the invitation because of the close personal relationship he had with many priests of the diocese, no permission had been given by the chairman of the Catholic Church Administrative Commission of the province. This was the explanation given to us by the government officials who were accompanying us. They also added that the area is presently without a bishop and Fr. Paul Lam, who was administering the diocese was just an ordinary priest without episcopal authority, and he could not act on his own in such a matter. The Bishop explained that he, himself had not taken the initiative but was strictly in a passive position. He reiterated his desire to adhere to all laws, and to observe the rules set down by China, even if those rules were unique to China and not found any place elsewhere in the world. He did suggest, however, that allowing him to offer Mass publicly would not only be to the benefit of the Chinese believers but would also add to the international reputation of China and bolster confidence among the people of Hong Kong with a view to 1997. With these factors in mind, he asked the officials to check with the pastor Fr. Luke Lu to find out if, in fact, he had obtained the necessary permission to invite him, and if not, would our hosts be kind enough to telephone Bishop Ye, Chairman of the Catholic Church Administrative Commission for Guangdong Province, in Guangzhou to request his permission. Our arrival in Beidouzhai was delayed. The traffic situation and lack of adequate arrangements were given as the cause. When we finally did arrive, we were met by a large and enthusiastic crowd of people who welcomed the Bishop to the sound of exploding firecrackers. We were told then that permission to say Mass had not been obtained. When asked if they had phoned Bishop Ye, the officials replied that they had not, because, as government officials, they were not allowed to interfere in Church affairs. While Bishop Wu was not allowed to say Mass in Beidouzhai, he was permitted to bless the crowd from a second-floor window and say a few words of greeting. Most of the people had not seen a bishop in over forty years and they were most eager to meet him. The Bishop was visibly moved by the warmth of their welcome, but when he asked if he might be allowed to mingle and talk with them, he was told that security reasons prevented it.[23]

The government thus won the battle to prevent the bishop from saying mass in Beidouzhai, but only at the price of being forced to resort to such patent doubletalk that it lost ground in the ideological war over the legitimacy of its stance toward Catholicism.

To win that war, the government will have to adopt more positive measures than legal coercion. To the extent that Catholicism believes that sanctity, manifested through self-sacrifice and even martyrdom, is the main sign of the authenticity of its faith, coercion is counterproductive to the government's purpose.

It is probably some recognition of this that is behind the government's recent moves to downplay coercion in favor of more subtle forms of co-optation and accommodation. On January 6, 1988, Bishop Gong had his civil rights restored after thirty years of incarceration that were followed by two and a half years of limited parole. Most other priests and bishops have now been released from jail. In some places priests who have never had anything to do with the Catholic Patriotic Association are allowed publicly to celebrate the sacraments in newly opened churches—provided that they will not speak against the association. "If you ask them why they participate under these circumstances," says a recent visitor to such newly opened churches, "they will say this is the only way." Catholics seem widely to accept such priests, especially if they have not married. In other places, though, only priests unambiguously associated with the Catholic Patriotic Association may openly celebrate the sacraments. Some Catholics may totally refuse the sacraments from such priests, but others may find these priests acceptable, especially if they have suffered some persecution for their faith.

There is an old Catholic saying that "The blood of martyrs is the seed of Christians." For an institution based on a faith that it can provide a transcendent answer to the problem of human suffering, that dictum makes good sociological as well as theological sense. In China, indeed, it seems that the suffering of local martyrs has strengthened the roots of a genuinely local Church. As a result, it may be argued, the tension between a colonial and colonizing Church no longer defines the primary way in which Chinese Catholics experience the contradiction between the particularity and universality of their Church. Though Catholicism is foreign in origin—like Buddhism—it is now understood in a way that is entirely consistent with the reverence for familial obligations that constitutes the mainstream of China's historical heritage. Though tied up in the last century with all of the baggage of cultural imperialism, the Church has now been freed from most of the baggage, as much because of what the institution has had to endure as because of initiatives it has chosen for itself. In the contemporary Chinese experience, the interplay between the particularity and universality of the Church now comes to a focus in the tension between the claims of religious community and the power of the state.

This is perhaps the main tension defining the experience of local Catholic churches throughout the modern world. Christian communities everywhere live in a world dominated by globe-spanning configurations of market relations and state power. Yet their traditions tell them that they cannot serve both God and money and that they cannot render unto Caesar things that belong to God. Catholic communities occupying positions with respect to international market systems and political structures different from those of Chinese Catholics have to reconcile these contradictions in different ways. For U.S. Catholics, perhaps, the main contradiction is between God and money; while for Chinese Catholics it is between God and Caesar.

CONCLUSION: CHINESE CATHOLICISM AND THE COMPARATIVE STUDY OF RELIGIOUS INSTITUTIONS

In this light, the fate of Chinese Catholicism can be seen as part of an enormously important worldwide public issue. To an unprecedented degree, the world is becoming economically and politically interdependent. Increasing academic interest in international political economy is but one reflection of this development. Yet the international dynamics of markets and states create profound moral dilemmas. As markets systematically turn humans into commodities and bureaucratic states turn people into objects for manipulation, the values that give meaning to human life—freedom, dignity, solidarity with others in community—become increasingly endangered. One source of resistance to these trends and affirmation of these values is religious institutions. The sturdiness of the Chinese Catholic church in the face of enormous political pressures offers potential lessons for everyone concerned about the survival of freedom, dignity, and community in the modern world.

Most of what little we in the West know about the Chinese Catholic church, however, comes from research carried out by Catholic priests and nuns writing for other members of the Catholic church. As the notes to this chapter indicate, most of the information used here comes from such sources. The problem with this information is not that it is inaccurate, but rather that it is framed in a theological language that mainly answers the questions of Catholic believers rather than those of people outside of the Church. In this chapter I have tried to frame this information in terms of concepts of the comparative sociology of religion and culture, in an attempt to answer questions posed not just by Catholic believers but by a broader audience of people interested more generally in solutions to some of the moral dilemmas of the modern world.

Even if this attempt were modestly successful, at best it would whet a more general appetite for a finer grained understanding of the Catholic experience in China and for a more subtle array of concepts for comparing the Chinese Catholic experience with that of other religious communities, both in China and throughout the world. In particular, it would stimulate a need for more knowledge about the range of individual and group responses of Chinese Catholics to the institutional dilemmas of their Church and for more of a sense of the dialectic between whole and parts within the Chinese Catholic church.

The Chinese Catholic church as a whole, however, is not simply the sum of its parts. The institution embodies a historical legacy, a doctrinal language, and a structure of ritual expression that give shape and meaning to the particular experiences of individual Chinese Catholics. If this chapter has been at all successful in conveying a sense of some of the dynamics of the Chinese Catholic church as a body, it should deepen our appreciation for the poignancy and hope embedded in vignettes like the following, which was recounted to me by a U.S. Catholic priest about a Chinese Catholic priest he visited recently in rural Guangdong.

Ordained before 1949, this Chinese Catholic priest is an old man now. Having refused to cooperate with the Catholic Patriotic Association, he was forbidden by the government to function as a priest for three decades. He worked a laborer in a small factory and is now retired with a small pension. He is in an area, though, where the government is allowing churches to reopen and allowing priests like him to rebuild the churches so long as they do not openly denounce the Catholic Patriotic Association. He is now working day and night, building churches and administering the sacraments to people who are flocking in. It is an enormously gratifying time for him. He told my informant that if he had done things his way, he would have lived a quiet life since 1949 as pastor of a small congregation. But after having seemingly lost everything, he is now busier and more active as a priest than he ever dreamed of being. This, he thought, seemed to be God's way.

NOTES

1. *To Taste a Hundred Herbs*, Carma Hinton, dir. (distributed by New Day Films, 1987).

2. Compare this figure with William Hinton's claim in *Shen Fan* that Long Bow is presently one-third Catholic (*Shen Fan* [New York: Vintage Books, 1984], p. 283).

3. William Hinton, *Fanshen* (New York: Vintage Books, 1964).

4. Hinton, *Shen Fan*, pp. 282–283.

5. Ibid., pp. 278–282.

6. The main statement about this was in Pope Pius XI's encyclical *Quadragesimo Anno* (1931). For a summary see Jean-Yves Calvez, "Economic Policy Issues in Roman Catholic Social Teaching: An International Perspective," in *The Catholic Challenge to the American Economy*, ed. Thomas M. Gannon, S.J. (New York: Macmillan, 1987), pp. 15–26.

7. For a good summary of Catholic church history in the first two decades of the People's Republic, see Eric O. Hanson, *Catholic Politics in China and Korea* (Maryknoll, N.Y.: Orbis Books, 1980), p. 670.

8. Jerome Heyndrickx, "Emergence of a Local Catholic Church in China?" *Tripod*, no. 37 (Fall 1987), p. 69. *Tripod* is published in both Chinese and English about four times a year by the Holy Spirit Study Centre, which was established by the Roman Catholic Diocese of Hong Kong in 1980. Staffed mostly by Catholic priests and nuns, of whom about half are Chinese and half foreign, the Holy Spirit Study

Centre aims to "help the Church of Hong Kong better understand the changes in the fields of religion and ethics taking place in China today," with the hope that such understanding will lead to "Christian concern, and eventually even to dialogue with our brothers and sisters in the motherland." These aims undoubtedly influence what kind of information is published by the Centre. *Tripod* is aimed at a rather broad audience of Catholics, so it features articles that are shorter and less detailed than typical social science journal articles. Since its ultimate goal is to promote dialogue between Hong Kong Catholics and Chinese Catholics, it tends to emphasize what it considers signs of hope in the situation of the Church in China, although it does not fail to mention problems with the Chinese church. Finally, it pays more attention to theological evaluation of events in the Chinese church than to sociological analysis.

From the point of view of a social scientist, therefore, *Tripod* is less than an ideal source of data. It is for now, however, the best single source available. In using *Tripod* for this chapter, I have assumed that the information contained in it is basically accurate, though selected according to different criteria than would have been used by a social scientist. I have tried to keep these differences of criteria in mind when using data from *Tripod* and attempted to translate theological concerns into sociological concerns. And I have been sociologically conservative: That is, I have refrained from basing any essential part of my argument on information that might be rendered unreliable by possible biases inherent in the Holy Spirit Study Centre's mission.

9. Ernst Troeltsch, *The Social Teachings of the Christian Churches*, trans. Olive Wyon (London: George Allen, 1931).

10. *Weixin Newsletter* (Hong Kong), no. 4 (June 1987), p. 3.

11. The general theoretical perspective used here is partially based upon the philosophy of Hans-Georg Gadamer. See his *Truth and Method* (New York: Seabury Press, 1975).

12. See Emily Honig, "Pride and Prejudice: Subei People in Contemporary Shanghai," chapter 9 in this book.

13. Aloysius Jin Luxian, "The Church in China: Today and Tomorrow," *Tripod*, no. 40 (Summer 1987), p. 74. For a description with photographs of these all-Catholic fishing villages, see Donald MacInnis, "Faith of Fishing Families," *Maryknoll*, April 1988, pp. 10–13. For interviews with Catholics from these villages, see Theresa Chu, *Learning from Christians in Wuxi*, pamphlet, Canada China Programme, Canadian Council of Churches, 1988.

14. This is apparent in a film on the Sheshan pilgrimages, made in Shanghai, that was shown by the delegation from the Catholic church in China at an international conference on Christianity in China, held in Montreal in October 1981.

15. *Tripod*, no. 38 (Winter 1987), p. 29.

16. John Tong, "With Bishop Wu in Guangdong," *Tripod*, no. 31 (Spring 1986), pp. 66–67.

17. Hanson, *Catholic Politics*, pp. 72–82.

18. This statement is in disagreement with the argument of Tu Wei-ming in "Christian Faith and Confucian Tradition: An Authentic Possibility of Creative Misunderstanding" (unpublished ms.). Tu suggests that the intellectual issues of the Rites Controversy have never been resolved. I would emphasize the sociological practice of the Chinese Catholic church and argue that at this fundamental level they have indeed been resolved.

19. Quoted in Hanson, *Catholic Politics*, p. 21.

20. Ibid., pp. 22–23.

21. The interviews cited in this chapter were carried out with representatives of Catholics in America Concerned About China, during their annual meeting in December 1987, at Maryknoll, New York.

22. Reprinted in *Tripod*, no. 39 (Spring 1987), pp. 78–83.

23. John Tong, *Tripod*, no. 31 (Spring 1986), pp. 69–70.

8

Recycling Rituals
Politics and Popular Culture
in Contemporary Rural China

HELEN F. SIU

Many visitors to rural China have noticed a spectacular flourishing of popular rituals in the post-Mao era and assumed, perhaps too hastily, that this phenomenon is best understood as the resurgence of traditional antihegemonic ritual practices that miraculously survived Maoism and now plague the socialist state. Yale anthropologist Helen Siu, looking at the social meaning of funeral and wedding rituals in Guangdong, doubts this interpretation. She argues that present-day rituals are new reconstructions of the 1980s and that their meanings are linked to new perceptions of power relations in rural society. The attack on popular culture launched by the socialist state in the 1940s destroyed most of the social bases for popular rituals and replaced their political functions. Rituals related to individual life-cycles were stripped of their wider social linkages and confined within the household. Thus, the resurgence of popular rituals in the 1980s represents the recycling of cultural fragments in a rural society that has been effectively penetrated by monopolizing state power. In Hong Kong and Taiwan the diluting of ritual practices is associated with the secularizing force of the market, but in mainland China the diluting is linked to state intervention.

—Eds.

CONCEPTUALIZING
POPULAR THOUGHT AND RITUALS

Scholars who observed the lack of color in rural social life in the Maoist era have also marveled at the liberalizing energies released by the recent decade of reforms. Unprecedented movements of goods, capital, and people across the rural landscape have been accompanied by a flourishing of popular rituals. The phenomenon poses interesting questions about culture change. Has Maoist politics ironically preserved the popular culture of peasant communities to the extent that, once the party-state attempted to retreat from society, popular culture regained its former momentum to influence the process of modernization? Or has peasant culture been so touched by the Maoist programs that what we observe today are new reconstitutions of tradition for coping with contemporary existence defined by the socialist state, rather than cultural remnants that survived the encounter with that state? On the basis of fieldwork carried out in 1986 in Nanxi (a pseudonym), a market town in the heart of the Pearl River delta known for the intensity of popular ritual activities in the past and the present, I will examine a set of rituals, especially those for funerals and weddings, and the meanings practitioners attribute to them in order to address the issue of cultural continuity and change in rural China today.[1]

At the methodological level, this chapter raises the issue of the interaction of culture, state, and society over time. Chinese anthropologists have long recognized that traditional popular culture in general fitted in with the imperial paradigm, although at times it was also used to subvert state ideology. But the major thrust was toward integration. It had always been the intention of the imperial state to co-opt potential threats from local society, both institutionally and ideologically, as is clearly indicated in its bestowal of imperial titles upon popular deities that had gathered substantial followings. Community and domestic rituals also showed that local society actively cultivated a symbiotic relationship with the state culture rather than opposed it.[2]

While past interpenetration between state and society in the realm of Chinese popular culture is readily assumed by scholars, the treatment of popular rituals in the postrevolutionary period lacks this perspective. Instead, the relentless efforts of the socialist government to suppress popular thought and rituals are posed in a mechanical fashion against their preservation and their recent renaissance. Viewed as inherently antistate and antihegemonic, popular culture is presumed to have survived the onslaught of Maoist politics only to come back in full force to plague the reformers today.[3]

There is ample evidence that what appear to be traditional ritual practices have re-emerged in China, especially in the rural areas.[4] During the year I spent in Nanxi, I was struck by the ritual intensity that was displayed. Eight years into the reforms, one would not have been surprised if the market town, traditionally known for its 393 ancestral halls, 139 temples, and monasteries that had been the scenes of rituals throughout the years, had resumed at least some of its customary ways.[5] Such usual religious items as paper money and incenses were sold not only in the markets by peddlers, but also in individually owned shops that conducted a prosperous business.

Moreover, contrary to observations elsewhere that public rituals are lacking,[6] community temples and secular festivals that were linked to the interests of overseas compatriots were actively promoted by the town government. When the residents eagerly pursued rituals related to the life-cycle of individuals, there was also an aggressive touch of public display that acknowledged the limits set by officials. The primacy of performance in these rituals, similarly observed by James Watson in those of the late imperial period, is significant here. If the socialist government today actively appropriates tradition in order to make cultural communications suit its political priorities, as the imperial state did, and if local society actively pursues them with such understanding, will the consequence be a unifying culture of "reritualization," to use Watson's term,[7] in which the state and society continue to give each other recognition?

Instead of arguing that traditional practices are being revived and are challenging the socialist ideology, this chapter maintains that the rituals today are reconstituted by a different cast of performers and that the process reproduces a much transformed rural society in which the power of the socialist state has long been taken for granted. This ritual revitalization involves the complicity of both the socialist state and the rural practitioners, and provides an important window on the changing meanings of rituals that highlights new perceptions of power and commitment in contemporary rural society. In this way, the effects of the thirty years of administrative history emerge from the analysis of popular culture in rural China today.

TRADITIONAL RITUALS IN NANXI

Major works in Chinese anthropology suggest that rituals, as cultural performances, reflect the ways in which practitioners order their sociopolitical reality, both symbolically and instrumentally.[8] To interpret what they mean to practitioners in Nanxi today, one needs to understand how rituals before the revolution created a compelling moral fabric for social living, and how the transformation of the traditional order gave rise to new contexts for ritual acts. Since the eighteenth century, the landlords and grain merchants who resided in Nanxi controlled the surrounding sands, which were vast areas of reclaimed alluvial land rented out to migrant tenant farmers. The rise to power of landlords and merchants in the regional economy was accompanied by intense ritual activities. Apart from compiling elaborate lineage genealogies that dazzled the eye with the names of imperial degree-holders, members of the three largest surnames of the town, He, Li, and Mai, put great energies into the ceremonies of their numerous ancestral halls as well as into the periodic community festivals centering around the major temples of which they were principal patrons. The year-round rituals helped to make explicit social connections and political distinctions. Family members participated in domestic rituals but were linked to a wider range of kin through the male members, who took their respective places in the complex of public rituals at the lineage halls and graves. Another network was constructed by their participation in the rituals of neighborhood shrines that delineated communal boundaries. At the same time, the neighborhoods that centered around a shrine, known as *she*, were the building blocks for larger scale religious events. As collectives, they made monetary and material contributions and provided organized manpower for temple festivals.[9]

The lineage and temple networks partly merged in communitywide festivities that centered on the five large temples and major ancestral halls in town. Through taking part in the rituals, the inhabitants sought affiliations that confirmed status and differentiated access to resources, claimed rights of settlement and tenure, forged political alliances, arbitrated conflicts, and secured social mobility.[10] The chrysanthemum festivals organized periodically by the literati members of major lineages are particularly noteworthy. Participants mimicked the civil service examinations by competing with poetry and flowers. The activities nonetheless involved intense manipulation of cultural symbols—lineage aggrandizement, community exclusiveness, wealth, and literati connections to political office. Together, such festivals delineated the changing configurations of power among local elites as the regional economy centering the town developed. The wealth and scholarship flaunted by the elites and the social networks that organizers employed revealed political agendas by which the language of imperial authority percolated downward and negotiated with local initiatives at the ritual arena. The process reproduced the values of kin, community, class, and politics among the town residents to guide social life in both the domestic and public realms.[11]

RITUALS AND THE SOCIALIST REVOLUTION

The socialist revolution of 1949 not only attacked popular rituals severely but also has destroyed most of their social bases and replaced their political functions. In accordance with official ideology—that popular rituals are feudal superstitions linked to the peasants' support of the imperial order—the town government carried out campaigns to destroy and discredit them. The public rituals were the first to be suppressed. As early as the period of the land reform from 1950 to 1952, estates upon which ancestral halls and temples depended to finance their activities were confiscated. The buildings were converted to schools, factories, and administrative offices. Managers of these estates were publicly discredited and some were killed for their "class crimes." During the high tide of the Great Leap Forward in 1958, the ancestral halls were dismantled and their bricks and stones transported to the surrounding villages under the party slogan to aid agricultural production. Notions of kin continued to exist but were weakened when the material evidence and the instrumentality of lineage solidarity were replaced by the priorities of the socialist government. In the late 1950s, old trees that stood above neighborhood shrines were also cut down to fuel the backyard furnaces; the disappearance of the physical symbols of the former *she* coincided with their reorganization under the fifteen neighborhood committees. By translating the political directives of the town government into the management of their neighborhoods, the committee directors institutionalized the power of the new state in everyday social living.

The temples were spared at the time because they were physically rather small-scale compared to the halls. With the 1960s even these remnants of cultural tradition were destroyed: During the Cultural Revolution, young students were mobilized to attack "the four olds," or traditional customs and habits; classic texts and genealogies were burnt, and the images of deities in temples were smashed. A former Daoist priest recalled that out of fear, he voluntarily took most of his ritual texts and tools to the brigade headquarters to be burnt and promised not to recruit apprentices for his trade. However, he managed to hide some of the ritual scrolls and a geomancy compass, and preserved a large copper bowl used for funeral rites by storing pig feed in it. The Buddhist monastery and the two convents in the area were closed down. The monks were sent away and the building converted to private living quarters. The nuns were made to return to secular life. With the religious specialists prohibited from their trades, the annual communal exorcism and the temple festivals that were tied to the agricultural cycle, together with the more personal funeral rituals, gradually faded from people's memories. Though there were rumors that the destroyers of the Chengwang temple had turned mad, which preserved the fear of the gods among the elderly, young skeptics who could not tell one deity from another regarded these tales as hearsay.

The suppression of popular rituals extended to the domestic realm as well. With the demise of the ancestral halls and the prohibition of burial, rituals related to individual life-cycles such as births, weddings, funerals, and memorial rites to ancestors were stripped of their wider social linkages and increasingly confined within the household. During the Cultural Revolution, not only was cremation strictly enforced, but also the large mound on the edge of the town that had served as the community's graveyard for centuries was appropriated for agricultural use. Some villagers grew crops in the midst of the tombstones. Most often, graves were dug up and the land converted to fish ponds and vegetable gardens. In the land-scarce villages close to the town, memories of the hungry years in the early 1960s lingered, and many villagers valued garden plots above other people's ancestors.[12] "In the political confusion of the period," an elderly friend added, "those who were daring did not care where their ancestors were placed, and those who cared dared not raise the issue." Furthermore, every street committee saw to the burning of domestic altars and ancestral tablets, fueled in part by the efforts of young students who were mobilized by the radical faction of the town government.

Elderly residents in Nanxi admitted that they hung onto their practices in the "privacy of their bedrooms," but lament that what was passed on to their children was fragmentary at best. I was told of a sadly comical episode that occurred during the period of the Cultural Revolution. The eldest son of a man who had died was given the task of performing *mai shui* (buying water to wash the deceased).[13] For this he had to fetch some water from the river. Traditionally, that water was used to wash the body of the deceased, but more importantly, the ritual had to be performed under the watchful eyes of kin and neighbors as it indicated important rights and obligations in inheritance. The basin in which the water was collected was to be lowered evenly into the river to allow it to be filled from all sides in order to signify the recognition of the equal status of sons in property division. As the chief mourner and heir, he must see to it that everything was done properly. However, the political circumstances at the time presented real problems. Instead, the son slipped out alone one night, scooped some water from the river and rushed home. Unfortunately he ran into a young cadre who asked why he carried a basin of river water in the middle of the night. After mumbling some excuses, he got away, but spilt most of the water out of fear. The incident reveals that for the younger generation, popular rituals have become a secretive, domestic affair because they were not linked to the wider social meanings of the rituals pertaining to lineage or community. It seems that the overarching ideological structure signified by the gods, ghosts, and ancestors that the residents of Nanxi used rituals to represent symbolically, to associate and negotiate with, and to guide practical action as well as spiritual needs were no longer dependable. Instead, that structure remained only in fragments, broken by the priorities of a new intervening political power.

The plight of the rituals reflected the social and political relationships in the corporeal world.[14] Since the 1950s, the livelihood of the town residents has become divorced from that of the surrounding villages. Resources confiscated from the ancestral estates were returned to the former tenants in the sands, while those of the merchants were transformed into collective enterprises increasingly linked to the state sector as ancillary industries. Corresponding to the decrease of alternative paths for economic and political advancement, people's lives were bureaucratized under the concerted efforts of their work units and neighborhood committees. The town government was staffed by local party cadres whose power over the life of the town residents was total. But unlike the local elites before them, they were cogs in a national political machinery that was highly organized. Their positions gave them less room for maneuver as far as implementing party policies was concerned. When political pressure from their superiors was applied, they transmitted it down to their constituents. To bolster its own power, the socialist government introduced a new set of rituals that the town cadres eagerly pursued. The public struggle meetings against the former corporate landlords during the land reform, the regimented euphoria of the Great Leap Forward and the communization movement, the influx of the poor peasant cadres from the sands during the Four Cleanups campaigns, the tabloids, the Mao quotations, the loyalty parades, and the factional fights among students and factory workers during the Cultural Revolution each in its own way introduced symbolic as well as practical statements of political authority to the residents of Nanxi in the postrevolutionary era.

AN INTENSIFIED RITUAL LANDSCAPE

Today, the ancestral halls in town remain closed. Cadres in the town government are adamant that "superstitious practices" in this former "fortress of feudalism" should not be publicly condoned or revived. On the other hand, they did allow the He lineage association from Hong Kong, whose membership is made up of powerful merchants and industrialists, to claim back their ancestral halls, which had been occupied by factories and government offices. But these halls remain cultural artifacts because lineage rituals are not activated.[15]

However, practically every household has restored its domestic altar, including several of the homes of leading cadres. In the central part of the sitting room, the tablet that used to represent the nine popular deities has been replaced by a large word *shen* (deity) written in gold against a red background. Though its exaggerated presence is no longer balanced by the simple, one-line ancestral tablet on its left nor the small tablet for the household god (*menkou tudi*) at the doorway, the trio is recognized as essential for the welfare of the members of the household.

Not only is the old carpenter who makes these tablets now taking in apprentices, but the street where his shop is located, known as Coffin street because it is the area where the trades catering to funerals used to congregate, is experiencing a new lease on life. Funerals, like weddings, have been conducted with ever-increasing extravagance to the point that some of the old literati in the town complain about the vulgarization. Gifts of condolence accompany the shiny wood coffins that are taken in procession through the main street, and the passersby, instead of avoiding them as they customarily would have in the past, eagerly stand around to comment on the number of wreaths and the size of the funeral bands. For families who have thrived in the decade of reforms or who have overseas connections, funerals are followed by a dinner of up to thirty or more banquet tables. Some even hire Daoist priests and nuns to perform the funeral rites that can extend for seven weeks. Taken together, the expenses easily amount to 10,000 yuan or more. For a market town where the average worker earns 200 yuan a month, the sum is extraordinary.

A similar extravagance prevails over weddings. What appear to be traditional ceremonies have once more become popular. The red bridal gowns with the embroidered flowers and the phoenix are rented for 10 yuan; hiring a ritual specialist to accompany the bride costs another 25 yuan. Then there are the two days of elaborate gift exchanges between the families of the bride and groom that involve up to 5,000 yuan, plus the thirty or so banquet tables for relatives and friends that cost 150 yuan each. While parents in town complain that marrying off a daughter is ruinous because of expensive dowry items such as a refrigerator, a washing machine, electric fans, and even a hi-fi system, those in the nearby villages protest against the runaway inflation of bridal gifts provided by the groom.

While subscribing to the ceremonies is expensive and difficult, especially when ritual specialists do not operate altogether publicly, they are nonetheless eagerly pursued.[16] One may expect that the older generation is delighted with the turn of events; to my surprise, some of my older friends are most vocal against what they term "the vulgarization of tradition." Their complaints are curiously juxtaposed with the uncharacteristic fervor of the young, who are taking an active part both in organizing and financing the rituals. In the past, there was much knowledge about the rituals, even though the young had not reached the stage in their life-cycles to be deeply involved. The revolution has eliminated a great deal of that knowledge, which begs the question: What fuels their enthusiasm today?

Young entrepreneurs are most concerned about geomancy, about which they know little, and are diligent in their offerings to Guandi (regarded as the god of fortune). A majority of those young people I interviewed had also gone on pilgrimage trips with friends and coworkers to the Longmu Temple up the Xi River in order to make personal appeals ranging from passing examinations to gaining a fortune and finding a spouse.[17] One can also see old trees covered with red paper on which names of young children are linked with tree spirits believed to be efficacious. At neighborhood entrances and street corners there are a variety of offerings to small stone slabs. The indiscriminate fervor leads one to wonder what meanings popular rituals are taking on for their practitioners today.

Furthermore, a singularly talismanic concern underlying the ritual behavior of the younger generation was brought home to me most vividly on a visit to a major Buddhist temple that has recently been reopened for tourists. In late 1986, I took a trip there with several former nuns to perform a *yankou* ceremony for their religious master, who had died during the Cultural Revolution. For three days, I was lodged at the temple and watched them perform the rituals in the evenings after the temple closed its doors to the public. In the quiet chilling nights of the mountain, they chanted with the monks to reach out to their deceased master. They wept quietly, communicating their regret that they had yielded to adverse political realities and had not come to relieve their master sooner. The world these nuns unveiled to me could not have been more different from that of the young visitors who occupied the temple during the busy hours of the day. The latter came in hordes, indiscriminating in the ways they placed their incense and in their ritual performances. They crowded the gift shops looking for an efficacious souvenir and patronized the temple canteen for a vegetarian meal. After posing for pictures at the grand entrance of the temple, they hurried off as noisily as they had come. They and the old nuns shared the same social space, but they seemed worlds apart.

Granted that rituals mean different things to different people, the divergent meanings they have assumed today are noteworthy. The prevalent attitude toward rituals for the younger generation is the following: Make offerings and go through the ceremonies when one has the free time. Who cares if there are spirits or not, but one should cast a wide net just in case. If there are spirits, it is too easy to offend one unknowingly, which may lead to misfortune. If the spirits in one's path are happy, they may even bring pleasant surprises.

FUNERALS AND WEDDINGS

Let us take a closer look at funeral and wedding rituals in Nanxi in order to evaluate the extent to which the content and the underlying popular perceptions about political and social relationships have changed during the last three decades. As suggested earlier, these changes can be particularly revealing because they carry a personal and domestic dimension and at the same time they are rituals performed publicly, involving the wider networks of neighborhood, friends, and relatives, and also the complicity of officials. Both of these dimensions have been severely attacked by the socialist government. For example, wedding feasts were condemned as wasteful, and an explicit rule forbade more than four banquet tables. There are of course generic reasons in China as well as elsewhere behind the complaints about ritual expenses, but in this case, there are also political motives. Except for community-based temple festivals, appeals to deities are relatively individualized; weddings and funerals, on the other hand, gather together the members of a large network of friends and relatives whose organizing principles are seen by the political cadres as threatening their authority and priorities. However, the recent decade of reforms has brought about the increased intensity and lavishness in these rituals.

Every day at noon, one cannot miss the funeral processions that proceed along the main road before turning into Coffin street at the end of which friends and relatives disperse while members of the deceased's family continue to the burial mound behind the town. The mourning dresses, the wreaths and the "longevity cloth" on display, the playing of the funeral band, and the coffin carried by eight peasants from nearby villages—all are novel features for those under twenty-five years of age. However, knowing elders in town also complain how differently these processions look today. They claim that many features have been simplified. In the prerevolutionary days, the route for the procession passed through three neighborhood shrines (*guo sanshe*) in order that the female mourners could notify the spirit of the shrines (*shetou gong*) and symbolically bid farewell to the community for the deceased.[18] Furthermore, it avoided routes where major surnames had their private roads and ancestral halls. Today it takes the most direct route to the main street because most of the halls and shrines no longer exist; and even if the halls continue to stand, the once cohesive surname groups who owned them have long lost their power to interfere.

At the head of Coffin street, a small temple was erected in the last century by a member of the local gentry of the He surname, in honor of his housekeeper and tutor. Known as the Sheren Miao, the temple had been a stopping point for the funeral procession to distinguish friends from close kin: Friends were given sweets and a packet of small change before they dispersed, while relatives followed to the end of the street where a bridge divided the town from the neighboring settlement of Yongding (a pseudonym). From then on, only the sons of the deceased attended the actual burial at the mound. This gradual dispersal of the funeral procession that symbolically revealed the social distance and the obligations of the participants to the deceased, as well as the degree of death pollution to which the participants are exposed, is no longer adhered to. In the first place, the temple is now a dilapidated building used as a hostel for the elderly homeless, and even middle-aged mourners cannot identify it. Most turn back at the bridge, but female members of the family now join the men at the burial site, because the taboo on their presence at these sites (which might lead to a lack of descendants) has become much less important.[19] The demise of the ancestral estates and their halls after the land reform seems also to have led to a falling off in the hierarchical, male-oriented public culture of the lineage and to have drawn family members closer together within households on the basis of their contribution to the domestic economy.

A similar flattening of hierarchy and differentiation based on kin and gender is seen in the mourning dresses. Formerly, a sharp-eyed bystander could immediately tell how many sons, daughters, in-laws, nephews, and nieces the deceased had from the type of cloth the mourning dresses were made of, from the layers of cloth that were worn, from the style of the headgear, and from the canes mourners carried.[20] But today most of the mourners either wrap a white sash around their waists, if they are close relatives, or wear a black armband, in the case of distant relatives and close friends.

Although there has been a telescoping of mourning categories, that does not mean concerns of kin and descent are fading in the community. Local residents have shrewdly allied themselves with surname associations overseas in their attempts to restore ancestral halls. There was even a recent case in which segments of a lineage came to blows at the gravesite of an ancestor, each accusing the other of illegitimate descent. What is happening is obvious: During the Maoist period, valuable properties were confiscated, in some of which overseas owners had an interest. The liberal united front policies that aim to attract overseas investment allow many to reclaim such properties; their relatives in Nanxi stand to gain. A local saying that has become very popular in recent years among the young runs, "Cast your kin net widely and you will find a big catch." On the other hand, older people lament that even cousins do not know one another, and certainly know the etiquette neither for greeting nor for the solution of conflicts. Practical concerns underlying the traditional claims of kinship affiliation are well recognized, but today these claims become more blatantly instrumental for personal gain. The imbalance is partly due to the fragmentation of the former overarching ideological structure, which used to mediate the concerns of kin, community, and class interests.

What most annoys my elderly friends are those features in the funeral ceremonies today that are more appropriate to festive celebrations. The plastic wreaths with their multicolor designs are uncharacteristically cheerful and represent a sharp difference from the days when only white and yellow chrysanthemums were used.[21] The young female mourners are often wearing their brightest Sunday clothes, especially those who are mere friends to the deceased. Even if they do not intend to show their best in such an occasion, they are dressed for the evening banquet.[22] In prerevolutionary days, a small number of relatives and helpers were given dinner at the end of the day. Now this token of thanks from the mourners has turned into an elaborate banquet for a wide network of people who have only slight connections with the deceased.

According to my elderly friends, this feasting is a result of two recent trends. More unrelated people now contribute to the funeral ceremonies by sending longevity cloth and wreaths or by giving a token of longevity money. The contributors are then invited to the evening banquet, making up the unlikely mixture of the coworkers of sons and grandsons of the deceased, of neighbors and street-committee directors, and of overseas business contacts. Quite contrary to what used to be an occasion to be avoided if possible, the funeral today has become a special event. It is as if everyone is eagerly contributing to it for socializing purposes and attending to the dead is but an excuse.

Moreover, the banquet has assumed a new meaning. It involves the ceremony of the *shang gao*, which used to take place 100 days to a year after burial, and also involves thanksgiving in the household, signifying that the deceased has now joined the ranks of the ancestors. The fact that such a celebration today takes place before the corpse turns cold in the grave gives the occasion a strangely disquieting character.

Why the mourners collapse the two occasions into one has its social logic. When burials were banned in the 1960s and 1970s, the ashes of the deceased were brought home and put at the family altar hidden in bedrooms. Funeral mourning and the ceremony of joining the ancestors took place almost simultaneously with little fanfare. Today, the two continue to be merged, but the ceremony is fueled by the new wealth and the new energies for networking, the result of which is to produce the incongruent lavishness, a phenomenon labeled by the town's elderly educators as grotesque. In 1986, the talk of the town was two elaborate occasions of this kind. The first was the funeral banquet of forty tables staged for the wife of a prominent man, formerly a landlord-merchant of the He surname, who, through the help of overseas relatives, has claimed back numerous properties from the town government. The other was financed single-handedly by the grandson of the deceased, who has become a successful private entrepreneur. The publicly advertised generation-skipping of the second funeral was quite unusual, but the young man, while criticized, was also praised by his friends for his shrewd business instincts. The eager complicity of relatives is understandable, since the networking process can probably be beneficial to them all.

Wedding ceremonies display changes of a similar kind, with the young taking an active part. An obvious example is the institution of *huiyou*, which used to be a brotherhood composed of a few lifelong friends who helped the bridegroom not only through the wedding but also at other important occasions in his life-cycle. The modern brotherhood has grown more extensive and now includes a few dozen people from the immediate circle of the bridegroom's friends, coworkers, and cousins, who disperse once the wedding is over. The ego-centered way in which the *huiyou* is formed and the transient nature of its functions mean that young men find themselves serving as *huiyou* for several friends during a busy season. Of course, they complain about the severe drain on their financial resources, as they are expected to contribute more than the normal standards of a wedding gift on account of the special relationship with the groom. Nevertheless, most are honored to be asked and feel compelled to participate. According to them, this act of networking is necessary for operating in this day and age. The utilitarian mode of the *huiyou* also caters to the groom's priorities as well. He can depend upon the brotherhood to call on friends to collect banquet tables and chairs, to secure foreign wines and cigarettes, and, most important of all, to supply minibuses and "taxis" for the bride and for relatives. These items are expensive and hard to come by, except with the right connections.

Despite the overtly pragmatic nature of the ceremonies, the symbolic aspects of the ritual are still important. The head of the brotherhood must be an older male, married, with living parents, and preferably have a son. The groom is expected to benefit from his good fortunes by association with him. However, the way the values behind the symbols are pursued do not convey the feeling that the practitioners subscribe to the traditional ideological structure. They are ignorant of the surrounding myths and legends, and they do not care one way or another. Without exception, none of the young married couples I interviewed in 1986 knew enough of the legends of the white tiger and the golden rooster to understand why an umbrella is an essential item for the protection of the bride. For them, it engenders talismanic effects similar to the pair of sugar cane and the head of lettuce that accompany the bride to the groom's house.[23] When asked about the meaning of these practices, respondents often gave vague answers. One friend after another told me, "I do not understand these rituals; nor can I explain or expect when they do or do not work. One supernatural power is just as good as another so long as it delivers. Everyone now carries out these rituals, so I feel I should do the same so that I am not left behind. One does not lose anything by doing what others do. If the power that be chances to fancy what you offer, all the better."

RECYCLING RITUALS

If one would be hard put to insist that the funeral and wedding rituals observed today in Nanxi are mere revivals of tradition, one may at least argue that they are but an aspect of a secularizing trend that is being experienced by the town residents. This of course assumes that changes in beliefs and ritual behavior correspond to particular transformations in political economies. But unlike such processes in Taiwan and Hong Kong where they are colored by the nature of industrial work, by westernized education, by general political liberalization, and by functional differentiation in economic activities, the transformations in Nanxi and the surrounding villages have undergone instead an enclosure of their social and economic worlds, which were dominated by a political organization based on patronage and on unequal access to privilege. Social life and values have been bureaucratized, but not in the way that so concerned the Weberians. Instead, the powerful control by the state accompanied the personalization of the authority of individual political leaders, so that all were subject to arbitrary interpretations.

Although the recent wave of reforms shows the sincerity of the national leaders in trying to separate the state from the economy and social life more generally, its omnipotent presence and the consequent relationships of control and dependency have been internalized by the actors and are taken for granted. These structural transformations have engendered cultural attitudes and social experiences different from those of the populations in Hong Kong and Taiwan, where the rhythms of a modern, internationally involved market economy dominate. Therefore, if one concludes that there is a general diluting of popular ritual practices in these Chinese communities in the course of the last three decades, the underlying causes have been different. The dilution in Taiwan and Hong Kong can be attributed partly to the secularizing force of the market, whereas that in rural China has been due to the intervention of a monopolizing state power.

Those who are optimistic about the recent reforms may argue that the last decade has finally allowed rural China to be exposed to secularizing market forces and that this process has resulted in today's proliferation of instrumental and individualized assumptions in ritual behavior. The proposed withdrawal of the state is certainly liberalizing for individual entrepreneurs, especially for the young generation who are desperately eager to make the best of their chances before another turn of the political wheel. It nevertheless leaves them with a great deal of uncertainty about the present and the future. For measures of the traditional networks of social mobility have disappeared with the older victims of past political vicissitudes. To break out of the cellular existence dominated by the party-state urgently requires the construction of new networks. Not only does the process need time and confidence, but also formal organizational means based on functional differentiations that at present are still subject to the scrutiny of a state bureaucracy known for its vindictive power. Informal networking is preferred over other organizational means that may be seen to threaten a political party already insecure in an era of ideological redefinition. Because popular rituals are now politically tolerated, especially if they involve overseas patrons, they become the surest context for new networking.

In fact, the town government itself has played a part in bringing about the recent renaissance of rituals. The explicitly political rituals of the Maoist era are a thing of the past. But the town government continues to monopolize the communitywide rituals. When the town government staged a series of chrysanthemum festivals beginning in 1979, during the course of which they feasted overseas emigrants in the name of the town, the political agenda was promoted in an unabashed fashion. Their efforts to show that they are liberalizing in earnest have successfully tapped new investment, which they use to claim credit from their superiors in the party in this age of reforms. When entrepreneurs shrewdly follow with their own lavish feasts in life-cycle rituals such as weddings and funerals, the cadres can hardly deny their legitimacy.

The practitioners of these rituals are not entirely utilitarian. Certain talismanic qualities of the rituals are particularly appealing to the young, who are uncharacteristically eager about practicing and financing the rituals. They believe that the umbrella, the sugar cane, and the lettuce in a wedding are objects invoking efficacy by association, but these views differ fundamentally from those of their elders, who appreciate the legends concerning the power of the spiritual forces in the form of the white tiger and the potential harm of the golden rooster. The intellectual justifications for these rituals by the Daoist priest in terms of the contradiction embedded in the forces of nature are even less relevant for the young.[24] A similar assumption lies behind their pilgrimages to deities about whose legendary power they are largely ignorant but with whom they nevertheless are eager to associate.

It appears that when traditional hierarchies of power are no longer relevant and when the socialist power structure that replaced them ceases to inspire confidence, social as well as moral existence becomes very much in flux. The ideological crisis of the socialist system affects the younger generation more so than the older, because they have no alternative worldview for comparison. In three decades of political vicissitudes, the gods, about whom they know little, and many of the party leaders, whose power they know all too well, have not been able to save themselves. The random ritual maneuvers of the young unveil to me a generation actively and desperately trying to anchor itself in a supernatural and a corporeal world they have little faith in.

In sum, I have tried to compare popular rituals in general and life-cycle rituals in particular before and after the socialist revolution in order to explore the underlying social bases and meanings. Rituals in the prerevolutionary period communicated meanings related to a supernatural power structure that was closely tied to an accepted corporeal social structure and morality. The repeated efforts of the party-state changed both drastically.[25] In today's ritual landscape, revitalized with an unusual intensity, the basic features of traditional weddings and funerals and their ideological assumptions continue to have appeal. But the practitioners are also most concerned with the mundane affairs of everyday social living where the power of the socialist state has long been internalized. The resurgence of these rituals in their transformed state represents cultural fragments recycled under new circumstances. In arguing that these are new reconstitutions of tradition, this chapter tries to make meaningful connections between cultural change and political economy. The ritual expressions today point to the fact that the power of the Marxist state has reached far into society; its proposed retreat triggers new anxieties as well as energies. To cope with this era, residents in Nanxi shrewdly reconstitute ritual fragments to interact with the encapsulating political structure, reproducing, improvising, and changing their cultural meanings.

NOTES

1. This paper is based on fieldwork conducted in the Pearl River delta in 1986 and 1987. I am grateful to the Committee on Scholarly Communication with the People's Republic of China, National Academy of Sciences, for financing the year of

research in 1986. I also thank the participants in the conference on popular thought at San Diego, California, in October 1987, and professors Jack Goody and Rubie Watson for their comments.

2. One can start with an article by Arthur Wolf, "Gods, Ghosts and Ancestors," in *Religion and Ritual in Chinese Society*, ed. Arthur Wolf (Stanford: Stanford University Press, 1974). Wolf describes major categories of popular religion as reflections of social relationships in the corporeal world. In *Chinese Ritual and Politics* (Cambridge: Cambridge University Press, 1981), Emily Ahern analyzes how the integrations of popular and state cultures actually takes place when notions about power and the etiquette of dealing with power are learned through ritual practices. On the issue of how cultural unity has been maintained through the centuries as a result of the attempts of the imperial state to standardize ritual performances, see James Watson, "Standardizing the Gods: The Promotion of T'ian Hou (Empress of Heaven) Along the South China Coast, 960–1960," in *Popular Culture in Late Imperial China*, ed. David Johnson, Andrew Nathan, and Evelyn Rawski (Berkeley and Los Angeles: University of California Press, 1985). With regard to funeral rituals, see the introduction and chapter 5 of *Death Rituals in Late Imperial and Modern China*, ed. James Watson and Evelyn Rawski (Berkeley and Los Angeles: University of California Press, 1988).

3. For statements about the antihegemonic nature of popular rituals in imperial as well as modern China, see a symposium of papers in *Modern China*, vol. 13, no. 1 (January 1987), organized by Hill Gates and Robert Weller; for socialist China, see the paper by Ann Anagnost, pp. 40–61. See William Parish and Martin Whyte, *Village and Family in Contemporary China* (Chicago: University of Chicago Press, 1978) on traditional ways of life that lingered despite the efforts of the new government to change them. In a paper presented at the Conference on the Social Consequences of China's Economic Reforms, at Harvard University, May 1988, Vivienne Shue posed popular culture against the socialist ideology by emphasizing the paradoxical preservation of the former in the Maoist era. For some opposing views, see Richard Madsen, *Morality and Power in a Chinese Village* (Berkeley and Los Angeles: University of California Press, 1984); and Helen Siu, *Agents and Victims in South China: Accomplices in Rural Revolution* (New Haven: Yale University Press, 1989), on how new socialist ideology and rituals intertwined with everyday social practice in the villages since the 1960s.

4. See the paper by Martin Whyte in Watson and Rawski, *Death Rituals*. Watson has similar observations in his fieldwork in rural Guangdong in 1985.

5. A manuscript written by He Yanggao in 1946, which I was shown during my fieldwork, lists the local temples, the lineage halls, and some of the neighborhood shrines. A draft of the Nanxi Zhen gazetteer compiled by a group of local historians (1984) contains similar information. For lineage history, see the genealogies of the He, Li, and Mai surname groups in Nanxi.

6. See Whyte in Watson and Rawski, *Death Rituals*.

7. James Watson, introduction in Watson and Rawski, *Death Rituals*.

8. See Wolf, "Gods, Ghosts"; Ahern, *Ritual and Politics*; and Steven Sangren, *History and Magical Power in a Chinese Community* (Stanford: Stanford University Press, 1987).

9. See descriptions of the importance of neighborhood shrines in Taiwan by Kristofer Schipper, "Neighborhood Cult Associations in Traditional Tainan," in *The City in Late Imperial China*, ed. G. William Skinner (Stanford: Stanford University Press, 1977).

10. The connection between notions of community and the rituals of community exorcism (*jiao*) is described vividly by scholars who worked in Hong Kong. See the works of David Faure, James Hayes, and Tanaka Issei.

11. See Helen Siu, "Recycling Tradition: Culture, History and Political Economy in the Chrysanthemum Festivals of South China," unpublished manuscript.

12. Most of this land was divided into private plots for the villagers. A few whom I interviewed admitted that they were apprehensive in the beginning, but that plots were valuable for supplementing the meager collective income and for adding variety in their diet. After a few years, they thought little of the graves. I saw that most of those standing in the fields today were marked by small stone slabs with nothing inscribed on them. Some families confronted with misfortune have tried to locate graves with the aim of appeasing their ancestors; their attempts are largely unsuccessful.

13. For an analysis of *mai shui* see James Watson, "Of Flesh and Bones: The Management of Death Pollution in Cantonese Society," in *Death and the Regeneration of Life*, Maurice Block and Jonathan Parry (Cambridge: Cambridge University Press, 1982), pp. 155–186. Also see Emily Ahern, *The Cult of the Dead in a Chinese Village* (Stanford: Stanford University Press, 1973).

14. For the transformation of the political economy of Nanxi, see Helen Siu, "Socialist Peddlers and Princes in a Chinese Market Town," *American Ethnologist*, vol. 16, no. 2 (May 1989).

15. Several of the halls were simply locked up after the factories moved out. In my travels in the Pearl River delta, I came across other ancestral halls being restored. When asked about installing the ancestral tablets, the caretakers were not sure when and how it would take place.

16. I interviewed a sixty-eight-year-old Daoist priest who was told to give up his practices during the Four Cleanups movement in 1964. He has resumed his trade in the 1980s but said that he would only perform rituals privately because he was still unsure of the political winds.

17. The temple used to be popular among local residents not only for personal appeal, but also because it was an important center where rituals were performed for calming the flood waters of the Xi River. Today, the town provides a special bus service that leaves once a week to make the ten-hour trip. One can also take an overnight boat up the river to the town of Yuecheng where the temple stood.

18. Important events in one's life-cycles, such as birth, wedding, death, are marked by offerings to the shrines. The spirit who resides in the shrine supposedly watches over daily living and is notified of these events.

19. James Watson (chapter 5 in Watson and Rawski, *Death Rituals*) mentions other reasons given by his Cantonese informants for not allowing women at the burial sites.

20. For a description of the elaborate differentiations in mourning dress in Taiwan, see Arthur Wolf, "Chinese Kinship and Mourning Dress," in *Family and Kinship in Chinese Society*, ed. Maurice Freedman (Stanford: Stanford University Press, 1970). See also Ahern, *Cult of the Dead*.

21. The symbolisms of flowers are deep-rooted in Chinese culture. Flowers are used for public rituals to communicate those well understood meanings.

22. In several cases, I saw helpers in the front part of funeral processions carrying an entire roast pig that was used for worship after the burial and distributed that evening.

23. The length of the cane symbolizes a lasting marriage; the lettuce is a pun on the word *shengcai*, which sounds similar to fertility and fortune. As to the story behind the golden rooster and the white tiger, elderly friends explain that the umbrella and rice carried by the wedding procession are to protect the bride from the golden rooster on the way to the bridegroom's house; the coat thrown over the bed after the bride enters the house is to distract the white tiger lurking in the bedroom that

would have harmed the bridegroom. According to the Daoist priest, these ritual acts had arisen from a battle between two mythical figures, Zhou Gong and Taohua Nu.

24. Responses to these rituals differ among the people I interviewed. As mentioned earlier, the Daoist priest was the only one who could provide an intellectual justification from Daoist texts with regard to the tension in cosmic forces symbolized by the battle between the two mythical figures. My older friends said that the supernatural powers would listen and would bestow their powers when the rituals were performed. The young couples, on the other hand, seldom believed in these powers. Instead, power is invoked by the objects themselves (such as having an umbrella), as if efficacy came from direct association with them.

25. Traditional rituals always had their practical and talismanic qualities, but the overarching ideological structure also provided checks and balances. This chapter focuses on the changes in their meaning when the restraints have been partly replaced by a different political power.

9

Pride and Prejudice
Subei People in
Contemporary Shanghai

EMILY HONIG

Shanghai was populated by immigrants in the nineteenth century. The social and economic elite came from Jiangnan, while people from Subei, a region stereotyped for its backwardness, formed the underclass. Prejudice against Subei people, a dominant feature of popular culture in Shanghai during the late Qing and Republican periods, thrives today— even though it is virtually invisible in official documents. Yale historian Emily Honig asserts that no self-respecting person of Jiangnan origin would marry someone with a Subei background. To be called a Subei ren is to be called poor, ignorant, dirty, and vulgar. Sexually promiscuous men are accused of "having a lazy cock, like a Subei person." Many Subei people in Shanghai are ashamed of their native place identity and go to great lengths to disguise their origins. But other Subei people deeply resent the discrimination and are involved in various "Subei pride" activities. Professor Honig argues that prejudice against Subei people cannot be explained simply in terms of the persistence of a historical legacy. Discrimination against Subei people is perpetuated and reproduced today by social and economic structures in the areas of employment, housing, and education that keep Subei people physically and economically marginal.

—Eds.

Native place identity has long been recognized as a major element in Chinese popular thought. A person's native place (*laoxiang*), more than their actual place of birth, immediately connoted personality traits, cultural practices, and social status. In Chinese cities, sojourners from the same native place clustered together in neighborhoods, where they could speak their hometown dialect, enjoy similar forms of entertainment, and help one another. The proliferation of native place associations in Republican-period China reflected the importance of local origins in defining self and community.

Hierarchy, too, was frequently structured according to native place identity. In Shanghai, a city whose population was initially composed primarily of immigrants, people from Jiangnan (the Ningbo/Shaoxing region of Zhejiang and the Wuxi/Changzhou area of Jiangsu) formed the economic and social elite. Migrants from Subei (the part of Jiangsu north of the Yangzi River, also called Jiangbei), a region stereotyped for its poverty and backwardness, formed the underclass.[1] And native place identity, not race, religion, or nationality provided the most significant ethnic distinctions in Shanghai.

Given its centrality in traditional China, surprisingly little attention has been paid to native place identity in the decades since 1949. Scholarly analyses seem to have assumed that it simply disappeared, perhaps because in the 1950s native place associations and guilds were abolished, migration from the countryside to the cities was prohibited, and extensive campaigns were undertaken to make Mandarin replace local dialects as the common language. Or perhaps it was simply invisible in the official documents, policy statements, newspapers, and periodicals upon which most analyses were based. Since the late 1970s, opportunities to conduct interviews and fieldwork within the People's Republic of China (PRC) have made it possible to explore aspects of popular thought, including native place identity, that were previously inaccessible. This chapter, focusing on attitudes toward Subei people in contemporary Shanghai, examines the persistence of native place identity in popular thought and culture.

METHODOLOGY

Subei people (*Subei ren*) are a group about which very little written information exists. Unlike intellectuals, peasants, women, or even factory workers, Subei people have rarely been recognized as a distinct social group, and therefore have not been the subject of surveys, investigations, or reports. Even census takers do not count the number of Subei people in Shanghai, making it impossible to know the exact percentage of the population they constitute. Moreover, like most non-elite groups, Subei people have written very little about themselves.

This has several implications for an attempt to study Subei people in Shanghai. Save for several limited surveys conducted by sociologists in the early 1980s, almost no information about the residential, employment, and marriage patterns of Subei people is available. Since the selection of marital partners is one of the most visible ways in which the prejudice toward Subei people is expressed, marriage registration records are a potentially valuable source, as they indicate the native place (*jiquan*) as well as the place of birth (*chushengdi*) of both the bride and groom. Yet it is difficult for foreign scholars to obtain access to these records, and I was able to use only those from one district. Information about employment is even harder to obtain, in part because few work units have ever calculated the number of workers of Subei origin whom they employ. Much of the information provided by officials is more impressionistic than exact: "Most of the workers here are from Subei," or "Oh, about 70 percent of our employees are Subei people."

If we focus, however, on *attitudes* toward Subei people (and their attitudes toward themselves), a wealth of information is available, primarily in the form of what people say. And it is the spoken word on which I draw most heavily in this chapter. I conducted formal interviews with a large number of Subei people in Shanghai during the fall of 1986, primarily to document their historical experience. Yet it was often the inadvertent comments or even the ways people behaved that were most revealing. For instance, a group of sanitation department workers from Subei were so delighted to be of interest to a foreign scholar that they welcomed me to their unit with heaping platters of fruits, nuts, and sweets in addition to the more common and simple cup of tea offered at units more confident of their respectability. A bath-house pedicurist from Yangzhou arrived at an interview dressed in a Western suit, while his coworkers originally from Yancheng dressed in more ordinary workers' clothes, underlining his attitude that though they were all from Subei, Yangzhou people were far more urbane and sophisticated. And many sessions that began as formal interviews, with interviewees answering my questions, turned into heated arguments among the interviewees about the nature of and reasons for discrimination against Subei people in Shanghai. The anger and indignation expressed in these spontaneous debates told me far more about their attitudes than did their responses to formal questions about what it meant to them to be from Subei.

Casual conversations are as important as formal interviews in exploring attitudes toward Subei people. Since the status of Subei people has never been a political issue (as was, for example, the status of the working class or national minorities), almost no sensitivity, embarrassment, or shame censors people's derogatory comments. The mere mention of my research topic, for example, inevitably elicited impassioned expositions on the character defects of Subei people (or, sometimes from Subei people, whispered admissions of their native place). Even conversations on topics completely unrelated to Subei people were likely to produce comments indicative of popular attitudes. Such was the case when a friend related to me the story of a teacher at her university who was allegedly involved in a number of extramarital affairs. "He was from Subei, of course," she observed, not knowing that Subei people were of particular interest to me. Likewise, a U.S. scholar, struggling to board a bus, had it explained to her that *all* people guilty of pushing and shoving on the Shanghai buses were from Subei. In yet another instance, when a train passenger betrayed his ignorance of the fact that Washington D.C. is the capital of the United States, fellow passengers quickly explained to the U.S. scholar riding the train that the man was from Subei, and hence exceptionally ignorant. In all these instances, comments about Subei people were spontaneous and unsolicited, and therefore particularly useful as an index to popular thought.

Although I draw most heavily on interviews and casual conversations, another source of information about attitudes toward Subei people has become available in recent years. For reasons discussed below, the prejudice toward Subei people has become particularly virulent in the years since the Cultural Revolution. In response, a number of Subei natives have written articles for local papers, voicing complaints about the inferior treatment accorded them. These essays are particularly useful for understanding the forms of prejudice most disturbing to Subei people themselves.

All these sources—the sociological surveys, interviews, conversations, and news articles—share one problem, and that concerns the definition of *Subei ren*. Although people in Shanghai use the term with great frequency and confidence, no standard definition exists. As will be seen below, while the most common definition is based on geography (and even the geographic definition is debatable), others are based on dialects and economics. An examination of attitudes toward Subei people in Shanghai must therefore begin with a discussion of what the term means.

THE MEANING OF *SUBEI REN*

The concept of *Subei ren* has its origins in the nineteenth century. The very notion that Subei exists as a coherent region was a product of Shanghai's development in the decades following the Opium War. Moreover, most people from Subei did not identify themselves as *Subei ren* until their arrival in Shanghai. Prior to that they most likely had never even heard the term. Instead they were identified as Yangzhou *ren*, Yancheng *ren*, Nantong *ren*, etc. And in their minds, each of these districts was vastly different: Each had what to its native residents were different dialects and each boasted an entirely different form of local opera. But in Shanghai these were homogenized into a single Subei dialect and Subei opera. (In contrast, no one in Shanghai spoke of *Jiangnan ren*, Jiangnan dialect, or Jiangnan opera; people were identified as Wuxi *ren*, Ninbgo *ren*, etc.) In other words, the idea that a place called Subei and people called *Subei ren* existed emerged from Shanghai's development as an immigrant city.

The term *Subei ren* has most commonly described people from Subei. Most literally, Subei refers to the part of Jiangsu north of the Yangzi River. Unlike the Jiangnan, famous for its production of rice and silk, most of the land in northern Jiangsu is used to cultivate cotton, wheat, and salt. The river creates not only a geographic boundary, but a linguistic one as well. While people in Jiangnan all speak variations of the Wu dialect (from which Shanghai dialect derives), the dialects spoken by natives in the northern part of the province belong to an entirely different linguistic family. Based on these differences, almost all geographers and linguists include only a portion of the northern area in their definition of Subei—from Nantong and Haimen in the south, through Yangzhou and Taixing, and then Yancheng, Funing, and Huai'an in the north. The most northwestern part of Jiangsu, including Xuzhou, is usually considered part of Huaibei, an entirely different geographic region. However, some Republican-period writers, wanting to paint an almost exaggerated picture of the poverty and backwardness of Subei, would quite carelessly draw on descriptions of Xuzhou despite their own observation that Xuzhou was not part of Subei; still others included Xuzhou as part of Subei.

To further complicate the definition of Subei, several areas south of the river—such as Zhenjiang and even occasionally Nanjing—are sometimes considered part of Subei, while several areas north of the river—such as Nantong and Haimen—are thought of as belonging to Jiangnan. This is usually because of dialect, but in some cases the confusion is an economic one. Poor areas south of the river are considered part of the north, while wealthy areas north of the river are considered part of the south. In other words, Subei sometimes refers to a particular geographic area, but is sometimes a metaphor for class: If it's poor, it must be Subei, particularly if the individual speaks something resembling (to speakers of Wu dialect, at least) Subei dialect. Thus, some people from parts of Anhui and Shandong are occasionally identified as *Subei ren*, even though they perceive themselves as Anhui or Shandong *ren*.

Throughout the first half of the twentieth century, being a Subei person in Shanghai meant being poor. Mostly refugees from floods or famine in their home districts, Subei people did the jobs in Shanghai that were the least lucrative and least desirable. They dominated the ranks of unskilled laborers, representing the majority of rickshaw pullers, dock workers, construction workers, nightsoil and garbage collectors, barbers, and bath-house attendants. In factories, which employed people from Jiangnan as well, Subei natives concentrated in the workshops where the jobs were considered most dirty, physically demanding, and low-paying. This regional stratification was even apparent among prostitutes: The highest class prostitutes, who worked in lavishly furnished brothels and catered to businessmen and officials, came mostly from Jiangnan; girls from Subei filled the ranks of "wild chickens" who roamed the streets of Shanghai's red-light district soliciting customers.[2] Given their economic status, it is not surprising that most Subei people resided in the slums located on the periphery of the city, where they built shacks from reeds, cardboard, or whatever other scrap materials they could find. So close was the association of Subei people with the slums that the areas were often referred to as "Jiangbei shack settlements."[3]

Partly because of their poverty, Subei people were the objects of prejudice and discrimination. They were laughed at for wearing "tasteless" gaudy red and green garments, shunned for the smell of garlic on their breath, and ridiculed for speaking Subei dialect. Subei culture, once considered a symbol of sophistication, came to be regarded as low-class and despicable. Such was the fate of Subei local opera, for instance, which was never performed in the major entertainment centers of Shanghai. One of the most common curses in Shanghai dialect was to call someone a Jiangbei person or a Jiangbei swine. It meant that the person, even if not actually from Subei, was poor, ignorant, dirty, and unsophisticated. Subei thus became a metaphor for low-class.

The historic prejudice against Subei people, however, was not simply a product of their economic status. Politics, too, contributed. Prejudice against Subei people, according to one Chinese scholar, began during the suppression of the Taiping Rebellion: Most of the soldiers in the Huai Army, notorious among Shanghainese of the time for the atrocities they committed, were recruits from Subei. This, he suggests, initiated their disreputable image.[4] Subsequent political events may have reinforced the prejudice. During the war with Japan in the 1930s and 1940s, for example, many Shanghainese believed that Subei people in Shanghai were collaborators with the enemy. The expression *Jiangbei traitors* appeared daily in the local newspapers.[5] Contempt for Subei people therefore turned into hostility, if not hatred— they were not only poverty-stricken, but traitors to boot.

Historically, then, the term *Subei person* had several meanings. Most literally, it referred to someone whose native place was in northern Jiangsu. More commonly, it described a person who engaged in menial labor, was poor, and lacked the urban sophistication and cosmopolitanism for which Shanghai prided itself. Finally, it described a people who were mistrusted and despised for the role they played in various political movements. Subei people were, in short, considered the scum of Shanghai.

PRIDE AND PREJUDICE
IN CONTEMPORARY SHANGHAI

What became of Subei people after 1949? One might initially expect the prejudice to have diminished and the negative connotation of the term *Subei ren* to have been forgotten. As noted above, migration from Subei to Shanghai ceased, and organizations based on native place identity no longer existed. Moreover, political campaigns attacked class inequality and ethnic prejudice. In spite of this, however, the problematic status of Subei people has continued to be basic to the social and economic structure of Shanghai; a consciousness of "we, the Shanghainese versus them, Subei people," has remained a central element in popular thought. Though scarcely evident in documentary sources, popular prejudice against Subei people thrives; its constant expression in casual conversation can be confirmed through more formal interviews as well as social surveys.

Before describing the ways in which popular prejudice toward Subei people is manifested, it is important to point out that the Subei population of present-day Shanghai is somewhat different from that of the pre-1949 past. First, the majority of the so-called Subei people in Shanghai today were not themselves born in Subei. Rather they are the children, grandchildren, and in some cases great-grandchildren of migrants. Indistinguishable from the rest of the Shanghai population by physical appearance, only language belies their identity. Although most contemporary Subei people speak Mandarin or Shanghai dialect, they grew up in families where Subei dialect was spoken at home and speak Mandarin with an allegedly Subei accent. Since language is the only recognizable marker of a Subei person, those with no accent can effectively disguise their native place origins—at least until friends visit their home and hear relatives speaking Subei dialect.

Another feature distinguishes the Subei population of current Shanghai from that of the pre-1949 past. Historically, the overwhelming majority of migrants from Subei were peasants fleeing natural disaster and poverty; notably few Subei people were to be found among the ranks of Shanghai's political and economic elite.[6] This changed in 1949: The communist soldiers who crossed the Yangzi River and liberated Shanghai, members of the New Fourth Army, came mostly from Subei. After Liberation many were appointed officials and cadres in the city government. So well recognized is the political prestige of Subei people (currently both the mayor and Communist party secretary of Shanghai hail from Subei) that when citizens are dissatisfied they commonly say, "No wonder we have so many problems—our leaders are all from Subei!" In the decades since 1949, then, the Subei community in Shanghai has consisted not only of manual laborers, but members of the political elite as well.

How are Subei people regarded in Shanghai today? To what extent is prejudice against Subei people an element of popular thought, and how can it be recognized? The most immediately visible evidence of popular attitudes toward Subei people is linguistic: Derogatory references to Subei people permeate the language of Shanghainese. The expressions *Jiangbei ren*, or the more insulting *Jiangbei lao* (old Jiangbei), *Jiangbei danzi* (Jiangbei egg), or *Jiangbei zhuluo* (Jiangbei swine), continue to rank among the most common swear words in Shanghai dialect.[7] These terms are used not only in reference to someone who is actually from Subei, but also to accuse someone of being low-class or unreasonable. Subei has become a metaphor for almost anything distasteful. People who speak crudely, for example, are criticized for "speaking Subei dialect"; individuals who fail to conform to standards of cleanliness are scolded for "being dirty and unsanitary, like Subei folk"; sexually promiscuous men are accused of "having a lazy cock [literally, *lan diao*], like a Subei person."

The prejudice toward Subei people extends to aesthetics: Anything smacking of Subei tastes is ridiculed or condemned. Purchasing a piece of bright red cloth or donning a red garment is likely to provoke friends or onlookers to comment, "That's so ugly—it's like what Jiangbei people wear." A young woman recalled that whenever a primary-school classmate wore a red ribbon in her hair, friends would inevitably mimick Subei dialect and call her Xiao Sanzi—Subei people allegedly named their children Xiao Sanzi (Little Three), Xiao Sizi (Little Four), etc.

Popular culture, too, reflects the prejudice against Subei people. Save for a brief moment of glory in the 1950s when Zhou Enlai (himself from the Subei district of Huai'an) dedicated a Huai opera theater in Shanghai, local opera from Subei has suffered a poor reputation. My own efforts to convince Chinese friends to accompany me to a performance of Huai opera were fruitless; foreign affairs office members, certain that Huai opera would disappoint me, offered me tickets to the more prestigious Shaoxing opera instead. Members of the Huai Opera Troupe in Shanghai speak bitterly about the low-class status accorded their art. "We only get to perform in theaters in Shanghai when they do not have good business," the well-known Huai opera singer Xiao Wenyan complained. "We are required to report all our new operas to the Cultural Affairs Bureau, but they always pick the Shaoxing operas for performances. They are the decision-makers, so there is nothing we can do about it." "Whenever it is opening night for one of our operas," a director for the troupe added, "we invite the city leaders to attend. If it were for a Shaoxing opera, they'd be glad for the invitation. But to get them to accept the invitation to our Huai opera we have to phone several times. And even if we send cars to pick them up, they still usually say that they are busy and cannot come." Officials in charge of local radio and television stations shared the scorn for Subei opera, granting priority to Shanghai, Shaoxing, and Beijing opera instead.[8] When I accompanied the troupe for part of a two-month tour of Subei, the performers were ecstatic—the presence of a foreigner conferred on them an almost unprecedented prestige.

The attitude of Shanghainese toward Subei opera is not simply disinterest in an unfamiliar art form, but rather represents hostility toward something considered base and unsophisticated. This was made most clear to me when I naively asked an old woman worker from Subei whether she ever went to see performances of *Yueju* (Shaoxing opera). An older male factory official present at the interview—himself from Shaoxing—indignantly interrupted to explain to me that "they [people from Subei] did not go to see *Yueju.* Most people in this mill are Jiangbei people, and so they would not go to see *our* Shaoxing opera. *Yueju*—that's something for us Shaoxing, Ningbo, and Yuyao people to see. Subei people would go to see *their* Jianghuai operas."[9] A similar attitude was expressed by one of the directors of the Shanghai Huai Opera Troupe. Himself a native of Shanghai, he recalled his anger and shame when he was assigned to the Huai Opera Troupe after graduating from a drama institute.[10]

Popular culture not only reflects the prejudice toward Subei people, but in some cases actively perpetuates it. This is most conspicuous in performances by comedy troupes in Shanghai. Evil characters are played by someone from Subei or someone who speaks with a Subei accent; Subei dialect is often the brunt of jokes; whenever the characters include a rickshaw puller or cobbler, they are called Xiao Sanzi or Xiao Bazi (see explanation above), which is pronounced by the other characters in imitation Subei dialect.[11]

The prejudice toward Subei people finds its most concrete expression in the search for marital partners. No self-respecting Shanghainese would consider marrying a Subei native, and most are unabashedly explicit in stating this preference. Individuals seeking introductions to prospective mates commonly remind their friends of the requirement that the person not be from Subei. Even the recently formed marriage introduction bureaus report that when young people in Shanghai register their preferences for a mate, many specify that they will not consider an introduction to someone from Subei. "Anyone but a Subei person" or "a southerner," "will refuse a Subei person," are commonly written on the registration forms.[12] That the forms include the question "What are your preferences for a spouse's native place?" itself underscores the continued importance of native place identity.

Many an otherwise satisfactory match has dissolved at the revelation of a person's Subei origins. The young woman writer Wang Xiaoying recalled the plight of a cousin whose girlfriend of two years was from Subei. When his mother heard the Subei accent she opposed the marriage, and the young couple separated. "You probably don't realize that Subei people are the most poor, vulgar, and low-class people," his mother proclaimed.[13]

A young Subei man angrily lamented his rejection:

> My mother had introduced me to a prospective mate. Before I met the girl we had exchanged photographs, and based on our "conditions," it seemed that this match would succeed. My mother took me to the Anhui restaurant at the corner of Shaanxi Road to have a meal with her family. After the meal, based on arrangements made by both our parents, I took the girl for a walk to the Bund. Several days later my mother heard that the girl did not want to continue with me. When I heard this I couldn't figure it out. I wondered whether my actual appearance was that different from my photograph. Several days later, I found out by coincidence that the girl broke it off because she heard my mother speaking Jiangbei dialect.[14]

Statistics confirm these attitudes. A 1984 survey found that approximately 70 percent of the younger generation of Subei people in Shanghai married other Subei people.[15] The 1986 marriage registration records for Shanghai's Zhabei district are even more extreme: Some 80 percent of the individuals who listed Subei as their native place chose spouses of Subei origins.

When asked to explain their strong objection to marrying people from Subei, Shanghainese offer several reasons. First is the association of Subei people with poverty. In the minds of Shanghainese, economic hardship leads to criminality and makes Subei people untrustworthy. As the director of the Huai Opera Troupe admitted,

> I am a Shanghainese and I looked down on Subei people. That was because all the Subei people I know had fled from a famine-stricken area. In my home in the Shanghai suburbs people were relatively wealthy. You could dry your clothes and shoes outside in the sun. But if a Subei person walked by, all your things would be gone. . . . Subei people were so poor that they "used their hands to snatch water snails and catch fish." That was what I learned as a kid.[16]

In many cases, then, the rejection of Subei mates is a class issue: Marrying someone from Subei is perceived as downward mobility.

Yet more than class is at stake, as suggested by the difficulty of finding mates encountered by officials of Subei origins.[17] The undesirability of Subei people as mates also involves beliefs about differences in habits and customs between them and Shanghainese. One Shanghai native, the head of the cultural affairs station in a predominantly Subei district of Shanghai, offered the following explanation of why intermarriage between Subei and Ningbo people was problematic:

> The habits of Subei and Ningbo people are very different. Ningbo people are much more picky. For example, when they make *tangtao* [sweet soup dumplings]: Ningbo people make very small, delicate ones, while Subei people make large, coarse ones. Or *kaufu* [wheat gluten]: Ningbo people deep fry it and use sugar and a lot of oil, while Subei people don't care about the flavor. The same with *suji* [mock chicken, made of bean curd skin]: Subei people just fry it and eat it, while Ningbo people add soy sauce.

These differences, he concluded, would make a couple incompatible.[18] A young woman concurred. She called off her engagement to a man from Subei after visiting his home and being served a platter laden with eight *pidan* (thousand-year-old eggs). "A Shanghai person would consider *pidan* a delicacy, and delicacies should be served in small quantities. I realized that if I married this man I would have to contend with things like this." Perceived character differences exacerbate the problem: Subei people are allegedly "frank and coarse," "talk very loudly," "like to argue a lot," and "are stingy with money."

From the vantage point of Shanghainese, then, Subei people represent something akin to a different ethnic order. Not only do they come from a different region and speak a different dialect, not only are they relatively poor and uneducated, but in addition they have different cultural practices and personality traits. Whether these differences actually exist or have instead been distorted and exaggerated by Shanghainese is less important than the fact that Shanghai residents believe in them.

Thus far we have been looking at the prejudice of Shanghainese toward Subei people. But what of Subei people's attitudes toward themselves? At first glance it seems that Subei people have internalized their inferior status. Their sense of shame is most obvious in their reluctance to admit their native place. When asked about their family's local origins, people from Subei typically reply, "Jiangsu Province." Even in formal interviews, when I asked which part of Jiangsu Province an individual was from, Subei people were reluctant to answer. Only when I asked them to show me their native place on a map would it become clear they were from Subei. (In contrast, people from Jiangnan places never hesitated to declare that they were from Wuxi, Changzhou, or Ningbo.) One of the relatively small number of students from Subei attending Fudan University in 1980 informed her classmates that her family was from Nanjing, although their native place was actually Nantong.[19]

Subei people in Shanghai often go to great lengths to disguise their identity. Most commonly they do not speak Subei dialect outside their home or neighborhood, partly to avoid the harassment described above, but also to ensure that no one will discover their identity as a Subei person. Members of the youngest generation do not want to speak Subei dialect even at home. "Our children don't want to speak Subei dialect," a director of the Shanghai Huai Opera Troupe complained. "Even at home they just want to speak Shanghai dialect."[20] A woman who worked as a street sweeper had a slightly different attitude: She was proud of her son's ability to disguise his background. "At home we spoke Subei dialect when the kids were growing up," she said, "but when we'd go out, we would speak Shanghai dialect. It was easy for our kids to learn Shanghai dialect because they grew up and went to school here. When my oldest son goes out, no one knows that he is a Subei person. He seems exactly like a Shanghainese."[21]

Language is the most conspicuous and common way in which Subei people attempt to disguise their identity. Less frequently, they disassociate themselves from other aspects of Subei culture. For instance, members of the Shanghai Huai Opera Troupe complained that young people of Subei families in Shanghai refuse to see performances of Huai opera. While this can be partly explained by the increasing availability of television and film, it is also an expression of their fear of being identified as Subei. "They feel they've lost face if they go see Huai opera," observed the well-known performer Xiao Wenyan. A director added that fights about Subei opera often erupt in the homes of Subei people: The younger generation violently opposes their parents' desire to watch opera performances on television, not only because it bores them but also because they fear the expression of "Subei culture" in their homes might be seen by others.[22]

In some cases, the shame of being from Subei is so extreme that young people raised in Shanghai disassociate themselves from their parents altogether. One young man recalled that although his mother was actually from Anhui, everyone called her a *Jiangbei ren*. By implication, he, too, was a Jiangbei person. "When I was a child I knew that in Shanghai this name was derogatory, so I was afraid to go out with my mother," he later confessed. "I did my best to avoid speaking with her because I feared that people would hear me and call me 'Little Jiangbei.'" His predicament was alleviated when he went to boarding school, where no one knew his family's background, and he was able to rid himself of the label *Jiangbei ren*. Occasionally, however, his determination to disguise his background forced him into painful predicaments. He recalled, for instance, a weekend that he had gone home but forgotten to take the money for his boarding fees at school.

I had no choice but to phone home and ask my mother to bring the money to school. That day when I went to class I watched carefully for my mother. I didn't want her to end up going all over the school using Jiangbei dialect to ask for me. During the third period I suddenly saw her. As soon as the bell rang I dashed out to where she was, grabbed the money, and quickly told her to return home immediately. I am sure my mother originally intended to say something to me, but she saw my panicked look and turned to leave.

He concluded the account with a description of the guilt he felt for having treated his mother so cruelly.[23]

Internalized inferiority may be the most obvious attitude of Subei people toward themselves, but it is not the only one. Anger, too, is expressed as they recount their experiences. Former rickshaw puller Chen Dewang, a well-known model worker, described his fury when well-meaning acquaintances would say, "Hey, Lao Chen, how can a Subei person be good like you? You don't really seem like a Subei person at all!" "I'd get angry when people said that and I would tell them why it made me mad," he indignantly recalled.[24] The female writer Wang Xiaoying's rage took a slightly different form. So outraged was she at the prejudice against Subei people that she publicly claimed Subei—where she was born—as her native place even though her family was actually of the more prestigious Ningbo origins. "My grandmother says that I am a typical Ningbo person because my great-grandfather was from Ningbo," she explained in an essay entitled "The Girl from Subei." "But even my father had forgotten what Ningbo looked like, and I had only seen it on a map." She described her fond memories of a childhood spent in the Subei county of Binhai, where her parents had been stationed as Communist cadres during the civil war of the 1940s. Nevertheless, her grandmother repeatedly warned her that if she identified herself as being from Subei she would never find a husband. Proud of her birthplace, and furious at her grandmother's shame, she proclaimed her determination to say "Subei" whenever asked about her native place.[25] A similarly defiant young man, who no longer lived in Shanghai, expressed his anger at the prejudice against Subei people by deliberately speaking Subei dialect whenever he visited Shanghai.[26]

Angry denunciations of the prejudice are accompanied by a burgeoning sense of pride among Subei people in their ethnic identity, not unlike that expressed by various ethnic groups in the United States beginning in the 1960s. The conviction that "Subei is beautiful" is expressed both directly and indirectly. That middle-aged and older people, despite the preferences of their children, persist in using Subei dialect at home and in Subei neighborhoods attests, among other things, to a quiet determination to preserve a cultural identity rather than assimilate. After complaining about the derogatory use of Subei dialect in comedy acts, a sanitation bureau worker declared, "But we like to speak our language!"[27]

The pride is more clearly evident in the refusal of some individuals to accept passively the popular notion of Subei as a poor, backward, and culturally impoverished region, but to instead search for and assert the richness of its history. A barber originally from Yangzhou spoke at great length about the famous writers and officials from his hometown. "And the Qianlong Emperor himself visited Yangzhou three times!" he proudly declared.[28] "Anyone with an even slight knowledge of history knows that Subei has always been wealthier than Jiangnan," a professor of literature at Fudan

University told sociologists investigating the status of Subei people in Shanghai in 1984. Challenging the pride of southerners, he pointed out that Subei had once been so prosperous that people from Jiangnan migrated to the northern half of the province. "There was no problem of discrimination against northerners by southerners at that time," he observed.[29] Others turned to the more recent past to find evidence of the glory of Subei. That Zhou Enlai hailed from the Subei county of Huai'an is one of the most frequently heralded claims. "It is well known that Shanghai was liberated mainly by the [New Fourth Army]," a cadre in the research office of the Shanghai Municipal Committee pointed out. "At present there are many Subei people among the leaders at the district, county, and bureau level. Subei people are scattered among the trades and professions of Shanghai, playing an important role in the construction of the Four Modernizations."[30] Yet another took his assertion of Subei pride to the press, challenging the inferior status often accorded Subei dialect. "Actually there is no such thing as a 'good' or 'bad' language," he wrote. "Subei and Shanghai dialect are six of one, half a dozen of another. . . . From the perspective of closeness to standard Mandarin, Shanghai dialect is actually inferior to Subei dialect." He concluded by demonstrating the influence exerted by Subei dialect on Shanghainese.[31]

EXPLAINING THE PREJUDICE

The pride, anger, and shame expressed by Subei people, like the popular prejudice, attest to the persisting centrality of native place identity in popular thought in present-day Shanghai. Yet given the changes that occurred after 1949—the abolishment of native place associations, the prohibition of migration, and the promotion of Mandarin as the common language—how is this persistence of native place identity, and more particularly the prejudice, to be explained?

The explanation most commonly offered in Shanghai is that the prejudice is simply a historical legacy, a remnant of the prerevolutionary past that will surely disappear with time. Many people, for instance, explain their contempt for Subei people by saying that "*before* 1949, they were the poorest people." Social reality, they imply,· had changed since 1949 such that Subei people were no longer actually poor; the association of Subei natives with poverty had simply not yet faded. There is certainly some power to this explanation, particularly given that social structures based on native place identity no longer exist, that the physical distinctions (such as dress) between Subei natives and other Shanghainese are no longer so clear, and that some people from Subei have become members of the political elite. All these factors support the notion that the prejudice must be a historical legacy. Closer examination, however, reveals that this explanation is inadequate, that the prejudice is not simply a deep-seated value that has failed to disappear. More important than the legacy of old values is the persistence of the very social and economic structures that initially gave rise to prejudice against Subei people—structures that keep them both physically and economically marginal.

Although no systematic data exist that correlate native place identity and job status, preliminary surveys conducted by Chinese sociologists indicate that the post-1949 Shanghai labor market, despite its radically changed nature, continues to be segmented along regional lines, at least to the extent that Subei people are still tracked into, indeed dominate, the unskilled sector. For example, a 1959 survey of pedicab drivers showed that 77 percent were of Subei origins. A survey conducted in the early 1980s indicated that the overwhelming majority of bath-house attendants and barbers were still people from Subei. And the majority of the city's sanitation department workers, even in districts where few Subei people live, continue to be people of Subei origins.[32] Surveys of the jobs held by various generations of members of Subei families suggest little upward mobility. According to one such survey, over two-thirds of the members of the younger generation worked at unskilled jobs.[33] Likewise, the 1984 records of job assignments for graduating secondary school students in a Subei district of Shanghai bore a remarkable similarity to pre-1949 patterns: The overwhelming majority joined the ranks of Shanghai's unemployed youth; those fortunate enough to secure employment, with very few exceptions, were assigned factory or construction jobs, or work in the city's sanitation bureau (as street cleaners or garbage or nightsoil collectors).[34]

An explanation of the continued concentration of Subei people in the unskilled sector of the labor market requires an analysis of labor allocation processes in post-1949 China that is beyond the scope of this chapter.[35] Education is at least part of the problem, for it appears that Subei people do not have the same opportunities for higher education enjoyed by other sectors of the Shanghai population. Unlike their parents, most of whom were illiterate, the majority of children of Subei families do attain an elementary school education. But less than half attend upper middle school, and only a scarce few are admitted to schools that require examinations, including universities.[36] University graduates dread the possibility of being assigned to teach in a school in a Subei district, where the students are reputedly "rough and not motivated to learn." In a semi-autobiographical short story entitled "The Poor Street," contemporary writer Chen Naishan describes the hardships she faced teaching in a Subei district school, where few students were on time for class and many never attended at all. She recalls another teacher explaining to her, "These students in the low-class quarters are not cut out for studying, so it's a waste of time to prepare your classes. Ours is a school to prepare the army of laborers. Most of the students will take their parents' jobs—they'll empty night soil buckets or sell *dabing* [wheat cakes]. How much do they need to learn?"[37] Under these circumstances, it is not surprising that disproportionately few Subei people are found in jobs requiring high levels of skill and education.

Residential patterns, too, contribute to the continued association of Subei people with poverty. Most Subei people live not in the downtown or central districts of Shanghai (the areas that formerly composed the International Settlement and French Concession), but rather in the old working class districts—Zhabei, Yangshupu, and Putuo. Although housing projects have eliminated the worst of the pre-1949 "shack settlements," these districts continue to be regarded as slums or, in contemporary parlance, the "lower quarters" (*xia zhi jiao*) of Shanghai. My research assistant, horrified by the conditions in one such district, asked whether "slums in the United States are this bad." "The Subei districts in Shanghai *are* worse than the black people's slums in the U.S.," declared a Chinese scholar visiting the United States. In "The Poor Street," Chen Naishan describes her first impressions of the Subei district where she taught: "The school was only a one-hour bus-ride from my home, but in that one hour it was as if I had gone from the first world to the third world. . . . [I] never would have believed that in Shanghai, the Number One city of the Far East, there existed such a corner, completely neglected by prosperity."[38] These areas, according to another writer, have "the fewest cultural and welfare facilities, the worst housing conditions, and the highest population density in the entire city."[39] Shanghainese who live in other districts perceive the Subei areas as rough and crime-ridden, and warn their children against going to these so-called Jiangbei villages.[40]

The continued concentration of Subei people in the unskilled sectors of the labor market, their inferior levels of education, and their residence in slumlike districts can help account for the continued prejudice toward Subei people. The prejudice is therefore not simply a remnant of the past, but rather one that is actively perpetuated and reproduced by contemporary social conditions. Political events, too, may contribute to the persistence of prejudice based on native place. Preliminary interviews suggest, for example, that Cultural Revolution factions in Shanghai correlated partly to native place, and that the most violent factions were composed of people from Subei. As was the case in the 1930s, when the belief that Subei people were collaborators with the Japanese fueled popular contempt for Subei natives, the popular perception of Subei people as the most violent in the Cultural Revolution is more important than whether they actually were or not. For it is such perceptions that contributed to and perhaps even consolidated prejudice.

It would be misleading to conclude that the prejudice against Subei people has been static throughout Shanghai's history. One must at least wonder whether the prejudice that is so clearly evident in Shanghai today has existed throughout the decades since 1949, or whether it is a recent phenomenon. While it is difficult to measure the extent of prejudice in the years immediately following the 1949 revolution, it quite possibly has become particularly virulent in the decade since the Cultural Revolution. Resentment toward the activities of working-class people during the Cultural Revolution, the post–Cultural Revolution contempt for cadres (many of whom in Shanghai, as noted above, were originally from Subei), as well as the increased attention to economic status that has resulted from the post-Mao reforms could all account for an intensification of prejudice against Subei people. The revival of migration from rural to urban areas in recent years might also contribute to a heightened prejudice. As peasants from Subei, which remains substantially less developed than Jiangnan, begin to migrate to Shanghai (usually on a temporary basis), they have once again begun to build shack dwellings on the outskirts of the city and perform menial tasks, such as collecting and selling garbage scraps, that few urban residents would do. This might reaffirm the association of Subei people with poverty and consequently intensify the extent to which Subei people are looked down on.

Prejudice, in other words, has a historical dimension. On the surface it appears that throughout Shanghai's modern development, prejudice against Subei people has been an unchanging element of popular thought. However, further research might well reveal that while the prejudice flourished during certain periods, it diminished at others. More important, the content of the prejudice has changed. At some times the prejudice against Subei natives has reflected a disdain for a people perceived as poor and backward; at other times it has also represented a contempt for people believed to be collaborators with the Japanese; during the Cultural Revolution it may have involved anger toward members of the working class; and more recently it has coincided with hostility toward officials. Contempt for the poor may be the most constant element in the prejudice, yet even that cannot be understood as something static, for the structure of their poverty has changed radically over time.

Popular thought, then, must be understood in a context. As the case of Subei people in Shanghai illustrates, although the ways in which prejudice has been expressed—the derogatory terms, the scorn for Subei culture, the refusal to marry Subei natives—have been constant, the meaning of the prejudice has changed. Calling someone a Jiangbei swine may be as popular a curse in contemporary Shanghai as it was in the early twentieth century, but the meaning is altogether different. Moreover, the curse remains popular not simply as a traditional expression, but rather because social, economic, and political conditions have created new bases for the prejudicial attitudes that the term *Jiangbei swine* reflects.

NOTES

1. Zou Yiren, *Jiu Shanghai renkou bianqiande yanjiu* (Shanghai: Shanghai remnin chubanshe, 1980), pp. 112–113. From 1885–1935, Shanghai natives accounted for an average of only 19 percent of the population of the International Concession, and 26 percent of the Chinese-owned parts of the city. It is impossible to know the exact percentage of the Shanghai population that was composed of people from Subei, since currently available population statistics that indicate native place specify only the province. Shanghai residents listed as being from Jiangsu were as likely to have come from southern Jiangsu as from the northern part of the province. According to the only available statistic, there were 1.5 million people from Subei in Shanghai in 1949. The entire population of Shanghai at that time was 5,062,878. Subei people thus accounted for nearly one-fifth of the population. See Xie Junmei, "Shanghai lishishang renkou de bianqian," *Shehui kexue*, no. 3, 1980, p. 112.

2. For a more extensive discussion of employment patterns see Emily Honig, "The Politics of Prejudice: Subei People in Republican-era Shanghai," *Modern China*, vol. 15, no. 3 (July 1989), pp. 243–274.

3. For a description of the shack settlements, see Shanghai shehui kexueyuan, jingji yanjiusuo, *Shanghai penghugude bianqian* (Shanghai: Shanghai renmin chubanshe, 1965).

4. This interpretation, held by Yu Xingmin, is summarized in "Miandui Pianjiande Tiaozhan," *Xinmin wanbao*, March 12, 1987.

5. See, for example, *Shen Bao*, April 6, 1932; April 7, 1932; April 13, 1932; April 19, 1932; and May 11, 1932. For a more extensive analysis of the association of Subei people with collaboration during the Japanese attack of 1932, see Honig, "Politics of Prejudice."

6. See, for example, *Shanghai geye gonghui lilingshi minglu*, ed. Shanghaishi shanghui (Shanghai: n.d.). Of the approximately 2,500 individuals listed in this commercial directory, published in the 1940s, only 175 were from Subei.

7. For a written description of the use of some of these terms, see "'Jiangnan' he 'Jiangbei,'" *Zhongguo qingnianbao*, March 30, 1982. Another derogatory expression used in reference to Subei people is *liang kuai tou*, literally, a "two-pieced head." This expression derives from the fact that in Subei dialect the words "here" and "there" are *zhekuai* and *lakuai* (Emily Honig interview with Qian Nairong and Ruan Henghui, Shanghai University, November 1986).

8. Honig interview with Xiao Wenyan and Wang Jianmin, Shanghai Huai Opera Troupe, October 30, 1986.

9. Honig interview with Chen Zhaodi, Shanghai Number One Cotton Mill, April 11, 1981.

10. Honig interview with Qi Yufan, Shanghai Huai Opera Troupe, October 30, 1986.

11. Honig interview with Chen Dewang, October 30, 1986; Honig interview with workers at Jing'an District Sanitation Bureau, November 18, 1986.

12. Chen Zhongya, Xu Zhuyuan, Ying Tingjia, and Wu Lijiang, "Guanyu qishi Subeiren qingkuangde diaocha," *Shehui*, no. 3, 1983, p. 23.

13. Wang Xiaoying, "Subei guniang," *Xinmin wanbao*.

14. Han Hufeng, "Mama shi 'Jiangbei ren,'" *Xinmin wanbao*, November 30, 1986.

15. Wu Liangrong, "Shanghaishi Subeiji jumin shehui biandong fenxi," in *Shehuixue wenji*, ed. Shanghai shehuixue xuehui (unpublished book, 1984), pp. 187–188.

16. Interview with Qi Yufan.

17. Honig interview with members of the New Fourth Army Research Institute, Shanghai Academy of Social Sciences, November 13, 1987.

18. Honig interview with Yang Zhangfu, Cultural Affairs Bureau, Zhongxing Street Residence Committee, November 4, 1986.

19. This phenomenon was also apparent on marriage registration records. A large number of individuals, rather than admitting their specific native place, wrote "Jiangsu" on the registration form. "You can count all those people as *Jiangbei ren*," the official in charge of the records told me with great certainty.

20. Honig interview with Wang Jianmin, Shanghai Huai Opera Troupe, October 30, 1986.

21. Honig interview with Ma Xiuying, Zhabei District Sanitation Bureau, November 3, 1986.

22. Interview with Xiao Wenyan and Wang Jianmin.

23. Han, "Mama shi 'Jiangbei ren.'"

24. Interview with Chen Dewang.

25. Wang, "Subei guniang."

26. Han, "Mama shi 'Jiangbei ren.'"

27. Honig interview with workers at Jing'an District Sanitation Bureau, November 18, 1986.

28. Honig interview with He Zhenghua, Xinxinmei Beauty Salon, November 12, 1986.

29. Interview with Zhu Dongrun, professor, department of Chinese language and literature, Fudan University, in "Zhe shi jianli xinxing shehui guanxi de banjiaoshi: Guanyu qishi Subeirende caifang jiyao," *Shehui*, no. 3, 1983, p. 27.

30. Interview with Mi Dianqun, in "Zhe shi jianli xinxing shehui guanxi de banjiaoshi," p. 28.

31. Peng Xiaoming, "Shanghaihua yu Subeihua," *Xinmin wanbao*, August 2, 1985.

32. See Wu, "Shanghaishi Subeiji jumin shehui biandong fenxi," pp. 180–184. The information about sanitation bureau workers is from Chen, Xu, Ying, and Wu, "Guanyu qishi Subeiren qingkuangde diaocha," p. 24; it is also based on interviews with workers and officials at the Zhabei District Sanitation Bureau, November 3, 1986, and at the Jing'an District Sanitation Bureau, November 18, 1986.

33. Wu, "Shanghaishi Subeiji jumin shehui biandong fenxi," p. 183.

34. Ibid.

35. Chinese sociologists commonly cite the *ding ti* policy of the late 1970s to explain the persisting patterns. Through this policy educated youth who had been sent to the countryside during the Cultural Revolution could return to Shanghai if one parent retired. The child would then be assigned to that parent's work unit. This, however, does not explain the employment patterns of the 1950s, 1960s, and most of the 1970s.

36. Wu, "Shanghaishi Subeiji jumin shehui biandong fenxi," p. 185. This finding is corroborated in Chen, Xu, Ying, and Wu, "Guanyu qishi Subeiren qingkuangde diaocha," p. 25.

37. Chen Naishan, "Qiong Jie," *Xiaoshuo jia*, no. 2, 1984, p. 8.

38. Ibid., p. 5.

39. Chen, Xu, Ying, and Wu, "Guanyu qishi Subeiren qingkuangde diaocha," p. 25.

40. The continued use of the expression *Jiangbei villages* in reference to these districts is documented in Wang Hongguang, "Laizi Shanghai 'xiazhijiao' de baogao," *Qingnian yidai*, no. 4, 1985, p. 56.

10

The Persistence
of Propriety in the 1980s

ELLEN JOHNSTON LAING

*University of Oregon art historian Ellen Johnston Laing is interested
in the visual manifestations of Chinese conceptions of propriety. The
main hall in nineteenth-century homes required formality of furniture
arrangement and a prescribed type of decoration, based on the principle
of "centralized symmetry." The most important items, the ancestral altar
and centerpiece paintings, were on the central axis. Secondary objects,
such as chairs and endtables, were arranged in balanced symmetry to
either side. The traditional New Year's prints that decorated all homes
depicted plants, creatures, and insects endowed with symbolic meanings
that conveyed Confucian ideals of happiness. Pines and cranes stood for
longevity, pomegranates symbolized the desire for many sons, and pairs
of ducks represented marital fidelity. Professor Laing finds that these
traditional visual expressions of what is proper have resurfaced in post-
Mao China, especially in rural homes. Furniture is still aligned with the
walls, a central display (reminiscent of the traditional ancestral altar)
dominates important rooms, and symbolically meaningful New Year's
pictures (such as a print of a chubby boy holding a carp) adorn the
walls. The "correct" arrangement of furniture and selection of decorative
paintings still attest to a family's understanding of traditional values.*

—Eds.

Chinese concepts of propriety, of what is proper and decorous, were
expressed in many ways in traditional China. Most familiar are the ideals

that shaped social and ritual behavior: observing the dictates of filial piety, venerating ancestors, perpetuating the family, and respecting the "five relations" between ruler and minister, father and son, older brother and younger brother, husband and wife, and friend and friend. But Chinese concepts of propriety were also given visual manifestations. This visual expression is especially apparent in certain aspects of the home and its physical appearance. There, the prescribed placement of furniture, the fixtures of the ancestral altar and their arrangement, and the subjects depicted in paintings used in the main hall and in New Year's prints all reflected established practices verified by widespread and continued usage to be "proper."

Analysis and evaluation of old interiors and pictorial decoration provide a basic knowledge of the nature of these traditional expressions of propriety. Once understood, these old concepts are still recognizable today as they sometimes determine, or at least affect, the appearance of domestic interiors in the People's Republic of China (PRC).

TRADITIONAL INTERIORS

In reception halls and other formal rooms in the traditional upper-class Chinese house, the placement of furniture followed a strict pattern. This arrangement consisted of repeated units of a chair on either side of a small table. The chairs and tables were set squarely one next to the other in a rigid row paralleling the walls. The sequence could be several units in length. Sometimes the unupholstered backs and seats of the hardwood chairs were covered with fabric "chair cloths." This dignified and regularized arrangement of furniture immediately made a visual announcement that demanded commensurately decorous behavior.

The main hall in the traditional Chinese house required formality of furniture arangement as well as a prescribed type of decoration (Figure 10.1). The main hall, called a *tangwu*, was at the back of the central courtyard. It contained the ancestral altar and served as a family shrine. Large elegant scrolls were hung on the back wall of this room, above the tables. Such scrolls were called *tanghua*, "hall pictures," or *zhongtang*, "centerpieces." They occupied the most conspicuous position in the hall. The centerpiece was flanked on either side by one or more long, narrow hanging scrolls of *duilian* calligraphy couplets (Figure 10.2). According to van Gulik,

> The religious significance of the place occupied by the *t'ang-hua* finds its expression in the custom, observed all over China, to suspend during domestic ceremonies or private religious services instead of the *t'ang-hua* another hanging scroll with a picture appropriate for the occasion. . . . When, for instance, a birthday is being celebrated, a large picture of the God of Longevity replaces the *t'ang-hua*, and incense is burnt on the table below.
>
> The *t'ang-hua* is generally considered as the hanging scroll *par excellence*, and mounted scrolls that qualify as such are designated in catalogues and other works on pictorial art by this special term.[1]

Figure 10.1. General view of the main hall in a Chinese house. Drawn by the Chinese architect Dai Nianci. (From R. H. van Gulik, *Chinese Pictorial Art, as Viewed by the Connoisseur,* Serie Orientale Roma XIX [Rome: Istituto Italiano per il Medio ed Estremo Oriente, 1958], pl. 19; courtesy Istituto Italiano per il Medio ed Estremo Oriente.)

There could be more than one scroll in the centerpiece ensemble. The subjects for all of them, which were set by convention, included landscapes, dragons and tigers, bamboo and pine, and plum blossoms and orchids. Sometimes there could be three types of flowers, or three famous personages. In sets of four, the subjects might be the four seasons or the four accomplishments of music, poetry, calligraphy, and chess.[2] Clearly, the subject or subjects of the paintings contributed to establishing the proper tone of the room and, by extension, attested to the family's understanding of traditional values.

The organizational principle observed in the *tangwu* was centralized symmetry. In a formal system of this kind, the most important item is in the center, on the central axis. Secondary objects are ranged in balanced symmetry to either side. The static and stable arrangement serves to direct attention to the most important central object.

The New Year's picture was another type of decoration in the traditional Chinese home. Often printed rather than painted, New Year's pictures were produced throughout China for sale at New Year's time, when the year-old pictures throughout the house were replaced with fresh ones. In general, New Year's pictures served three basic purposes: Protective door gods kept

Figure 10.2. The decoration of a back wall. (From R. H. van Gulik, *Chinese Pictorial Art, as Viewed by the Connoisseur*, Serie Orientale Roma XIX [Rome: Istituto Italiano per il Medio ed Estremo Oriente, 1958], pl. 5; courtesy Istituto Italiano per il Medio ed Estremo Oriente.)

evil out of the house; other figures, embodying an array of auspicious wishes, brought good fortune and prosperity into the house; and yet other pictures, such as theatrical scenes, story illustrations, landscapes, or pretty women, simply served to brighten up the rooms. A New Year's print of the kitchen god, complete with a calendar for the coming lunar year, was mandatory.[3]

Before 1949, New Year's and other traditional paintings depicted dozens of plants, creatures, and insects endowed with symbolic meanings that conveyed Confucian ideals of happiness. Peonies stood for wealth, pomegranates (because of their many seeds) for many male offspring, pines and cranes for longevity, willows for springtime, pairs of mandarin ducks for marital fidelity and happiness. Images of tigers helped protect the house, and pictures of red roosters guarded against fire. Sometimes the symbolic significance was based on a rebus or pun. Cats and butterflies, because their names (*mao* and *die*) suggest the Chinese words for segtuagenarian and octogenarian, conveyed wishes for long life; bats signified happiness because the sound of the word for bat, *fu* is identical to that for happiness.[4]

These ideals of wealth, happiness, longevity, and the like were summed up in the most popular of New Year's images in traditional China: a chubby boy holding a carp (Figure 10.3). Here the fish signifies abundance because

Figure 10.3. Anonymous, *Boy Holding a Goldfish*, nineteenth-century New Year's print. (From *Banhua congshu*, vol. 1, *Yangliuqing banhua* [Taibei: Xiongshi, 1976], pl. 25.)

the pronunciation for the word fish, *yu*, is identical to that for abundance. The imagery also expresses hopes that the boy will successfully pass the all-important civil service exams—the key to an official position (likened to a carp leaping the falls to become a "dragon"), which in turn would bring honor, prestige, fame, and perhaps additional wealth to the family.

Paintings and prints of such subjects were largely representational so that the motifs could be easily identified and the messages readily grasped. New Year's pictures ranged in quality from elegant to crude, but they had certain elements in common. In particular, they tended to have all available space covered with motifs—colored with bright, unmodulated red, green, yellow, and blue. Their busy and colorful appearance contributed to the atmosphere of *re'nao*, the cheerful noisiness regarded as a positive indication of the socially well ordered, happy Confucian family.

For nineteenth-century China, the strict rows of furniture, the centralized symmetrical arrangement of the centerpiece paintings along with their proper subject matter and representational style, and the brightly colored, auspicious New Year's pictures provide visual evidence of some of the characteristics of what was considered appropriate and correct in the house and its decoration.

CURRENT INTERIORS

Many of these attitudes have survived into the 1980s. They affect the appearance of both urban and rural domestic interiors in contemporary China, although the persistence of the traditional ideals is stronger in the villages.

Figure 10.4. A worker's flat. (From *China Pictorial*, May 1981, p. 16.)

In present-day Chinese cities, the housing shortage has severely restricted living space. The small quarters allotted to families in urban apartments do not permit a luxurious use of space. But even when space would allow, for example, an informal placement of chairs on a slight diagonal so occupants could converse easily with each other, it seems this is never done. Instead, all furniture is almost inevitably aligned with the walls. It is still customary to find one chair flanking each side of an endtable (Figure 10.4). Thus the decorous formal arrangement of furniture persists, although it may now be reduced to a single chair-table-chair unit.[5] The arrangement of a chair on either side of an endtable is also seen in the rural areas (Figure 10.5). The countryside continues the traditional use of the chair cover, protecting the back and seat cushions of upholstered easy chairs by draping over them a cloth that resembles Western toweling.[6]

Although urban dwellers today seem reluctant to put pictures on their apartment walls, representations that are hung share with the pictures displayed in rural areas a preference for old, established themes. The views of famous places both old and new (the White Pagoda or the Foxiang Ge of the former imperial palaces; the Nanjing Yangzi River bridge), the pictures of pretty women, and the depictions of opera characters are all similar to the repertoire of New Year's prints produced during the nineteenth century.[7]

One motif found today in both the city (see Figure 10.4) and the country is the tiger.[8] In traditional China tigers were depicted in New Year's prints as well as in painted scrolls. The tiger conveys many meanings in popular lore. It is a symbol of military courage and of sternness and dignity; as lord

Figure 10.5. The central room of a peasant house. (From *China Reconstructs*, October 1983, p. 53.)

of the land, it is paired with the dragon (lord of the waters), and the two creatures occupy an important place in *fengshui* workings; the tiger is considered a protective figure capable of frightening away evil spirits; and it sometimes represents the god of wealth.[9] Any of these attributes might provide a rationale for hanging a tiger image in the house.

A rooster on a rock amidst peony plants in a contemporary rural home conveys a number of traditional meanings.[10] The rooster represents the *yang* element and has five virtues: a literary spirit, a warlike disposition, courage, benevolence, and faith. A picture of a red cock "is often pasted on the wall of a house in the belief that the bird is a protection against fire."[11] The cock also drives away ghosts at dawn with his crowing.[12] A depiction of a cock (*ji*) on a rock (*shi*) conveys the meaning of good luck (*ji*) in the house (*shi*), as in the phrase *shishang daji*.[13] Another rebus is composed of a crowing cock and a peony to wish success and honor: *gongming fugui*. *Gongji* (the cock) suggests the word for merit, *gong*, while *ming*, to crow, suggests name, or fame. The peony, like the cock associated with the *yang* principle, is also called *fugui hua*, the flower of riches and honors.[14] Many of the pictures in urban apartments appear to be cut from calendars, and, indeed, calendars themselves with large-scale pictures are often displayed.[15]

With their greater reliance upon older traditions, people in the countryside continue to use the picture of a boy holding a carp or a goldfish (see Figure 10.3).[16] Yet this sentiment continues to be expressed by the city dweller in allusive fashion, for although the urban dweller may not post a picture of a chubby boy holding a golden fish, the same idea is often conveyed by live goldfish in glass bowls or tanks.[17]

It is of interest to note the survival, sometimes directly, sometimes only as an echo, of the ancestral altar in the rural areas. This place of honor is accentuated by means of a large-scale central image or object surrounded by a symmetrical arrangement of objects. There is no doubt about the echo of an ancestral altar in Figure 10.5. Hung in the center of the back wall is a large and imposing depiction of the god of longevity. On either side is a couplet (duilian) inscribed in black on red paper. On the table below, amidst a clutter of objects, the symmetrical arrangement of a central glass case and two large porcelain vases of flowers is discernible. Below the table are two incense burners and two placards with gold or black inscriptions on red paper. All of this suggests the traditional altar. In another example, the ancestral altar is clearly demarked above an ornate painted cabinet. Here the central object is a large mirror in a heavy frame, in front of which stands a clock in a glass case and to the sides of which, to carry through the symmetry, tall white porcelain vases designed with large pink and white peonies hold feather dusters.[18] The mirror is often the central element in echoes of the ancestral altar. In yet another example, a couplet written in gold on red flanks a large mirror, and the calligraphy in turn is flanked by lithographed images of opera scenes.[19]

After 1949, removal of the family ancestral altar was undoubtedly part of Communist party efforts to eliminate "superstitions" and shift loyalties from family to state. However, in 1983, in accordance with the dictate, enunciated in 1980, that art should serve the people instead of politics, the government recognized the important role played by the centerpiece painting in traditional Chinese life.

PEASANT RESPONSES TO CURRENT PICTURES

On January 5, 1983, an exhibition of scrolls by professional, trained artists, entitled "Centerpiece Pictures," opened in the village of Zhuoxian, Hebei Province.[20] Done in an array of different styles, from the meticulously detailed to the splashy and the colorful to the monochrome, the scrolls in the centerpiece exhibition offered a wide variety of subjects. Some drew upon traditional motifs, such as *Tiger Roaring* or *Pines and Cranes* or *Cats and Butterflies*. There were depictions of immortals and illustrations of legends and historical figures. There were landscapes and decorative characters. Other pictures represented modern themes, such as *Poultry-Raising Girl* and *Girls of the Sea*, or portraits of people like Lu Xun and Zhu De. At the opening of the exhibition in Zhuoxian some of the artists met with peasants from the Dongguan Brigade of Zhuoxian for an informal discussion. At this time the peasants gave specific evaluations and opinions about several of the artworks.[21] A few months later, when the exhibition was shown in Beijing, the opinions of the peasants were posted next to the works. A selection of thirty-five pictures plus comments was reproduced in the art journal *Meishu*.[22]

The comments attributed to the peasants are couched in relatively unso-phisticated vocabulary, lending credibility to their authenticity. However, it is impossible to know whether what was printed in *Meishu* is a full or partial record of the total commentary on a given work, whether it represents the criticisms of one individual or several, or whether the responses were elicited on the basis of biased questions. Also unknown are the age and sex of the respondents. In addition to these drawbacks, only a few of the works in the exhibition were adequately reproduced in sources available in the West, making it difficult to get a grasp of the visual appearance of most of the pictures. Despite these obstacles, the reports in *Meishu* provide additional dimensions demonstrating the persistence of concepts of aesthetic propriety in China.

As will be evident from the examples of peasants' commentary on the centerpiece pictures given below, the aesthetic taste of modern peasants is largely conditioned by the artistic conventions familiar to them from the old New Year's prints: They prefer auspicious wishes conveyed through visual symbols rendered in a representational approach and bright colors, preferably filling all available space of the format.

The comment reported for a triptych depicting *Fish Playing in a Lotus Pond* (Figure 10.6), in which the fish (*yu*) stand for abundance and the lotus (*lian*) bring to mind the word for "connected"—composing the message of "continuous abundance"—is typical of the peasant critiques: "The fish are well painted, but the flowers do not look real (*yu huade hao, hua buxiang*), lotus flowers do not have long pointed petals, the painting is too small, and empty spaces are too many, peasants would not spend money to buy this much blank space. One picture divided into three is no good."[23] The major faults of the fish-and-lotus scene, according to the peasants, were the inadequate use of surface and the inaccurate drawing of the blossoms. In addition to this painting, many others in the exhibition were considered deficient in representational terms. One work was criticized because some of the people looked alike,[24] others because the human figures were stiff.[25] It was noted in a portrait of Lu Xun that his hand appeared to be crippled.[26] Scenes where animals were not lifelike were panned.[27]

The peasants' traditional love of color also determined their acceptance or rejection of a picture. Some peasants found colors unattractive when they were not "fresh and clear";[28] others complained that the mechanical use of bright red and bright green was "vulgar."[29] One person insisted, "Today's peasant does not much like bright red and bright green [*dahong, dalü*]."[30] However, pictures with no color whatsoever, or with very somber color schemes, were disasters as far as the peasants were concerned.[31]

A splashy, monochrome ink rendition of *Eight Steeds* had, to the peasants' eye, a major defect: Its imagery verged on the abstract. On the other hand, the peasants recognized that this feature (and no doubt the monochrome ink style) appealed to other segments of society: "This painting is for intellectuals," was a peasant opinion of the work.[32] The portrait of Lu Xun was not appreciated by the rural audience: "We don't recognize the person

Figure 10.6. Niu Zhongyuan, *Fish Playing in a Lotus Pond*, dated 1982. (From *Hebei huaniao huaji* [Shijiazhuang: Hebei meishu chuban she, 1984], pl. 42.)

in this picture." Another peasant said, "Hearing he was a great writer, I bought a copy of the picture and took it home. My spouse took it down, asking me where I got this figure to hang on the wall—it was appropriate for an intellectual to hang and has an intellectual's type of elegant air about it, so don't hang it up."[33]

Just as in the past, when the New Year's images of door gods and kitchen gods had assigned positions in the house, so too in 1983, the peasants had definite ideas about what sorts of images were appropriate for certain parts of the house. A depiction of *The Legend of the Anqi Bridge* showed the eight immortals with the sun and the moon and the five sacred mountains testing the strength of the bridge. This scene elicited the following comment, as peasants claimed they "had seen this type of painting when children, and it was not new. As a centerpiece, it is a little lightweight and might better be placed on the *kang*; youngsters do not understand this kind of story."[34] Similarly, a doubled character for happiness (*shuangxi*) composed of various birds was dubious as a centerpiece picture and best for a *kang*; "Young people getting married buy this kind of picture," was one statement about it.[35] Exactly such an image is seen above the bridal bed in a modern rural interior.[36]

Some pictures barely made the grade as centerpieces. Included in this group are the *Pine and Cranes*, ancient symbols conveying wishes for longevity (which one peasant thought would be fine to hang at New Year's time),[37] and the painting *Peonies and Two Doves*, considered "not bad for a centerpiece."[38]

Only two paintings were specifically pointed out as appropriate centerpiece works. One of these was *Drinking Horses* (Figure 10.7). The subject perhaps involves a rebus: *yinjun* "drinking horses" being similar to *yingchun* "welcome spring" makes it suitable for New Year's and, by extension, a proper "centerpiece" picture. The peasant commentary on *Drinking Horses* was: "This painting is definitely right for a centerpiece. People over fifty as well as youngsters all like to see horses; if it were done again, a few more horses should be added, then it would be even better."[39] The second painting explicitly thought apt for the centerpiece was the equestrian portrait of *Commander-in-Chief Zhu De in the Taihang Mountains* (Figure 10.8). The peasants made the following remarks about it: "Peasants like this painting; it has a forceful spirit. The horse is well painted, the figure also looks like old General Zhu. Hung in the central hall, it would be able to 'keep things under control.'"[40]

The peasants' comments make it evident that they still adhere to old aesthetic preferences as embodied in the traditional New Year's picture. They want representational pictures wherein the subject is immediately identifiable, clearly delineated, and accurately detailed. They prefer colored pictures, although there may be some difference of opinion over whether the color should be bright or soft in hue and intensity. The peasants have definite ideas about what is proper and correct imagery and style for pictures in various rooms of a house; some pictures are all right for the *kang*, but not

Figure 10.7. Ci Xu, *Drinking Horses,* done in 1982. (From *Meishu,* March 1983, p. 30.)

Figure 10.8. Quan Zhuming and Zhang Xinguo, *Commander-in-Chief Zhu De in the Taihang Mountains*, done in 1982. (From *Meishu*, April 1983, p. 44.)

for the formal hall centerpiece. It is also interesting that the peasants have specific notions about what, to them, is intellectual and what is peasant, in both style and subject. A splashy, semi-abstract approach is intellectual, while a more descriptive and meticulous method is always accepted by the peasants. Lu Xun is the intellectuals' giant, but Zhu De is the peasants' hero.

Since 1949, many efforts have been made by Chinese Communist party authorities to break with the past. The traditional standards of rectitude and propriety, however, are deeply rooted in the Chinese mind, even though some visual expressions of these traditional ideals are conscious while others are not. As an example of the less-than-conscious, it is doubtful whether today either the Communist officials or the masses truly recognize the visual effect of the old, strictly regularized furniture arrangement sufficiently to verbalize it. Perhaps for this reason, it was never censured. An example of conscious persistence of tradition is that both the authorities and the people have been well aware of the import of the ancestral altar and of the auspicious imagery derived from the traditional centerpiece and New Year's pictures. When movements against such "superstitions" became strident (as during the Cultural Revolution), the use of old images and ways to express these ideals evaporated only to reappear when more lenient policies prevailed.

NOTES

1. R. H. van Gulik, *Chinese Pictorial Art, as Viewed by the Connoisseur,* Serie Orientale Roma XIX (Rome: Istituto Italiano per il Medio ed Estremo Oriente, 1958), p. 18.

2. Ibid., p. 20.

3. A sizeable literature on these prints, and many volumes of reproductions, have been published in both Taiwan and the PRC. Among the most recent are *Zhongguo meishu quanji, huihua bian,* vol. 21, *Minjian nianhua* (Beijing: Renmin meishu, 1985); Tianjinshi yishu bowuguan, *Yangliuqing nianhua* (Tianjin: Wenwu, 1984); *Banhua congshu,* vol. 1, *Yangliuqing banhua* (Taibei: Xiongshi, 1976); *Zhongguo chuantong banhua yishu tezhan* [Special exhibition collector's show of traditional Chinese wood-block prints] (Taibei: Council for Cultural Planning and Development, Executive Yuan, 1983).

4. The following studies are extremely useful in decoding such auspicious messages: Terese Tse Bartholomew, "Botanical Puns in Chinese Art from the Collection of the Asian Art Museum of San Francisco," *Orientations,* September 1985, pp. 18–34; Edouard Chavannes, *The Five Happinesses,* trans. Elaine Spaulding Atwood (New York: Weatherhill, 1973); Alfred Koehn, "Chinese Flower Symbolism," *Monumenta Nipponica,* vol. 8, pp. 121–146; Nozaki Nobuchika, *Kisso zuan kaidai* (1928; reprint, Taibei: Guting, 1979 as *Zhongguo jixiang tu'an*); C. A. S. Williams, *Outlines of Chinese Symbolism and Art Motives,* 3d ed. (1941; reprint, New York: Dover Publications, 1970).

5. Comments about contemporary urban and rural interiors are based upon illustrations published in China from 1979 until 1985. I wish to thank Professor Norma Diamond at the University of Michigan for her generosity in lending to me some rare materials for my use in preparing this chapter. Other examples of the chair-table-chair unit in urban settings are illustrated in *China Pictorial,* August 1983, p.

26; *China Reconstructs*, December 1983, p. 19; *Women of China*, July 1980, inside front cover; July 1980, p. 5; July 1985, p. 37.

6. Another example of the chair-table-chair used in the countryside is published in *China Pictorial*, April 1981, p. 25. Use of the traditional chair cover in the countryside is seen in ibid.; in *China Pictorial*, January 1984, p. 15; and in *Women in China*, May 1984, p. 29.

7. Photographs of rooms with these pictorial subjects on the walls are published in *China Reconstructs*, October 1980, p. 8; January 1983, p. 16; *Shandong huabao*, February 1984, p. 26; *Women of China*, June 1983, p. 23; May 1984, p. 14.

8. For a depiction of a tiger hung in a rural room, see *Shandong huabao*, April 1983, p. 5.

9. Williams, *Symbolism and Art Motives*, pp. 398–400.

10. For a picture, see *Shandong huabao*, April 1983, p. 5.

11. Williams, *Symbolism and Art Motives*, pp. 199–200.

12. Ibid.

13. Nozaki, *Kisso zuan kaidai*, no. 177.

14. Koehn, "Chinese Flower Symbolism," p. 133.

15. See photographs of urban interiors published in *China Pictorial*, May 1980, p. 42; August 1983, p. 26; *China Reconstructs*, December 1983, p. 19; and *Women of China*, August 1980, inside front cover.

16. Other rural pictures of a boy holding a fish (or closely related imagery) include those illustrated in *China Pictorial*, May 1985, p. 20; *Women of China*, February 1979, p. 42; August 1984, p. 31; Ronald C. Knapp, *China's Traditional Rural Architecture: A Cultural Geography of the Common House* (Honolulu: University of Hawaii Press, 1986), no. 10.

17. Goldfish bowls or tanks are seen in photographs of urban interiors published in *China Reconstructs*, October 1980, p. 15; *Women of China*, August 1980, inside front cover; February 1986, p. 3. Photographs of interiors with fishbowls from rural areas are published in *China Pictorial*, April 1981, pp. 25, 26; *Women of China*, May 1984, p. 29.

18. *Women of China*, May 1984, p. 29.

19. *Women of China*, June 1983, p. 23.

20. It was a major art event. High-level provincial party and cultural leaders, along with representatives from the press and members of the Chinese Artists' Association from Beijing and Tianjin, attended the opening ceremony. As Hebei's effort to respond to the new government policy, the exhibition began in March 1982 when the theme "Centerpiece Pictures" was decided upon and then won the support of the provincial leadership and of the head of the Chinese Artists' Association. Subsequently, a centerpiece picture creative research office was organized at every local, city, and district level in the province to promote the exhibition and to provide opportunities for appraisals and study of drafts. Ultimately, more than 100 scrolls were selected from some 300 works. Twelve works were given awards as outstanding and 42 as excellent ("Hebeisheng zai Zhuoxian juban Zhongtanghua zhanlan," *Meishu*, March 1983, p. 1). The event was reported in *Renmin ribao* on January 23, 1983 (Zhong Zhihong, "Hebei huajia gei nongmin hua zhongtanghua," *Renmin ribao*, January 23, 1983, p. 5). Apparently it was believed necessary to explain the centerpiece for the benefit of modern readers since another article in *Renmin ribao* was devoted to this topic (Jing Zhuo, "Zhongtanghua," *Renmin ribao*, January 23, 1983, p. 5).

21. "Hebeisheng zai Zhuoxian," p. 1.

22. "Nongmin dui zhongtanghuade juti yijian," *Meishu*, April 1983, pp. 42–47.

23. Ibid., p. 42.

24. *Welcoming Spring,* by Xia Lianyu, Zhou Hecen, and Chen Hongliang (ibid., p. 43).

25. Lan Ruishan's *Poultry-Raising Girl* (ibid., p. 44); Zheng Shuangtian's *Duck Herder* (ibid., p. 46).

26. Portrait by Zhao Chengxin (ibid., p. 44).

27. *Ode to the Fatherland,* by Xu Shiqin and Li Qin (ibid., p.. 43).

28. For example, in Zhang Huimin's *Four Immortals of Green Waves* (ibid.).

29. For example, in Guo Zhongguang and Wang Guiqing's *Happy Yuanshao Festival* (ibid., p. 45).

30. See commentary under *Peonies and Two Doves,* by Fang Shijun (ibid.).

31. Hao Zhiguo's print, *Eastern Song and Dance* (ibid., p. 47); and Yang Zhongyi's print, *Doves at Beidaihe* (ibid., p. 47).

32. *Eight Steeds,* by Zhao Guide (ibid., p. 44).

33. Ibid.

34. *The Legend of the Anqi Bridge,* by Hu Guilin (ibid., p. 46). The famous Dashi Great Stone Bridge (also known as the Anqi Bridge), built in the seventh century, spans the Xiao River at Zhaoxian (formerly Zhaozhou). It is considered a major engineering achievement. According to the legend, the bridge was built in a single night during the Warring States period; its durability was tested by the eight immortals, one of whom rode a mule and carried the sun and moon, while another hauled the five sacred mountains in the wheelbarrow for additional weight. The bridge withstood the test, although the builder had to support it; the marks of the mule, the wheelbarrow, and the maker's handprints are still visible. (Huang Mengping and Li Jinshuan, *Zhongguo Zhaozhou qiao* [Shanghai: Science and Technology Press, 1981]; see also *Nagel's Encyclopedia-Guide: China* [New York: Nagel, 1968], pp. 691–692).

35. *Double Happiness,* by Zhang Wenqian (*Meishu,* April 1983, p. 47).

36. See illustration of rural bed in *Women of China,* May 1984, p. 14.

37. *Pine and Cranes,* by Yang Hongshu (*Meishu,* April 1983, p. 46).

38. *Peonies and Two Doves,* by Fang Shijun (ibid., p. 45).

39. *Drinking Horses,* by Ci Xu (ibid., p. 46).

40. *Commander-in-chief Zhu De in the Taihang Mountains,* by Quan Zhuming and Zhang Xinguo (ibid., p. 44).

PART FOUR

Social Currents

11

Guerrilla Interviewing
Among the Getihu

THOMAS B. GOLD

One of the most interesting social groups to emerge in post-Mao China is comprised of urban private entrepreneurs, known as getihu. They value private interest over public, the individual over the collective, competition over cooperation, risk-taking for personal gain over submission to party leadership, and freedom of movement over membership in a restrictive state work unit. In short, they represent everything that Maoism opposed. Party reformers believe the economy needs getihu, but Thomas Gold, professor of sociology at UC–Berkeley, argues that the contributions of the entrepreneurs are undermined by resentful cadres, a distrusting public, and the getihu themselves, who suffer from low self-esteem. Getihu are squeezed by corrupt officials and widely regarded as a degenerate underclass who cheat their customers, flaunt their wealth, and engage in questionable sexual activities. In reality, Professor Gold asserts, getihu are caught in a difficult political and economic bind, most are not rich, and many have ideals that go beyond money-making. The official and popular discrimination against getihu is, in part, a function of Marxist-Leninist-Maoist values that still retain their appeal, but it is also a product of traditional Chinese attitudes toward private business.

—Eds.

A decade of reforms has led to increased differentiation within Chinese society. Whereas previously the party stressed eliminating the "three differences" (rural versus urban; agricultural versus industrial; manual versus mental work) and unifying thought and behavior under party leadership, in the late 1980s the leaders acknowledge that Chinese society has a complex structure: Just as everyone does not do the same job, everyone does not see the world in the same way; everyone does not have the same immediate or even medium-term interests, although, of course, everyone supports communism in the long term. The leadership positively values differentiation now, arguing that specialization, comparative advantage, individualization, and even inequality—all up to a point—will stimulate healthy competition, helping to achieve the Four Modernizations for society and an improved life for all Chinese.

New social forces have emerged in China over the past decade, one of which is urban private entrepreneurs. This chapter, based primarily on observational field research in several Chinese cities, discusses how this new social group sees Chinese society and its role in that society, and also how the group is perceived by fellow Chinese.

In addition to presenting a substantive discussion of the urban private business class, this chapter addresses the matter of doing fieldwork in China. China's open-door policy has extended to research scholars as well as foreign businesses. Although there are many formal and informal limitations on conducting fieldwork in China, the imaginative fieldworker can still learn a great deal about Chinese behavior and thought without violating either Chinese law or the ethical standards of particular disciplines.

THE *GETIHU* PHENOMENON

The urban private entrepreneur is one of the newborn aspects of socialism with Chinese characteristics. At its Thirteenth Party Congress in the fall of 1987, the Chinese Communist party (CCP) officially declared that China was still in the immature stage of socialism: China is socialist in that the state sector dominates the economy, the plan takes precedence over the market, and distribution is according to work,[1] but because the productive forces are backward and the standard of living low, only a mixed economy can bring China to the level of abundance that forms the foundation for socialism, according to Marx's scientific prediction. A central component of a mixed economy is a private sector. In the official view, the private sector will always remain supplementary to the state and collective sectors, but will play an indispensable role for the indefinite future. The rise of the private economy is part of a pronounced trend in recent years for the party to retrench from its direct control over most aspects of the lives of Chinese (party and nonparty members), granting, and in some cases foisting, responsibility onto individuals for their own lives.

In 1978, when the party reaffirmed the legitimacy of private business, it envisioned very small operations. the term for private entrepreneurs, *getihu*, literally means individual households.[2] As Table 11.1 illustrates, for most of the succeeding years, these enterprises were one- or two-person undertakings, officially not permitted to hire more than seven nonfamily employees. In

TABLE 11.1
Individual Enterprises and Employees

Year	Number of Enterprises (million)	Number Employed (million)
1949–1950	4.14	8.26
1956	0.43	0.51
1957	na	1.04
1978	0.30	0.33
1979	0.56	0.68
1980	0.89	1.56
1981	1.50	2.57
1982	2.64	3.19
1983	5.86	7.55
1984	9.30	13.00
1985	11.69	17.57
1986	12.11	18.46
1987	13.72	20.16
1988	14.13	26.24

na—not available

Sources: Zhongguo shehui kexueyuan jingji yanjiusuo, Zhongguo zibenzhuyi gongshangye di shehuizhuyi gaizao [The socialist transformation of capitalist industry and commerce in China] (Beijing: Renmin chubanshe, 1978), pp. 228–229; Eilly Kraus, "Private Enterprise in the People's Republic of China: Official Statement, Implementations and Future Prospects," in China's Economic Reforms, ed. Joseph C. H. Chai and Chi-Keung Leung (Hong Kong: University of Hong Kong, Centre of Asian Studies, 1987); Beijing Review; China Daily; Liaowang; Renmin ribao (People's daily), overseas edition.

reality, family members and friends regularly help out in enterprises, so the figures for "number employed" vastly understate the count of people directly involved. The figures in Table 11.1 do not specify rural or urban; estimates of the percentage of rural private enterprises or specialized households (zhuanyehu) range from 65 to 80 percent of the total.[3] There are also countless others who engage in various forms of income-generating unlicensed private business. Some are purely illegal, while others, such as "Sunday engineers"—moonlighting technicians helping township enterprises—are actually encouraged.

The scale of private enterprises expanded beyond the individual level and, after some debate, the government decided to legitimate this trend. At 1988's Seventh National People's Congress (NPC), the state created a new social category, "private enterprises" (siren qiye), for those ventures having eight or more (in some cases, several hundred) non-kin on the payroll. While still numerically small (225,000 firms employing 3.6 million workers in mid-1988),[4] they illustrate a trend of an expanding private sector and a leadership tolerant of such a phenomenon—at least for the time being. As the reforms take hold, the public/private dichotomy is breaking down somewhat and labeling becomes a delicate task. Individuals and families subcontract state or collective enterprises and run them as private firms. Should they be categorized by asset ownership or by management form?

In 1987, officially registered private operators accounted for 17.2 percent of total retail sales, up from 2.9 percent in 1982. This came at the expense of state shops and collective outlets.[5] At the end of 1986, 53.1 percent of individual enterprises were engaged in commerce; 12 percent in industry, 10.3 percent in catering, 8 percent in transport, 7.2 percent in repairs, 6 percent in sideline industries, and 0.4 percent in construction.[6]

Why would the CCP allow and even encourage a private sector? First, I would cite the economic stagnation and disarray of the late 1970s. Trying to run the economy directly on the Stalinist model was draining state finances. A private sector would not take state funds and could even generate revenue through taxes. By channeling private monies into particular sectors, notably commerce and services, the state could concentrate its resources on heavy industry and those ventures requiring large amounts of capital and technology. The private sector could contribute to a central reform goal—enlivening the economy (gaohuo jingji).

Second, improving services and the quality of life could mitigate some of the widespread popular frustration and antipathy toward the party.

Third, the stagnant state sector could absorb no more workers, so the private sector became a key route to employment. Youths finishing school and awaiting job assignments in the absence of a labor market, and rusticated urban youths just then returning in droves to the cities, could be directed to the private sector, lightening some of the burden on the state, which could then claim that these people had been placed.[7]

Fourth, as shown by Taiwan and Hong Kong, if people are kept busy working for themselves, they will have less time and energy for political activity (troublemaking).

Fifth, if some people get rich at private business, the clear link between effort and reward might stimulate improved efficiency and productivity throughout the economy. State workers' bonuses could thus keep pace with private incomes, mitigating possible conflicts resulting from income inequality.

From the reformers' point of view, then, getihu could relieve the overburdened state, enhance revenues, raise popular support, absorb surplus labor, and motivate workers. If the reforms failed, inflation took off, inequality worsened, social disorder increased, and morals declined, the private entrepreneurs could serve as convenient scapegoats.

The emergence of a private sector in the 1980s virtually from scratch is thus a direct result of the reforms. Its expansion has implications for future structural change in the economy and society more generally. The attitude of Chinese citizens toward private business is a function of their attitude toward the reform program more generally. The self-image of getihu and their views of society will influence a crucial component of the reforms.

This chapter focuses on urban entrepreneurs. They represent a different social phenomenon from their rural counterparts, and studying them offers a different cut into the nature of Chinese society. The rural sector never achieved the same degree of socialization as the urban economy. Except for a few state farms, the land has remained, nominally, collectively owned and managed. Through most of the socialist era, although unable to migrate off the farms, peasants still retained some control over their economic lives, both through private plots (collective land allocated for private use) and access to rural markets with fluctuating degrees of freedom. The shift to a contract-based responsibility system builds on latent structures never completely eradicated. Participation in household enterprises and markets is a mainstream activity for rural families.

By contrast, the urban economy after 1956 was virtually entirely socialized (see Table 11.1). Privately owned assets were almost all bought out by the state or merged into collectives under close state control. All new enterprises were state or collective ones. The state substituted bureaucratic job allocation for a labor market. The re-emergence of private enterprises and a measure of individual say in career choice is thus a more radical phenomenon than the rural reforms. Although the "small producer mentality" of peasants received criticism, it was not as virulent or sustained as the attack on private business and the glorification of the socialist sector in the cities.

The private entrepreneur represents a range of values and behavior antithetical to ideals promoted by the CCP for decades. *Getihu* promote private over public, individual over collective, competition over cooperation, aggressive risk-taking for personal gain over unquestioning submission to party leadership, and freedom of movement over restrictive membership in a totalistic unit (*danwei*). In spite of a decade of reforms, many of the values that held sway under Mao still retain their appeal. *Getihu* violate these by their daily public activity, and hence exist as a rather marginal element in Chinese urban society, embodying many of the contradictions of the reforms themselves.

Their marginality, tenuous social and political status, self-doubt, and the disdain which many officials have for them make *getihu* at once an attractive and somewhat inaccessible subject of research. How can a foreign scholar go about studying *getihu*?

GUERRILLA INTERVIEWING

China's reforms have been a boon to social scientists. As part of the nation's internal relaxation and broadbased opening to the outside world, China has begun to publish reams of data on the economy, population, and society. A public-opinion poll fever has resulted in surveys of popular attitudes toward a wide range of phonomena.[8] There has been an explosion in mass media, with the establishment of numerous newspapers and journals known for their unprecedented frankness. Even the stodgy older publications now provide what Westerners would consider hard news. None of this is unproblematic, of course, but compared with the days of detective-like piecing together of clues as to what was happening in China, we are now positively deluged with relatively straightforward information that provides insights below surface generalities and off-scale models.

Literary works, including drama and film (for theaters and television), have also penetrated numerous former forbidden zones. All told, these various time-proven sources of data for research into a society one off-limits for firsthand fieldwork retain great value for foreign scholars and must not be ignored.

At the same time, access to China has introduced a new implement into the research tool kit, which was formerly almost exclusively dependent on refugee interviews for a sense of Chinese popular thought and daily behavior— namely, field research.

Some scholars have taken advantage of official exchange programs to conduct interviews, collect data, and visit research sites. These provide valuable information, in particular, a firsthand feel for the object of inquiry that was previously unattainable. However, officially arranged research usually involves some sort of supervision that risks compromising the data. Most conspicuously, interview subjects become noticeably cautious and evasive in the presence of a foreigner, especially if attended by an entourage of Chinese cadres.

Beside these official programs, the ability to travel on one's own to over 200 locations and opportunities to work as an expert or as a professional afford additional avenues for primary research.

In my study of the private sector, I have availed myself of both kinds of field research situation, in addition to documentary and archival study in China and elsewhere. Under the sponsorship of the Committee on Scholarly Communication with the People's Republic of China (CSCPRC), I have interviewed officials, scholars, and entrepreneurs, resided in a village, and visited other sites to observe private business activity. I have paid an interview fee for subjects brought to my venue (and supplied tea and cigarettes), but was not charged when I visited them at home or at their workplace. In fact, they had the short end as they felt obligated to proffer tea, sweets, and endless amounts of watermelon on me, a situation I found very embarrassing.

I want to focus in this chapter on the second type of primary data gathering, what I call "guerrilla interviewing." I define it as unchaperoned, spontaneous but structured participant observation and interviews as opportunities present themselves.

An ironic aspect of the private sector is that many of its activities are carried out in the public realm. This means, at the very least, that opportunities for observational field research are plentiful. Strolling through free markets, engaging in transactions, and receiving services for fees all afford chances to observe and participate in at least some key aspects of the lives of private businesspeople. This is far from the whole of their lives, of course. Application for a license, procurement of materials, payment of taxes, and other dealings with officialdom are important activities not open to casual observation; understanding them comes from conversational interviews. How private operators spend their leisure time is partially observable; what they think of their lives and of society is another key area that is largely off-limits and requires probing. Guerrilla interviewing comprises a variety of techniques to observe behavior and probe beneath the surface to achieve a more well-rounded understanding of *getihu*.

I initiated a study of the urban private sector in 1984. I was actually researching the process of socialist transformation of capitalism during the

1950s but became sidetracked by the increasingly widespread resurgence of private businesses. Although I had noted evidence of private activity as a student in 1979–1980 and during a brief trip in 1982, the sector did not really take off until 1984. That summer, during my first visit to the Minnan region of southern Fujian province (Xiamen and Quanzhou), I began to seek out markets and chat with operators of small businesses. Most striking to me at that time was the similarity to markets in small towns in Taiwan, a subject I had investigated in some detail.

Formulating a new research project on the emerging private sector, I prepared itineraries and questions and tried to master the relevant jargon prior to subsequent visits to China in 1985, 1986, and 1988 (of one or two months' duration each), based on reading the press and talking with Chinese in the United States. I have combined delegation trips with independent travel, attempting for the latter to visit a diverse sample of locations. I have thus combined multiple visits to some sites with single trips to others. For any city I try to get to the same markets or commercial districts more than once.

Upon reaching a city, I learn the location and times of major free markets and shops, and note them on a map. These are my primary fields.[9] In addition, the peripheries of big-name tourist destinations are now swamped with private operators (a high proportion of whom are from nearby rural areas), making it possible to combine sightseeing with work. (Confucius would not be pleased at the rows of carts set up all around the three top Confucian attractions in his hometown of Qufu, Shandong.)

At a site, I first station myself or meander slowly to get a sense of the types of enterprises, how business is conducted, and the degree of supervision. I make mental notes of the age and gender composition of the people behind the counters. I also make an effort to examine the operating license to check whether each is really a *getihu* and not the outlet of a competing collective or state enterprise, and observe whether the vendor is the person whose picture is affixed to the license. In tightly controlled cities like Beijing, the license is prominently displayed, but in many other locations it is nowhere to be seen, as *getihu* wish to present a macho image of independence. In Beijing and Shanghai, markets are orderly; there are numerous people on duty (*zhiqin*) as evidenced by their red armbands, and in permanent markets, such as Shanghai's Huating Road, uplifting slogans about moral business practices adorn the lintels of the stalls.

After a spell of pure observation, I start to participate, thereby initiating a relationship. I present myself as nothing more than a consumer. In some instances, usually after being spotted as a foreigner, I am called out to and offered items or services or, very frequently, asked to change money. More commonly, I begin by inquiring about particular merchandise and let the conversation evolve. If it appears promising, I ask a series of questions about the operator and the enterprise, to establish facts. If that succeeds, I probe matters of opinion. Interspersed are questions about the merchandise and, commonly, a discussion about myself and life in the United States. I answer these as completely as possible. I never take notes at the time and usually do not carry a notepad. I never carry a tape recorder. I try to repeat information to make sure I have understood it correctly, and only write things down far out of sight or back at the hotel. At the time, I also review prepared notes and questions to uncover gaps in my understanding or data.

Results vary, as might be expected. In some places, people are very willing to talk, especially if we do not draw a crowd. If a crowd does gather, I sometimes carry on a general discussion with the masses. In other instances, I adopt good guerrilla tactics and move on to a situation where I can regain control. At times, *getihu* are reticent about talking at all. Some ask, "What paper do you work for?" or, "Are you interviewing me?" but it does not necessarily spell an end to the conversation. I usually reply, "I'm a professor; I'm trying to understand what's going on in China." This frequently elicits an even more spirited discussion.

I am sensitive to the good chance that someone in a supervisory role is also observing my movements, and that people I speak with might be called to account. I try to keep my questions noncontroversial, although the answers are often quite pointed, even in a group free-for-all when crowd dynamics take over. I also try to be as nondisruptive as possible, since I might influence a businessperson's livelihood in a negative way by taking up his time. On the other hand, if business is slow, the entertainment value of a Chinese-speaking foreigner often provides welcome relief.

Because I do not want the episode to be exploitive, when possible I reciprocate for the information by purchasing an item, eating something, having my hair cut, or whatever is appropriate. In some cases, I take photographs of the market or particular establishments (if things have gone especially well), but more commonly I do not even carry a camera.

In addition to the type of field research just described, I also avail myself of the opportunities to collect relevant data. Drivers of taxis, pedicabs, and other conveyances are often private entrepreneurs (especially in smaller towns) and, like their counterparts worldwide, are very prone to sound off on a wide range of topics. Travel on trains, buses, and ships affords numerous chances for extended contact with traveling businessmen, who now seem to constitute the majority of passengers. Places frequented by *getihu*, such as coffee shops, bars, small eateries, and dancehalls, also offer opportunities to chat.

The thrust of my research is an effort to understand the position of legitimate private business in a self-styled socialist economy and society. I have working assumptions that *getihu* tend to be marginal; see themselves as vulnerable to greedy, jealous, and resentful officials; enjoy their relative liberty from the stifling *danwei;* and are out to make money and consume it quickly, as they assume the political line permitting private business may soon change. In my line of questioning, I try to place the *getihu's* background and motives and learn about the conduct of business and his plans. In a larger sense, I am using private business as an indicator for more general privacy in socialist China.

I also interview officials to round out my picture. In addition to prearranged sessions, I have had some luck with guerrilla forays into relevant government offices, where the occasional cadre will speak even with someone bereft of an all-powerful letter of introduction from a *danwei*.

Finally, in the company of friends or other acquaintances I bring up the subject of private business if appropriate, to gauge the popular attitude. Since these people tend to be intellectuals and professionals, I ask them about the thinking of nonintellectuals in their worksite and I also try to broaden my own sphere of respondents by approaching people of other social strata.

Guerrilla interviewing as a research methodology is a unity of opposites: Its strengths are also its weaknesses. On the plus side, it offers a way to flesh out an important type of Chinese microsocial process in the reform period; it offers immediacy beyond the picture presented in the official media. Like all ethnography, it is strong on description, provides rich anecdotal material, and offers spontaneity. Because, in my case at least, I am studying a very public activity, the participants have to carry on their business in spite of my presence, so I can assume that I am observing authentic behavior and not a rehearsed performance. Visiting many sites conveys China's regional (spatial and cultural) and ethnic diversity. Observing over time illustrates the effects of changes in policy, social structure, and values. While not as rigorous as a questionnaire, guerrilla interviewing is based on a great deal of prior preparation and a memorized set of questions, and is therefore superior to casual uninformed conversation that leads to disorganized general impressions.

Negatively, because of the short duration of each observational stint and high percentage of single visits, there is a sacrifice of depth. The approach is not rigorously systematic, activities are non-replicable, and it is possible to forget key facts if they are not recorded immediately. There is an element of deception involved and the risk of hurting someone; people are seen as data to collect and relationships are overly commoditized. The results are anecdotal and, for various reasons, not attributable without a bit of disguise. This might make some readers skeptical as to their validity.

My own conclusion is that as a supplement to official interviews and the study of documents and other printed material, data derived from guerrilla interviewing enlivens, enriches, and deepens our understanding of and writing about Chinese society.

THE WORLD OF THE *GETIHU*

In this part of the chapter, I will present aspects of the world of the urban private entrepreneur from his or her perspective, from that of the party-state, and from that of society at large.

Motivations

Individuals are both pulled and pushed to become *getihu*, and in many cases it is a combination of the two. They come from a variety of social backgrounds; very few are from a capitalist class background or former businesspeople themselves.

The first criterion for receiving a license is that one not have a present job. For new school graduates or dropouts, or those not assigned jobs prior to the elimination of the job assignment system (fenpei), this does not pose an additional problem. Those currently employed must either take unspecified leave (tuizhi), take leave without wages but still pay into benefit funds to maintain these and one's seniority in the event of returning (tingxin liuzhi), or just quit (cizhi). Quitting is not easy and, as those who want to work for themselves are often the most capable and industrious, leaders particularly resist releasing them.

Aspiring entrepreneurs must also pass a test demonstrating facility with the trade they plan to pursue. This might be a written aptitude test or a practical exam. If cadres in the geti office know a particular trade, they administer the test; otherwise they call in skilled workers to do it. A number of private and public training programs have sprung up in cooking, tailoring, furniture-making, hair styling, and so on to satisfy demand.

Attractions that pull urbanites onto the private road include:

- Money, as the potential earnings far exceed those of wage plus bonus.
- Freedom from bureaucratically managed enterprises and organizations, and from the smothering, womb-like danwei, for a career where one can set one's own hours and travel freely.
- Bringing one's talents into full play (fahui caineng) by choosing one's own career instead of submitting to the arbitrary and favoritism-riddled job assignment system. This is becoming particularly appealing to recent university graduates, postgraduates included.[10]
- Supplementing pensions, as the cost of living rises.
- Entering an ongoing family business. Some are actually fronting for relatives employed elsewhere who are the real force in the endeavor. At any one time, the person actually working in an enterprise is very likely not the one whose photograph is on the license, but rather a relative or friend who is helping out. In this category I would also include the children of high-level cadres (gaogan zidi), who use money of unclear origin, provided by their parents, for private gain. Often, such enterprises are solely involved in brokering and middleman operations, what the Chinese call "briefcase companies" (pibao gongsi) where the only tangible assets are business cards and briefcases.
- Creating social wealth and contributing to society. One may scoff at this stock phrase as a genuine motive, at least in the initial stages, but many getihu really do say, "At first I was in it for the money, but now I do it to serve society."
- Surplus rural labor operating in urban areas.

Some Chinese become getihu after exhausting other alternatives:

- Waiting for work (*daiye*), that is, they did not receive a job placement.
- Did not get into secondary or postsecondary school.
- Fired from current job.
- Former prisoner not wanted by other work units.
- Former Red Guards who return to the cities. Officially, they settled in the rural areas for life. If they return to the cities, the state takes no responsibility for their welfare, but will not send them back out.
- Handicapped citizens not taken by other work units.
- Elderly who never worked (primarily housewives) and who have no other source of income.

The state labels many of these with the derogatory term *socially idle people* (*shehui xiansan renyuan*), meaning they have no fixed status or *danwei*.

Getihu *as a Career and Lifestyle*

As a new social force, *getihu* lack role models and a domestic reference group (pre-Liberation capitalists are not viable). They have thus had to create a lifestyle more or less as they go along.

A major evolution over the years has been in the *getihu's* attitude toward his or her career and lifestyle. In the early 1980s, those I spoke with suffered low self-esteem. They had been pushed to this lot because of personal inadequacies and lack of either an effective network (*guanxiwang*) or powerful family members who could get them a plum job assignment. In the late 1980s, the state sector holds less appeal. This is in large measure the intentional result of policies to "smash the iron rice bowl" of lifetime job security, benefits, and pensions, to compel more effort by workers. Many available state jobs are physically arduous and dirty and not attractive to young people solely because they are in the state sector. The pervasive heavy hand of the party and bureaucracy, rules and regulations, pressures to be politically active, and so on that characterize state units repel the youth of the second half of the 1980s. In fact, many *getihu* hold state employees in contempt for their lower wages, political toadying, lack of control over their own lives, and absence of entrepreneurial gumption. To a certain extent this is a defense mechanism, but I think they actually believe it, too. Many also believe state sector jobs will be available in the future, and that while they are young they should earn as much money as possible and enjoy their freedom, then later go conformist and settle down. Naturally, attitude is a function of one's motives for embarking on the private road, one's success to date, the attitudes of others, the type of enterprise, and the location. In Beijing, the bureaucratic heartland, I still sense more defeatism and resignation by many stall-keepers, whereas in Wenzhou, where the line between private and public is difficult to discern, *getihu* exude an infectious exuberance.

The *gethihu* I spoke with in Wenzhou (definitely an extreme case) had plans to expand operations and saw themselves as committed to at least this life if not a particular occupation. They consumed aggressively but saved as well. In other cities, *getihu* consumed more out of distrust for the longevity of the policy toward private business and also because they had no other outlet for their accumulated profits. In any event, they enjoy flaunting their wealth.

Everywhere, *getihu* spend money flagrantly. They purchase the latest popular items and fashionable clothes. They regularly patronize dance halls, restaurants, and bars. Successful *getihu* in Beijing flocked to the bowling alley, dancehall, and swimming pool at the Lido Holiday Inn until new rules made it off-limits to them late in 1986. The Rive Coffee Shop at Shanghai's Jin Jiang Hotel is another popular hangout; gambling and womanizing are common leisure-time pursuits.[11]

They also try to support each other. They congregate at privately owned restaurants and coffee shops, sit for hours in private barbershops and beauty parlors, and prefer to deal with private wholesalers. This is not tantamount to conceiving of themselves as a particular class (most decidedly have no political ambitions), but there is a definite consciousness of being a private businessperson in the PRC. It is too early to tell whether or not this consciousness can override the diversity in social backgrounds of the *getihu* and create a foundation for political activity.

Attitudes to the Party and State

Individual operators see the supervisory bureaucracy—the Industrial and Commercial Administration and Management Bureau (*Gongshang Xingzheng Guanliju*)—and its *geti* department (*ke*) at each level as so many mothers-in-law (*popo*) constantly hassling them. On both scheduled and impromptu occasions, bureaucrats check up on adherence to the licensed scope of operation, proper bookkeeping, sanitation, cleanliness, and who is actually working. They collect administrative fees (*guanlifei*) and assess fines. Tax collectors from the tax bureau (*Shuiwuju*) calculate sums owed, often after a certain amount of "discussion."

The *getihu* must pay these monies for security and to avoid additional trouble, but are also expected to provide certain favors for cadres (*qingke songli*). These vary by location and trade. Food purveyors, for example, have to offer meals and liquor for free or at a nominal rate. Others give merchandise or sell it at deep discounts. Cigarettes and alcohol are exchanged as a matter of course. There are also contributions to society—schools, playgrounds, public works, services for the elderly, and so on—that are another form of squeeze, although they might yield dividends in mitigating popular resentment toward these nouveaux riches.

Besides officials in a regulatory capacity private businesspeople also must deal with state enterprises, primarily for supplies. This involves a great deal of corruption, fueled by the state enterprise's own need to show a profit; that is, the enterprise and its salesmen both benefit from supplying *getihu* with scarce goods, obscuring the line between corruption and competitiveness. In China's emerging market economy, where monetary power has broken the monopoly of political power, officials have been actively supplementing their wages by reselling goods under the plan to other state enterprises or to private operators. They take advantage of the dual price system, obtaining goods at the low fixed price and selling them for whatever the market will bear. This bureaucratic speculation is called *guandao*.[12] One reason *getihu* prefer to deal with other private enterprises is that they feel less exploited.

Private entrepreneurs can apply for loans from state banks, a process involving collateral, official backing, and connections. Most rely instead on their relatives or friends for startup capital, which is repaid with interest.

Many *getihu* chose their career to escape the close supervision not only of their work but of their personal lives as well, which characterizes the *danwei*. They avoid being organized and mobilized by the party and state and have little interest in joining the CCP or Communist Youth League (CYL). However, membership in the Self-Employed Laborers Association (*Geti Laodongzhe xiehui*; SELA) is nearly universal and virtually compulsory. A handful become active in the SELA, CCP, or CYL as a route into the bureaucracy or to accumulate political capital.

Younger entrepreneurs live for the moment, but older ones, particularly those with families or on the verge of marriage, look to the government to help them solve problems whose solution remains a state of monopoly. These include housing, daycare, health care, insurance, and pensions. The state, meanwhile, is commoditizing most of these for its own workers as well and is unlikely to provide them for private households.

Individual businessmen remain skeptical about the sincerity of the party and state toward the private sector. Pronouncements at the 1987 Thirteenth Party Congress and laws promulgated after the 1988 Seventh National People's Congress allayed fears somewhat. Nonetheless, a number of private enterprises try to register as collectives or cooperatives, due to their more socialist nature, higher social status, and lighter tax burden. Much terminological confusion surrounds these categories. Formerly, collectives (*jiti qiye*) were set up and administered by urban neighborhood (*jiedao*) offices, usually to absorb housewives and youths. Cooperatives (*hezuoshe*) were rural entities. In today's collectives, shares are issued in proportion to the amount of capital contributed by each investor. State units might invest as well as private individuals. These shares are not publicly traded. Such enterprises are variously called *jiti, hezuo* and *hehuo* enterprises, the latter emphasizing that there are partners. The key is that individuals and not the state initiate and run them, and determine the distribution of profits. One famous example is the Stone Group of Beijing, started by scientists who quit jobs in state research units.[13] Reportedly, several high-ranking cadres back the Stone Group politically and financially. In Wenzhou, where privatization has gone quite far, the common practice is to register enterprises as collectives. I dropped in on the Zhenhua Municipal Bank, one of several banks (*xinyongshe*) in Wenzhou whose shareholders include individuals and, in this case at least, the Wenzhou Labor Service Company. The bank has 225 shares; the chairman, a former manager of a collective factory, is the largest shareholder.

As mentioned above, many *getihu* do not take a long-term view or plan to expand operations. Their objective is to make a lot of money as quickly as possible, consume grandly, then extemporize. Distrust of the party and state is at the root of this attitude.

The common *getihu* believe they are on an uneven playing field. They not only must deal and compete with powerful state and collective enterprises, and with what they perceive as a hostile and rapacious bureaucracy, but they see a number of children of high cadres (as well as ex-cadres themselves) using connections and influence for loans, contacts, materials, and so on beyond the reach of the average Zhou.

The Official View

Dealing with a legitimate private sector is a new challenge for local Chinese government officials. They not only need to approve and supervise activity but are also expected to improve the business climate and encourage some people to embark on the private road. Cadres in the relevant industrial and commercial departments are feeling their way as much as their charges are. Privatization of the economy reduces the monopoly of cadres over key aspects of Chinese life, threatening their power and privileges. It also violates the fundamental beliefs of many committed communists. With a legacy of a Stalinist planned economy, Maoist anticapitalism, and traditional anticommercial attitudes, plus the Leninist impulse to control all aspects of society, both older cadres and those raised during the Cultural Revolution must make a fundamental shift in attitude. In a wide-ranging guerrilla interview in a district industrial and commercial office in Shanghai, the cadres emphasized that changing their own thinking was as big a problem as the actual regulation of private business. They had to achieve a balance between a lively but not chaotic market and regulating things to death (*huo er bu luan, guan er bu si*)—not an easy task, and one with no real precedents to follow. Officials constantly study new laws and policies and one of their responsibilities is raising the legal consciousness of all parties involved.[14]

The central government sends mixed signals that are partly a reflection of its own ambivalence and partly a function of the balance between various political factions.[15] Party and state leaders have received private entrepreneurs with much fanfare, praised their contributions to socialist construction and the reforms, and accorded them laborer status. Since the Thirteenth Party Congress and Seventh NPC, the leadership has encouraged private business and begun to pass legislation that further protects it. But at other times, particularly in early 1985 and the middle of 1987, there have been anti–private business actions.[16] At these times, there will be raids on markets and "speculators" (*daoye*) will be shut down with much fanfare. The media will counter fears by claiming that this sort of crackdown is not aimed at private business per se, just at a small handful of illegal operations. Nonetheless, it raises the level of tension. There is a very real gap between policy and actual implementation, especially because local cadres stand to lose so much as the private sector expands. There have been well-publicized cases of cadres parasitically feeding off of successful legitimate entrepreneurs, eventually driving them out of business.[17]

Administration is only part of the local bureaucrats' job. They also are required to serve (*fuwu*) the private sector: provide information, ensure adequate electricity and water, assign suitable locations, help peasants in the city, etc. Most of these services are free. The bureaucrats also check to ensure that there are no extortion or protection rackets.

They guide (*zhidao*) the SELA at the appropriate level. Membership dues (50 fen to one yuan a month in Shanghai) and administrative fees help to pay for a secretary whom the bureau sends into the SELA, although each group picks its own leaders. The cadres hold discussions on taxation and other official matters, help *getihu* exchange information, arrange competitions, transmit teachings on proper business practices and ethics as well as ideals in life, organize healthy social activities, and advise on the selection of models. They also try to recruit CYL and CCP members.

In all markets, uniformed cadres and plainclothes supervisors (usually retired workers) are much in evidence, maintaining order. On occasions when I walked with officials through markets, they behaved in a friendly and solicitous manner toward entrepreneurs. They deny any corruption ("We've heard of cases elsewhere, but there haven't been any here"), contradicting what the businessmen say.

In one city, I visited a very active market with two uniformed industry and commerce officials. One of the biggest *getihu* there provided us with cold cans of Jianlibao, then asked us to lunch at a private restaurant in the suburbs. He paid the cab. We enjoyed a lavish repast, and when I asked the senior cadre how the payment was to be made he said, "Little Wang will pay. Don't worry, he has plenty of money!"

The Societal View

As China's society becomes more differentiated, it is hard to speak of a single attitude toward any matter. Nonetheless, I have found a striking uniformity of thinking toward the private sector that extends across class lines and involves varying degrees of prejudice and resentment. The former derives from a traditional anticommercial bias reinforced by decades of strident anticapitalist rhetoric. Chinese urban dwellers assume that anyone who becomes a *getihu* suffers from some sort of personality defect: In a self-styled socialist society, only a deviant would become a licensed capitalist. In spite of studies that show otherwise, most Chinese I spoke with are convinced that the majority of *getihu* are ex-cons, juvenile delinquents, or riffraff unable to do anything else. Or, in a variation, many are seen to be the children of high cadres, taking advantage of their parents' power and the openings provided by the reforms to use public funds for private gain.

In any case, popular thinking has it that in order to succeed, *getihu* must bribe officials and set up various sorts of networks and rackets to get around the state-dominated economy. Reportedly, they routinely cheat their customers and engage in a dissolute lifestyle, patronizing dancehalls and bars. They lead degenerate sex lives as well, especially on the road. (This is one reason among many that numerous parents shun *getihu* as marriage partners for their children.)

A story making the rounds in Shanghai in 1988 concerned two men in a coffee shop who had a contest to see who had the most cash to burn—literally. Although the *Jiefang ribao* (Liberation daily) article[18] did not explicitly say they were *getihu*, the description of their clothes (denim jacket, Western suit), foreign cigarettes, obsession with money and profligacy clearly imply they are *getihu*.

Jealousy and resentment ("red eye disease") reinforce prejudice. The fact that many *getihu* become wealthy and flaunt their wealth galls workers, low-level cadres, and intellectuals on relatively fixed incomes. In their minds, *getihu* and high-cadre children are birds of a feather, equally despicable. When the party urges workers ("masters of the country") and intellectuals strapped for cash to take second jobs, this rubs salt into the wound.

At another level, urban dwellers see *getihu* as symptomatic of and fueling the downside of the reforms: inflation, corruption, declining morals, and inequality. A word I heard repeatedly in 1988 was *suzhi* (moral or inner quality), usually considered conspicuously absent among cadres and their families and among private businessmen. People I spoke with readily ignored the way in which the private sector has provided a number of goods and services previously unavailable. The common response was, "They're too expensive!"

Although China's media is a handmaiden of the party and cannot be said to reflect independently the thinking of the masses, on the *getihu* issue it has been remarkably forthright. In the past, we took Chinese popular art, for example, as a mirror—it reflected the opposite of the truth. At present, though, it often is directly on target.

Films about *getihu*, such as *Yamaha Fish Stall* (Yamaha yudang) and *Zhenzhen's Hair Salon* (Zhenzhen no fawu)[19] reflect the attitudes cited above. I do not think they shape popular thought, in this case, so much as incorporate what is already there. In both films, the *getihu* protagonist is some sort of social idler. Even when they try to be honest, corrupt officials, jealous customers, and resentful citizens badger them to the point of physical abuse. Hu Yuyin of the novel and film *A Small Town Called Hibiscus* (Furongzhen) is an upstanding figure nearly martyred by the ultraleft but vindicated under the reforms.[20] The fact that the unmarried mother protagonist of *Under the Bridge* (Daqiao xiamian) is a *getihu* is not crucial to the film but does little to dispel the common assumption about *getihu*'s moral depravity. These works plead for sympathy for *getihu*, emphasizing the bind they are in, the fact that most are far from rich, and that many have higher ideals beyond making money.

CONCLUSION

The emergence and evolution of a private business class in China's cities is closely related to the post-Mao reform program. It comprises people who, for one reason or another, have either withdrawn from the socialist sector or never entered it. It introduces a new element into Chinese society, a stratum of people much more on their own in crucial aspects of their lives than has been permitted since the founding of the PRC. Their existence and activities, accorded legitimacy by the CCP, represent a challenge to ingrained ways of thinking and behaving, as well as to institutions established and maintained by the Communists. I conclude, based on observing *getihu* and the reactions of officials and citizenry to them, that they are still marginal to the mainstream of Chinese society and values. Many *getihu* do not see this as ostracism, relishing what they consider their freedom, while others— probably the majority—would prefer to be more securely anchored to the dominant society.

To me, a striking result of my fieldwork has been the resonance of *getihu* behavior and especially responses to it with traditional Chinese attitudes toward private business. The deep mutual distrust between businesspeople and officials, the payment and expectation of squeeze, the popular condescension toward those who focus their lives on pursuing profit, the assumption that *getihu* are dishonest, the general disdain toward nonconformity, the desire of some *getihu* to purchase respectability through philanthropy (however involuntarily contributed) or to use business status to enter the bureaucracy are fundamental Chinese characteristics reinforced but hardly created by Marxism-Leninism-Maoism.

Part of the revolutionary accomplishment of capitalist East Asia has been the rise to prominence of private businessmen and the redirection of state power, away from pervasive control toward the creation and maintenance of a good investment climate. The rise in the PRC of a private business class, along with the other aspects of reforms, makes it increasingly difficult to reproduce the traditional-cum-socialist social structure. This is what occurred elsewhere in East Asia; for the mainland, the transition has only just begun.

NOTES

1. We might also add to the essential components of Chinese socialism that the Four Basic Principles are in command. These are: adhering to the socialist road (an obvious tautology), leadership by the Communist party, Marxism-Leninism–Mao Zedong Thought as the guiding ideology, and the People's Democratic Dictatorship (current form of the dictatorship of the proletariat) as the basis of the state.

2. They are also called *geti laodongzhe* or individual laborers, which emphasizes their status as non-exploiting workers.

3. Not all rural households officially register as private enterprises. If they have a permanent operation in a city they are supposed to have a license, but do not necessarily obey. Table 1 in Kraus breaks down urban and rural enterprises but I have not been able to check this. See Willy Kraus, "Private Enterprise in the People's Republic of China: Official Statement, Implementations and Future Prospects," in *China's Economic Reforms*, ed. Joseph C. H. Chai and Chi-Keung Leung (Hong Kong: University of Hong Kong, Centre of Asian Studies, 1987), pp. 64–97, 70–71.

4. *Beijing Review* (hereafter *BR;* all citations from North American edition), no. 26 (June 27–July 3, 1988), p. 11.

5. *BR,* no. 23 (June 6–12, 1988), p. 40.

6. *BR,* no. 18 (May 4, 1987), p. 8. There is no explanation as to why this does not add up to 100 percent. Perhaps a service sector, including things such as barbers, bath-houses, tailors, hotels, and so on is missing. Also see Kraus, "Private enterprise"; Xia Zhongrui, Wang Wanzhen, and Jin Zhi, "Strengthening Guidance and Management; Expanding Individual Economy," *Chinese Economic Studies,* part 1, vol. 21, no. 1 (Fall 1987), pp. 102–117, esp. p. 103; and Marcia Yudkin, *Making Good: Private Business in Socialist China* (Beijing: Foreign Language Press, 1986), pp. 82–83 for examples from specific locales.

7. See, for example, Chen Jian, "An Effective Way to Increase Employment," *Chinese Economic Studies,* part 1, vol. 21, no. 1 (Fall 1987), pp. 43–71.

8. For more on surveys see Stanley Rosen, "Value Change Among Post-Mao Youth," chapter 12 in this book.

9. I have utilized the topic order in Leonard Schatzman and Anselm L. Straus, *Field Research* (Englewood Cliffs, N.J.: Prentice-Hall, 1973) to organize the material that follows.

10. See *BR,* no. 24 (June 13–19, 1988), pp. 12–13 for an example of a Ph.D. setting up on his own.

11. Problems of dealing with wealth are discussed in Ding Zhiyong and Lu Feiyun, "Zhifu yihou" [After getting rich], *Shehui* [Sociology journal], no. 4, 1987, pp. 11–13.

12. Julia Leung, "Beijing Purge of Profiteers Sparks Alarm," *Asian Wall Street Journal,* October 7–8, 1988, p. 1.

13. Daniel Southerland, "Two Firms Take Fight Public Inside China," *Washington Post,* June 19, 1988, p. H2.

14. For articles that disucss the complex position of cadres see the series under the general title, "Rang geti gongshanghu jiankang fazhan" [Let individual industrial and commercial enterprises develop in a healthy way], *Liaowang* [Outlook weekly], no. 9 (March 3, 1986), pp. 24–27; and Lu Zhonghe, "Shanghai geti jingji fazhan di chengjiu, wenti ji guanli yijian" [The accomplishments, problems and administrative opinions of the development of Shanghai's individual economy], *Shanghai jingji,* no. 2 (March 30, 1988), pp. 55–58.

15. For an essay emphasizing such ambivalence, see Linda Hershkovitz, "The Fruits of Ambivalence: China's Urban Individual Economy," *Pacific Affairs,* vol. 58, no. 3 (Fall 1985), pp. 427–450.

16. This is discussed in Thomas Gold, "China's Private Entrepreneurs," *China Business Review,* vol. 12, no. 6 (November–December 1985), pp. 46–50.

17. For the case of Geng Qui, see "Corrupt Officials Force Out Success," *Sunday Morning Post* (Hong Kong), June 5, 1988, p. 3. On Guan Guanmei, see "Cabbages and Capitalists," *Newsweek,* July 20, 1987, p. 37.

18. "Sichaopiao bisai" [Shredding cash contest], *Jiefang ribao* [Liberation daily], May 21, 1988, p. 6.

19. The script for the latter film, written by Xia Lan, is published in *Dianying xinzuo* [New film], no. 1, 1987, pp. 2–26.

20. The English version of the novel by Gu Hua was published by Panda Books of Beijing in 1983.

12

Value Change Among Post-Mao Youth

The Evidence from Survey Data

STANLEY ROSEN

Not only has social differentiation been accepted by the authorities in post-Mao China, but the "bourgeois" social sciences have been revived and legitimized as a means of understanding new social patterns. Stanley Rosen, professor of political science at the University of Southern California, argues that the first wave of survey data generated by Chinese researchers, when handled carefully, sheds interesting light on value changes among post-Mao youth under the impact of economic reform. Compared to the 1950s and 1960s, for example, college students express a greater hostility toward cadres and political leaders and place greater emphasis on independence of thought and a patriotism that does not take its cues from the party. Prosperous young peasants join the military not for ideological reasons, but in order to acquire political clout and access to networks that will benefit the family's new economic interests. As the urban economy expands, young women workers are earning more money, becoming more independent, and engaging more widely in pre- and extramarital sexual activity. Finally, attitudes toward education are changing in the 1980s, especially in the rural sector. The number of school dropouts increased once money became the standard for measuring success; families are willing to sacrifice their children's schooling if early employment is available.

—Eds.

In the 1980s, survey research emerged as a major new source of information on Chinese society. As in so many other areas, the decisions of the

Third Plenum of the Eleventh Central Committee (December 1978) marked a turning point for Chinese social science. By shifting party work away from class struggle and toward socialist modernization and by abolishing the practice of discriminating against people of "bad" class backgrounds—including intellectuals—this seminal meeting set the stage for a revival of the "bourgeois" social sciences in China. At the same time that Chinese social scientists were permitted once again to ply their trade, the authorities accepted and even encouraged social differentiation among the populace. Personal goals no longer were viewed as necessarily in contradiction with public values and competitive efforts began to be endorsed and rewarded.

These changes greatly aided the development of Chinese survey research. Indeed, investigators have sometimes marveled at the willingness of respondents to reveal attitudes that could not have been openly expressed a few years earlier. In turn, the surveys provide a fascinating picture of a society in transition that is groping toward a vaguely defined future called "socialism with Chinese characteristics." Moreover, one could argue, it is precisely this lack of clarity over both policy ends and means that allows social scientists and their respondents such additional freedom of thought and action.

This chapter looks at survey research on youth, the group that has been most extensively surveyed in China. It presents two primary concerns, one methodological and one substantive. Substantively, how can we characterize youth attitudes in China's transitional society? Have attitudes changed under the impact of reform policies? Methodologically, can we use survey research as a reliable guide to probe such attitudes? What are the strengths and weaknesses of this new (for China) methodological tool?

METHODOLOGICAL PROBLEMS
OF CHINESE SURVEYS

The most fundamental question one must ask in analyzing Chinese survey research is: How reliable are the results?[1] Theoretically, there are four likely sources of methodological error: (1) those that might stem from traditional Chinese political culture, which have been encountered on Taiwan;[2] (2) those that might be due to the constraints of a socialist political system governed along Marxist-Leninist lines, which have been encountered in the Soviet Union and Eastern Europe;[3] (3) those that are the result of a lack of sophistication in social science research methods; and (4) those that may be inherent in the survey research enterprise itself, which have been encountered in surveys done in the West. Given space considerations, we cannot undertake to characterize each problem in terms of these four types of error. It will be useful, however, to distinguish explicitly between methodological problems encountered at the data gathering stage and those arising at the data analysis stage.

Problems in Data Gathering

Putting aside criticisms of survey research that are generic to the enterprise itself, let us focus on the particular difficulties one faces in the Chinese context. There is little basis in Chinese traditional political culture to suggest that citizens will reveal their true feelings in a questionnaire, even one in which respondents may omit their names. Data collection of this sort, in China's political history, has been used in governmental attempts at social control. Nothing in post-1949 China, marked as it is by radical political movements, has altered this picture. Requests from the party to reveal openly one's true feelings in written form—for example during the Hundred Flowers era (1956–1957) and the Cultural Revolution (1966–1976)—have been followed by stern reactions from the party. In each case, one's "black materials" (hei cailiao) were used to justify the ensuing crackdown. Although recent years have seen a vast improvement in this pattern, those with long memories warn the young and overeager to exercise caution when writing or stating their views.[4]

Many of those conducting survey research are well aware that respondents are likely to play it safe and choose the "right" answer, the response the official surveyors want to see. Interviews with students and teachers who had participated in survey questionnaire projects revealed a similar awareness. As one leading educator, whose research institute had conducted many surveys, put it: "I'm very skeptical of using surveys, particularly with middle school students. The answers they give sound great, but we know from the actual situation in the classrooms that they are not telling the truth." Since many surveys of students contain political questions (e.g., Is socialism superior to capitalism? Is communism inevitable in China?), results should be interpreted cautiously. It is worth noting that the number of non-respondents tends to increase as survey questions become politically sensitive.

Aware that respondents may be less than completely truthful, Chinese researchers have designed their questionnaires to anticipate the problem. For example, some feel that a forced-choice form questionnaire may cause respondents to seek the correct answer, as if it were a multiple-choice examination. Open-ended questions, which allow more freedom to express opinions, can lead to more honest responses. This method, of course, presents coding problems; the researcher must fit a narrative into a predesigned category. The problem is complicated by the fact that often the researcher is as desirous as the respondent that the result be correct. Seeking positive results, the researcher has his or her Procrustean bed in which to fit wayward answers. Alternatively, some surveys fit open-ended answers into several categories, so that total percentages in the reported tables may be over 100 percent.

Another method of eliciting honest responses is to probe beyond the expected answers. An example of this can be seen in a survey of 1,109 new military recruits done by the General Political Department of the People's Liberation Army.[5] A subgroup of 628 had been engaged in the production or trade of commodities before their enlistment; their income levels in civilian life had ranged from 700 yuan a year to more than 7,000. Thus they were not typical poor peasants seeking an escape from rural poverty. When asked why they enlisted, 528 (95 percent) had as their primary motive "to defend the motherland" and "fulfill one's duty." Perhaps anticipating that rural traders—96 percent of the subgroup were from the countryside—would be less than completely forthright, the researchers also asked for secondary motives. These were more revealing. Of the 628 recruits, 237 (37.7 percent) enlisted to "enhance their social status," with about 90 percent of these seeking a route to party membership. Another 255 (40.6 percent) expected to learn a trade in the army that was not readily available in the countryside. Close to 80 percent of this group wanted to learn truck driving, a lucrative profession under China's newly relaxed rural economy.

Beside the problem of respondent veracity, a second major problem with surveys conducted in support of a political agenda is that they are often designed to affirm a predetermined conclusion. This is a problem at both the data gathering and data analysis stages. Rather than taking a hypothesis and testing it with survey data, some Chinese social scientists start with the answers and then look for evidence to demonstrate that their conclusion is, indeed, correct. The hypothesis becomes inseparable from the conclusion. Researchers have sometimes wanted to confirm broad support for a given state policy, be it the open policy (*kaifang zhengce*) or the Four Modernizations; other times, they have wanted to show that their young charges are being properly socialized. Surveys of students are expected to confirm their desire for knowledge, their moral rectitude, and their belief in collectivist values. Homeroom teachers and school principals are quite concerned that their students fill out survey questionnaires correctly. In part this is a question of "face"; incorrect answers reflect badly on teachers and school officials. Interviewees have reported numerous cases of results that were suppressed because of too many incorrect answers. As will be shown below, at the data analysis stage these pressures may lead researchers—perhaps even subconsciously—to manipulate data in order to report appropriate conclusions.

Political agendas also appear in questionnaire design. As we know from long experience in the United States, it is not difficult for commercial or political interests to generate results favorable to the product they are marketing. By using general buzzwords such as reform, modernization, socialism, and so forth, one set of (positive) responses will appear; a different set of buzzwords such as inflation, corruption, and capitalism will elicit negative responses.[6]

In addition to eliciting correct answers, surveys can be used—even inadvertently—to train students at an early age. One very revealing example is a survey, published in 1985, entitled "Research on Improving the Moral Education of Primary School Students."[7] Students were asked a series of questions, each one with two choices. The questions were as follows:

1. What kind of life is happiest?
   a. learning and engaging in life collectively
   b. eating, drinking, playing, and enjoying life
2. What represents beauty in a person?
   a. beauty of mind
   b. physical beauty
3. How should one handle the relationship between individual and collective?
   a. think of the collective first
   b. think of the individual first

In each case, before the lesson by the teacher, more than two-thirds of the thirty-nine students tested chose *b* over *a*. After the lesson, when told the correct answers, more than four-fifths chose *a* over *b*. Putting aside some of the difficulties in the design of this questionnaire, in which primary school students are forced to choose between traditional moral virtues taught in school and more natural responses based on what is presumably being learned in the home and from peers, there is the more basic issue stated above. While one can praise the necessity to instill proper socialist values in young children, it should also be clear that the children are at the same time learning that surveys require proper responses in order to win praise from adults.

There is a third major problem at the data gathering stage. The sensitive quality of much survey research, combined with the nature of Chinese society, makes it difficult for the researcher to choose an appropriate sample. Access to organizations containing one's targeted respondents appears rarely to be based on principles of probability sampling; it is most often based on personal relations (*guanxi*). The researcher must convince the organization to provide access. Therefore, university researchers are most likely to survey students on their campuses or at the university's attached middle and primary schools. Neighborhoods sampled will often be in the vicinity of the university. This tendency, of course, raises questions of generalizability of the results, even across one's district, not to mention across the whole city, or to other cities. The reliance on personal contacts rather than on scientific methods of sampling makes it difficult to produce impartial findings. A problem of face is involved when writing up results on one's own unit; more practically, acceptable results may be needed to guarantee continued access. But the problem is even more serious. Much of the published survey research, far from merely constituting a poorly chosen, unrepresentative sample, represents no sample at all. It is quite common simply to hand out questionnaires to everyone. As one Chinese social scientist who teaches classes on statistics put it: "Many Chinese researchers are proud of their large 'samples.' If N = 10,000, they feel their work must be ten times more valid than if N = 1,000. They don't know how to choose a random sample (*suiji chouyang*) or a representative sample. They don't understand that a carefully selected sample of 1,000 is better than their indiscriminate survey of 10,000." But the message may be getting across. In some of its crossnational studies, the United Nations has been compelled to reject data gathering by Chinese social scientists because of its limited and unrepresentative nature.

Problems in Data Analysis

The problems marking Chinese survey research at the data gathering stage are matched at the data analysis stage. At least four problems are common. First, reflecting the lack of sophistication in sampling procedures, there is the danger of overgeneralization. Sweeping conclusions are sometimes drawn from a very limited or unrepresentative sample. Researchers who argue that the results of their local studies apply to a larger universe (the whole district, city, or region) are seldom convincing. Second, there is often a confusion regarding the differences between, and proper use of, descriptive and inferential statistics. For example, one study sought to determine whether male and female college students had distinct and different views of the personal qualities of ideal mates. Quite naturally, there was some difference in male and female responses to the various questions in the survey. The authors then felt compelled to explain the different responses by reference to the physiological and psychological differences between men and women. Had they subjected these same results to a chi-square test, they would have discovered that the results were not statistically significant. Resorting to broad, highly general qualitative analysis to explain even very minor differences revealed in questionnaire results is not uncommon.

A third problem of data analysis stems from the above-mentioned necessity to reach a positive conclusion. Many surveys aggregate the responses of individuals to specific questions into larger, all-encompassing categories. One survey on the motivations for junior high students to study grouped the answers into three categories devised by the authors: individual motivation, tending toward societal motivation, and societal motivation. By combining the answers "for the Four Modernizations," "to serve the people," and "for communism" together, the authors could argue that approximately 54 percent of the respondents—thus, the mainstream or *zhuliu*—had merged their individual interests with broader social goals. But such essentially nonpolitical, catch-all terms as Four Modernizations, which have different connotations for different respondents, are too imprecise to be accurate indicators of motivation. More revealing are the disaggregated figures, which show that only 27 of 883 respondents (3.06 percent) chose "communism" or "serve the people" as their motivation for studying. While such questions of word use reflect another typical problem of survey design, the more serious issue is the necessity to use surveys to show support for the nation's policies. Unfortunately, the majority of published surveys do not provide enough detail to allow for such a reinterpretation of the results.

Fourth, the forced overaggregation of data is part of a more general problem. Although Chinese surveys commonly gather relevant and important sociological data such as sex, age, marital status, educational level, income, political manifestation, and so forth many surveys tend to disregard such sociological distinctions and simply report their findings on the group as a whole, setting out the respondents' beliefs, opinions, attitudes, motivations, or behavior as an aggregate. Thus, the interrelations between the sociological and psychological variables are not fully explored. In some cases, the disregard of these distinctions may be traced to the sensitive nature of the issue. Thus, a very detailed study of the qualifications of Tianjin schoolteachers did not report any distinctions between city-key, district-key, and ordinary schools. Similarly, a detailed study of middle-aged intellectuals in Wuhan—in which 240 of the 514 respondents were party members—did not take the important sociological variable of party membership into account in reporting results of the survey.

Having delineated a number of reasons that invite skepticism regarding Chinese survey results, it is necessary to add that the methodological flaws suggested by no means negate the use of surveys to study youth attitudes. In analyzing these surveys, one can quickly learn to avoid the most obvious pitfalls, which may include dismissing the large majority of the most accessible surveys. For example, because the function of much of what is widely disseminated in China is ideological,[8] it is important to note the means through which surveys are disseminated. Generally speaking, surveys published in professional journals are superior to those published in widely circulated newspapers and magazines; those published in internal (*neibu*) journals are more frank than journals that are openly distributed; and those that appear in Chinese are less colored by face than those that are selected by the Chinese authorities to be translated into English. As might be expected, the surveys that find their way into organs such as *People's daily* are primarily published for educational reasons, to show the widespread support for a given policy. Moreover, survey results disseminated in this form often are severely truncated, again to reflect the message the survey is meant to convey to the paper's readership (e.g., public acceptance of a bankruptcy law; the gradual development of "a civilized, healthy, and scientific lifestyle"; the effectiveness of price reform, to cite some recent examples).

One recent survey done in Sichuan, entitled "Survey of the People's Views on Reform," is a good example.[9] The survey was conducted by the Sichuan Economic Reform Office and Economic Research Center, but included over 580 students from the Southwestern University of Finance and Economics as surveyors. Judging from the brief account published in *China youth daily*, one purpose of the survey may have been to convince student skeptics that the reforms really were working. Several passages from the report have that flavor: "when the computer . . . displayed the final data . . . the . . . students . . . taking part . . . were convinced by the rational figures before their eyes"; "The information obtained by means of the 'Gallup Poll' method of survey raised the students' understanding of the national reform situation to a new height."

POST-MAO YOUTH AS REVEALED IN SURVEYS

Literally hundreds of surveys on the attitudes and behavior of youth have appeared, primarily in journals on youth, sociology, general social science, and psychology. Given space considerations, only a few representative surveys in a limited number of issue areas can be sampled.[10] The surveys described all derive from restricted (*neibu*) circulation journals, which are published for a specialized audience of professionals. While some of the concerns expressed above do bear upon them, the findings appear to be generally consistent with information available from more traditional sources such as documentary research and interviews.

Still, some caution regarding the interpretation of surveys on youth is in order. Because they began to appear only in 1979, we have little in the way of time series data. Chinese social scientists have sought to compensate for this by offering their impressions of the Maoist period when reporting attitude and opinion data from the 1980s. The most numerous and reliable surveys tend to come from large cities—particularly Beijing, Shanghai, Tianjin, and Guangzhou—making it difficult to draw conclusions about the vast interior of the country. Local surveys of outlying areas and national surveys—for example, on peasant youth attitudes—do exist. However, national surveys often present findings that are not sufficiently disaggregated to be sociologically revealing, while the quality of local studies tends to be questionable. Still, a couple of broad generalizations can be gleaned from this vast survey output.

First, support for established regime values—e.g., the Four Basic Principles, confidence in the achievement of the Four Modernizations, desire for party or youth league membership—tends to be higher in rural secondary schools and lower in large urban universities, particularly in Beijing. Second, in coastal areas where economic development has been rapid, youth have a variety of options unavailable to those in the interior.

In addition to the lack of time series data noted above, some readers may also protest that we are only measuring norms, not values, that in post-Mao China it is finally acceptable to report openly what one has always believed. Moreover, there is the seeming volatility of youth—particularly college student—opinions. Surveys done while political reform is a hot topic or soon after student demonstrations tend to exaggerate the political commitment of respondents. Surveys done prior to the large demonstrations of 1985 and 1986 tend to show much less interest in political commitment. The most recent surveys have shown a marked decline in student desire to study, and a commensurate interest in making money. Despite such caveats, Chinese social scientists are surely correct in asserting that youth values in the 1980s are very different from those of their counterparts in the 1950s, 1960s, and 1970s. Indeed, when one combines survey results with interview data and actual behavior, a strong case in favor of value change can be made.

Value Change Among College Students

There is strong evidence from the surveys that in post-Mao China political commitments and unquestioning loyalty toward the Communist party have

TABLE 12.1

Attitudes of Youth on Proper Standards for a Good Youth in the 1980s

Responses	Percentage[a]
Has talent and dedication to work	52.2
Is patriotic and able to preserve national dignity	46.5
Shows independent thought and creativity in work	27.5
Has Communist ideals	25.8
Is quietly immersed in hard work	11.0
Is united with the masses and finds it a pleasure to help people	10.0
Puts the public interest over private interests	9.0
Upholds truth and dares to struggle against evildoers and evil deeds	6.7

[a]Because the total percentage exceeds 100, it appears that sudents may have filled in an open-ended questionnaire and that the researchers then compiled the answers and devised the various categories. Student responses might have fit into more than one category. This is not made clear in the article.

Source: Geng Xiaolin and Zhu Yuejing, "Dangdai qingnian zhuiqiude 'lixiang xingxiang' yu daode bangyang jiaoyu" [The "ideal image" sought by contemporary youth and moral education], *Shanghai qingshaonian yanjiu,* no. 3, 1984, p. 6.

TABLE 12.2

What Ideological Qualities Should University Students in the 1980s Possess?

Responses	Percentage[a]
Love the country and love the people	16.5
Dare to think and be good at thinking	58.6
Honest and fair-minded	35.9
Listen to what the party says and be a revolutionary successor	3.0

[a]Because the total percentage exceeds 100, it appears that students may have filled in an open-ended questionnaire and that the researchers then compiled the answers and devised the various categories. Student responses might have fit into more than one category. This is not made clear in the article.

Source: Geng Xiaolin and Zhu Yuejing, "Dangdai qingnian zhuiqiude 'lixiang xingxiang' yu daode bangyang jiaoyu," *Shanghai qingshaonian yanjiu,* no. 3, 1984, p. 7.

declined at the expense of independence of thought and judgment, respect for talent, and a patriotism separated from party leadership. Table 12.1, from a survey conducted in late 1982 on the values and ideals of college students in Shanghai, documents this change. While noting that respect for talent, patriotism, and creativity were admirable and in accord with the goals of the Four Modernizations, the researchers expressed concern that students, particularly in their early university years, lacked proper recognition of the importance of communist ideals. A follow-up study was done in March 1983 on 630 young students in the entering class of 1981 from more than ten Shanghai universities. The results are presented in Table 12.2. As the authors pointed out, the fact that 58.6 percent chose "Dare to think and be good at thinking" while only 3 percent chose "Listen to what the party says and be a revolutionary successor" as the standard for university students in the 1980s indicates the striking change in student values compared to the 1950s and 1960s. Other studies also found that "students were concerned with talent and ability rather than ideals; knowledge rather than politics; and independent thought rather than obedience." The authors warned that this trend among freshmen and sophomores "should not be ignored."

More recent surveys–of college students on both famous and more obscure campuses–have shown similar results; patriotic sentiments and intellectual values win out over socialist ones. Asked to choose their ideals, 61.7 percent of Qinghua University students sampled chose "the revitalization of China"; 40.1 percent chose "the progress of mankind"; 32.3 percent chose "communism"; and 20.3 percent chose "individual and family happiness." Those who chose communism were primarily party members and party activists. Similarly, when asked the main historical responsibility of contemporary Chinese college students, 80.6 percent chose "Studying hard, and surpassing advanced world standards"; 26.9 percent chose "Arouse the masses and inspire a nationalistic spirit"; and 31.3 percent chose "Be of one heart and mind with the party and promote reform."[11]

A survey conducted among students at the Shandong Maritime Institute showed a suspicion of cadres and political leaders generally.[12] When asked whom they most venerated, the forty names chosen ranged from Marx to Einstein, and included Hitler, Kissinger, Jesus, and Chiang Kai-shek. Over 70 percent of the students chose positive, noncontroversial figures. Zhou Enlai received 27 votes, which was the highest total. Mao Zedong and Napoleon each received 10 votes, Deng Xiaoping got 5, and four students chose themselves.

The attitudes expressed toward approved political thought and the political cadres who control their lives—those who decide job allocations, screen applicants to the party, compile dossiers, and so forth—were particularly negative. When asked their deepest impression of current cadres, the largest number (41.9 percent) chose "contemptible, hateful, and detestable," followed by "other" (41 percent), and then "frightening" (10.2 percent). Only 2.5 percent chose "worthy of respect and approachable." Finally, a survey among college students in Sichuan showed that many students who support the reform policies see a contradiction between the initiatives of the Third Plenum (December 1978) and Mao Zedong Thought.[13] Fewer than 50 percent of the humanities and social science students queried thought the "correct" reform policies "adhered to and carried forward Mao Zedong thought."

Interviews conducted at colleges and high schools in China support the conclusions from these surveys. For example, interviews with students at Guangzhou's best high school revealed at least two very different strategies among top students. One type of student planned to go to a local key university, like Zhongshan or South China Engineering, and major in a field like construction engineering or computer science, both of which are in high demand. Then, upon graduation, they would be able to make up to 300 yuan a month from rich suburban townships or rural enterprises. There was no need to try to get into the nation's top universities, such as Beijing or Qinghua University. Their second choice, quite often, was Shenzhen University, again because of chances to earn more after graduation. Another group of top students was very committed to the reforms and modernization, and very independent in thinking. They wanted to attend one of the nation's best universities and play an important role in the reform process. In neither case was there any interest in politics courses as they were being taught, nor a great respect for the youth league or the party.

A discernible impatience with the pace of reform also revealed itself in interviews with university students in Beijing. While graduate students and young teachers felt the reform process to be quite rapid, many younger students thought the opposite, that few meaningful changes had yet taken place. The surveys done by the Research Institute under the Economic System Reform Commission back this finding for university students more generally. A 1986 survey showed that university students and graduate students made the highest demands on the reform process, but gave a very low rating to the results of the reforms.[14]

Military Recruitment and the Ideology
of Young Soldiers

The impact of economic reform has had a demonstrably negative effect on the ability of the People's Liberation Army (PLA) to attract qualified recruits.[15] Even with a substantial increase in pay for ordinary soldiers—a decade ago pocket money was fixed at between 6 and 12 yuan a month; now it is several dozen yuan—military allowances cannot compare to the earnings of enterprising youth in either city or countryside. Moreover, joining the military no longer confers a high social status. The Chinese press has frequently noted that youth have become indifferent to serving in the military, with stories on the low educational and moral quality of many recruits. One *Renmin ribao* report noted that a group of 150 new recent recruits in northern China turned out to be largely made up of criminals, including a murderer, an escaped prisoner, and the head of a criminal gang. Moreover, the report continued, "the deaf and sick have also joined the services" and "schizophrenics and epileptics are not uncommon." The recent extension of the conscription age limit for urban Chinese youth by one year, to twenty-one, is not likely to have a major impact.

In part of course the low quality of the recruits reflects the decline of recruitment standards. In some areas the quota can only be filled if no written test is given and the medical checkup is perfunctory. Moreover, the military itself has been forced to adjust to the prevailing economic winds. While bemoaning the influence the economic reforms have had on "commercializing the comradely relationship," the army is responsible for raising 30 percent of its food expenditure. Only 70 percent is provided by the state. The typical new recruit appears to reflect commercial over spiritual values. Thus, a recent Fudan University survey found that 33.3 percent of the armymen sampled maintained that "studying is useless," and many opted for "engaging in trade at the expense of studying."

Not surprisingly, many surveys on military recruitment explicitly take the new economic reforms as their starting point. Perhaps because of the difficulty of recruiting soldiers from wealthy rural areas, a seemingly disproportionate number of these surveys analyze the motivations, attitudes, and behavior of those who joined despite their economic success at home. Although presumably not representative of the majority of recruits, PLA officials have explicitly recognized the potential advantages of attracting these beneficiaries of the economic reforms. The most intriguing is the 1986 survey of 1,109 new recruits referred to previously (see note 5). The authors of the survey focus on the subsample of 628 "business-oriented" peasants, since they represent a potentially great change in the recruitment base of the PLA.

The findings are very revealing. First, we have already noted that the military has begun to attract well-to-do peasants who hope to parlay military service into enhanced status or wealth. Some of the recruits were particularly forthright, as the following passage shows:

> A new recruit of a certain regiment had been in the transportation business at home. The village cadre extorted money from him and they were at odds with each other. His purpose in enlisting was to gain admission to the party so that he could stand up against the village cadre when he returned home after discharge. A soldier of rural origin was enlisted to a certain regiment in 1986. He had been driving a truck at home, but had been unable to obtain a driver's license despite his many efforts at finding connections and giving out gifts. He declared: "My purpose of enlisting is to get a driver's license." What is new is not that soldiers joined partly for personal desires but that they could now openly disclose their personal intentions.[16]

Second, influenced by their business practices, these recruits explicitly placed a high value on building a network of connections. Some would offer cigarettes to superiors in place of a salute. When the larger sample of 1,109 recruits was asked, "What kind of people do you admire most in society?" 28 percent responded: "Those who are able to cultivate relations." The majority of those offering this response were from the business-oriented subsample. As one soldier noted on the back of his questionnaire, "I admire heroes and models, and I admire even more those who are able to make money and cultivate relations, because they fare well wherever they go."

Third, given their specific purposes for joining the military, it was not uncommon for the new recruits to become disheartened if they felt they had "over-invested" in becoming a soldier, endured more hardships than the gains they derived. Among the 628 surveyed, 113 (17.9 percent) had developed an unfavorable impression of the army. The large majority of them had either not been assigned to tasks that would allow them to acquire the skills they desired (e.g., driving a truck), felt they had no chance to be admitted to the party, or could not get along with their leaders. The survey also showed that 53 percent had not been assigned tasks which utilized their talents and were unhappy with their jobs.

Fourth, despite the low level of education of the recruits, they had little desire to upgrade their formal educational level. When asked, "Do you want to learn a skill or study some culture?" 99.3 percent opted for learning a skill.

While recognizing certain obvious shortcomings, the authors of the survey argue that these economically independent recruits "are the biggest contingent of talent in the history of our army." But many cadres within the military criticize new-style rural recruits arriving from a more prosperous countryside as "slick, speculative operators," "the dregs of society," "profiteers," and imbued with a "merchant mentality."

Another survey, contained in a lengthy collection of essays analyzing conditions among young soldiers in the Nanjing military district, sheds additional light on the attitudes of new military recruits from the countryside.[17] In a study of 127 such recruits—supplemented by discussions with more than 20 cadres—several disturbing trends were noted. The level of dissatisfaction with military life was high: 54.3 percent wanted to return before the end of their three-year tour of duty. "Several years earlier," the equivalent figure had been 20 to 30 percent. Interest in learning a specialty or technical skill had increased but concern with politics decreased. Company-level cadres reported that in the early 1980s more than 80 percent of the young soldiers wanted to join the party or receive certificates of merit. But survey results show that only 52.8 percent desired party membership and only 30 percent were seeking to obtain such moral awards as certificates of merit. The soldiers' families reinforced the recruits' lack of commitment: 41.7 percent of family heads wanted the recruits to return home as early as possible. Although the survey does not correlate opinion with income level, by providing detailed tables on the rising income levels, occupations, ownership of agriculture machinery, and so forth of the soldiers' families since the December 1978 plenum, it does make the more general point that the above changes in outlook were closely related to the flourishing economic conditions in the home areas of the recruits. Peasant youth no longer relied on the military just to leave the countryside. Another survey, on the material demands of soldiers, showed both a strong desire for material goods and a dissatisfaction with the quality of food, clothing, housing, and so forth provided in the army.[18]

A number of surveys have investigated the characteristics of soldiers from very rich peasant families. One of these, done by the political department of the Jinan military district, studied 100 soldiers from "10,000 yuan households."[19] Several of the findings are of interest because of the trends they reveal about military recruitment. First, the number of recruits from specialized (*zhuanye*) and key (*zhongdian*) households had been increasing each year, so that by 1985 (the time of the survey), such recruits made up around 40 percent of the infantry battalion sampled. Of those from 10,000 yuan households, 7 percent had joined in 1982, 17 percent joined in 1983, 30 percent in 1984, and 46 percent in 1985.

As in several other surveys, the recruits generally had a junior high school educational level. As the interviewees put it: "After we got out of school, we studied technical matters with our fathers and brothers. In general, all we needed was a junior high level." This helps explain why agricultural middle schools, strongly pushed by the government, remain relatively unpopular in the countryside.

While the large majority wanted to enter the party or youth league (8 percent were already party members, 64 percent were league members, 60 percent of league members applied to join the party, and 96 percent of nonparty, nonleague members applied to join the league), the researchers noted that their motives were not always pure. In some cases their families had been concerned that the party's policy of allowing the peasants to get rich would change, so that they might need a political safety umbrella that joining the army would provide. Others stated, "We have already become rich economically, now it is necessary to become red politically." As in other surveys, some dissatisfaction with the discipline and material sacrifices of military life was noted.

Attitudes and Lifestyles of Women Workers

Economic reforms have also had a major impact on the attitudes and behavior of young women, particularly with regard to employment and lifestyle issues.[20] With Chinese enterprises now responsible for their own profits and losses, putting productivity and economic efficiency at a premium, many factory directors have been reluctant to hire women. At the same time, there has been an effort to eliminate surplus employees, estimated to number as many as 20 million. In areas of increasing economic prosperity, many Chinese women have given up jobs to take care of family and household chores. An open debate has been raging in the Chinese press over the past several years regarding the relationship between the number of women in the work force and the successful realization of women's liberation.

The All-China Women's Federation and its local affiliates have been highly critical of attempts to ease women out of the labor force, although their arguments tend to appear mostly in journals and newspapers for women. General, large-circulation newspapers like *Renmin ribao* for the most part have published articles in support of a more realistic approach to women's liberation, noting that "many young women are exchanging ill-paid and unsatisfying menial and manual work for the challenges and satisfactions of taking care of their children."[21] Other reports cite experts who note that "the high proportion of China's female employment resulted from the intervention of governmental bodies and the neglect of working efficiency in the enterprises and institutions."[22]

Many surveys have addressed the employment issue from the perspective of young workers. For example, a survey on female "youth waiting for work" (*daiye qingnian*) in Shanghai revealed that the improved economic situation has led to several changes in the outlook of young women regarding employment.[23] They are no longer so eager to find a job. In a sample of 63 such youth interviewed in Shanghai, 75 percent came from families where the average per capita income exceeded 30 yuan; 40 percent were from families where average per capita income was over 40 yuan. Sixty percent of them felt no financial pressure from home to work; 40 percent felt only slight pressures. Furthermore, they have become more selective. Most of the 63 interviewees rejected jobs which involved hard work (textile work), unsanitary conditions or occupational hazards (hospital work), or long distance commuting (suburban factory work). They preferred jobs with high pay but light work (salesperson or bus conductor); 16 percent preferred technical or skilled jobs. Factory work has become less attractive, commercial and service work more attractive. Of the 63 women, 22 percent wanted factory jobs (a big drop from previous surveys) and 32 percent wanted service jobs. The latter figure rises to 40 percent if one includes those who wanted to set up private business operations.

Studies of the changing labor market done in other cities show similar results. For example, many surveys have been done on young textile workers.[24] In Suzhou, there had been no problem recruiting textile workers before 1983. Beginning in 1984, textile companies were notably unsuccessful in recruiting new workers, even after lowering their qualification requirements many times. Vocational schools have had to shut down classes for lack of applicants; graduates have been turning down assigned mill jobs to seek work on their own. First the mills went to nearby rural areas to recruit; when they still could not meet hiring quotas, they recruited contract labor from the more distant countryside. However, given the improved rural economy, rural women have not been enthusiastic about becoming urban textile workers. For example, two Suzhou factories hired 250 contract workers from local counties in 1985. Within three months most had left, some without waiting to get back the deposits they had made when signing their contracts. The transfer and absentee rates among the remaining workers showed an equally dismal picture. The situation has not been improving. A large textile mill in Wuhan planned to hire 500 new workers in 1987, but was only able to recruit 5. A mill in Beijing had 400 vacancies, but could only sign up 36 women, despite two months of canvassing.[25]

The impact of reform on lifestyle issues is equally striking, suggesting a clear decline in the ability of the state to dictate morality. A study done in Harbin, where 80 percent of the 14,800 young textile workers are apprentices, or 1st- or 2nd-grade workers averaging under 38 yuan a month, revealed that most of the single women spent at least half their income on clothing, accessories, cosmetics, and hair-styling. Very few saved anything from their salaries. Many of the married women reported being unhappy; for example, of the 210 married women workers at the Harbin No. 2 Knitwear Mill, 50 percent admitted to unhappy marriages.[26]

More details on love and marriage patterns are provided in a survey of three plants in Wuxi. The comparison with the 1970s is striking:

> In Wuxi, textile mills have traditionally had a rule that new worker apprentices may not engage in romantic activities during their apprentice periods, or their apprenticeship will be extended and they cannot become reguler workers on schedule. Most members of the highest age-group had entered the mills in the

mid-1970s and had had no boyfriends during their apprentice period, or, if they had, were quiet about it. Now, however, most apprentices come in with boyfriends. At the No. 2 Silk Reeling Mill, this was true of 80% of the newcomers, who made no secret of the fact. The regulation was impossible to enforce. Co-habitation and pre-marital pregnancy were almost unknown among the highest age-group when they came in during the mid or late 1970s. The few who had had problems of this type suffered much public censure and felt great shame. Now it is no longer a rare phenomenon among the lowest age-group. According to information provided by the offices concerned, 80% of current hospital abortion cases are of unmarried girls, 3 times the number before 1980. Co-habitation is even more common. 79 women workers between the ages of 18 and 22, or 9.4% of that age-group, are living with boyfriends without the benefit of marriage. This is a 70% increase as compared to the mid or late 1970s.[27]

Among the reasons given for this change are the influence of "unhealthy Western ideas such as 'sexual liberation,'" which the women are likely to accept uncritically; greater financial independence and less reliance on families; and low educational levels. Given the difficulty of recruiting textile workers, entrants need only score minimally on a test to be accepted. Most are junior high graduates or senior high dropouts. They generally have no interest in furthering their educations; rather, they "set high sights on material betterment and stimulation." As the researchers noted, "Many of the youngest group told us that, with so much time on their hands, what better way to spend it than playing around with the opposite sex? They called this 'living a more fulfilling life.'"

Other surveys—both in urban and rural areas—show similar new trends on the question of sexual activity. Premarital abortions increased greatly in the early 1980s. In Beijing, the total number of abortions performed was 157,000 in 1980; 189,000 in 1981; 234,000 in 1982; 251,000 in 1983; and 246,000 in 1984. Premarital abortions made up 27.9 percent of the total number in 1981; a 1984 survey of two hospitals showed a rate of 23.1 percent (although the rate in one of the two hospitals was over 40 percent), which would mean a total of 57,000 such abortions. In Shanghai, premarital abortions totaled around 39,000 in 1982; 50,000 in 1983; and 65,000 in 1984. In Dalian the proportion of premarital to total abortions was 22 percent.

Drawing on the above statistics, authors of a survey on abortions among unmarried women in Beijing explained the phenomenon as follows:

Traditionally, Chinese people had a very conventional attitude toward sex. People cared about their reputations and women were expected to be "chaste." After the founding of the People's Republic, new concepts on sex were based upon socialist morality. Romance, marriage, and birth became the unalterable legal sequence. Whosoever reversed this sequence was subject to prosecution by law and censure by public opinion. In the past few years, however, with the policy of opening to the world while invigorating the domestic economy, many ideological influences have infiltrated China from abroad, and new trends have appeared among a part of the Chinese youth, especially urban youth, on the question of sex. Apart from the few who were out to enjoy Western "sexual freedom," many other young people—90% or more in our survey—began to have sex before being lawfully wedded. This shows a breakthrough of the legal confines of socialist morality on this question. Sociologists should study this attitude change. In the past, due to "leftist" influences, few people made it a topic of research.[28]

School Dropouts

The impact of a hierarchical and two-track educational system and a more open job market has contributed to a set of new attitudes—and new options—among high school students. The dropout rate among primary and secondary school students became a serious problem as early as 1979, and by 1983 it had become a common theme in the Chinese press. The situation is especially serious at schools where students, with little hope of advancing up the educational ladder, consider early entrance to the job market an attractive alternative. The issue has been frequently discussed in forums in newspapers for youth, under such titles as, "Is it True that Studying Is not as Good as Selling Popsicles?" and "Is it Worth it to Leave School to Go into Business?"[29] A letter to the editor from a group of high school students illustrates their confusion amidst China's rapid social change:

> We are students from an ordinary middle school in Jiabei district. Last semester, two classmates who had poor study achievements, and felt they could not catch up, dropped out of school. Now, one works as a contract worker in a barber shop and makes about 90 yuan a month. The other has set up a fruit stall and makes about 150 yuan a month. When this news reached us, our whole class became excited. A great many became disheartened about studying, asking, "What's the use? Those who are uneducated can follow this model to make money, and make more than the intellectuals!" The study atmosphere in the classroom has become worse and worse. As class cadres, seeing more and more students failing, we have become very worried, and have tried our best to persuade everyone. But we are at a loss as to what to say to them.[30]

The official response, of course, is to urge students to stay in school; however, the reasons given—e.g., to improve one's spiritual life or to give one a greater competitive advantage in the job market—often seem unconvincing. As one letter writer put it, "Even those who love to read books can't buy them on low salaries . . . teahouses where they play music tapes and other such [entertainment] places belong to the world of the private entrepreneur. Therefore, we can see that the happiness of the higher spiritual life is inseparable from money."[31]

Student perceptions are reinforced by China's changing job market. Table 12.3, covering the years 1979–1984, shows the reasons for the high dropout rate in Beijing. The largest single number of dropouts—close to 60,000 out of 292,000—went back to the countryside to labor. As contemporary press reports made clear, the economic reforms in the countryside put a premium on labor power. Parents were simply pulling their children out of

TABLE 12.3
Reasons for Primary and Secondary School Students to Discontinue Their Studies or Drop Out of
School in Beijing, 1979 to 1984

Reason	Primary School	Junior High	Senior High	Total
Joined the military	874	1,095	1,664	3,633
Moved to another province or municipality	22,586	12,062	5,155	39,803
Died	1,225	651	250	2,126
Became ill	12,417	11,257	2,585	26,259
Experienced economic difficulties	8,906	22,561	6,945	38,412
Took a job	3,062	20,002	17,483	40,547
Returned to the countryside to labor	13,637	37,369	8,259	59,265
Had poor grades	10,419	34,673	7,321	52,413
Expelled from school	239	1,287	1,514	3,040
Ordered to leave school	1,766	532	147	2,445
Voluntarily withdrew from school	402	664	802	1,868
Other	7,409	10,682	4,332	22,423
Totals	82,942	152,836	56,457	292,234

Source: Chen Xianrong, "Beijingshi zhong xiao xuesheng liushi yu weifa fanzui diaocha baogao" [The phenomena of dropping out and criminal delinquency among middle and primary school students in Beijing], Shehuixue yu shehui diaocha, no. 2, 1985, p. 28. Translated in Chinese Education, vol. 20, no. 3 (Fall 1987), p. 87.

school and putting them to work in family enterprises, including farmwork. Even those who remained in school had to help out at home. One middle school teacher in Beijing's Chaoyang district noted that the majority of peasant children in his classroom were working an average of three hours a day on family production, some up to six hours. They had little enthusiasm for their lessons, some sleeping through the first class period.[32]

In areas where economic development has been rapid, labor power has often been particularly scarce. Wenzhou, in Zhejiang province, has been nationally publicized for its innovations in private economy and family industry. To fuel economic development in Wenzhou, however, it became common to hire child labor. According to surveys, children accounted for 20 percent of the workers hired in the countryside around Wenzhou. About 85 percent of these ten- to sixteen-year-olds were girls. Their families were reportedly quite satisfied to sacrifice their schooling, even their literacy, for early employment.[33]

As Table 12.3 shows, close to 80,000 dropouts in Beijing from 1979 to 1984 left either because of family economic difficulties or because they could immediately enter the job market. The largest number of senior high dropouts by far—over 17,000—left to go to work. Indeed, some units have gone directly to high schools to recruit graduating students before they graduate.

TABLE 12.4

Reasons for Dropping out of Junior High School in Guangzhou[a] (N = 253 teachers; 86 school dropouts)

Reason	Teachers' Perceptions		Stated Reasons of Dropouts	
	Number	Percentage of Total	Number	Percentage of Total
Bad grades, cannot make it academically	191	62.0	80	53.7
Want to go to work and make money	93	30.2	22	14.8
Violated school regulations	24	7.3	18	12.1
Feels no pleasure in going to school	—	—	29	19.5
Other	2	0.6	0	0.0
Total	310	100.0	149	100.0

[a]Respondents could choose three categories.

Source: Joint Investigation Group of the Guangdong Provincial Educational Studies Research Association and the Guangzhou Municipal Educational Studies Research Association, "Cong Guangzhou shiqu zhongxue chuzhong 'liusheng' wenti kan geng xin jiaoyu sixiangde zhongyaoxing" [Using the problem of junior high dropouts in Guangzhou to see the importance of updated educational thinking], Zhongguo jiaoyu xuehui tongxun, no. 2, 1987, p. 33.

In Guangzhou this became serious enough that the Labor Bureau and the Education Bureau issued a joint notice opposing the practice.[34]

The number of dropouts due to poor grades is likewise very high—over 52,000 in the Beijing survey. In fact, there has been some controversy over whether economic or academic reasons are the major cause of the high dropout rate. Taking issue with the many reports that link the dropout phenomenon to a more open economy and the development of the private economy, researchers in Guangzhou conducted a survey among teachers and dropouts to determine the major causes of the problem. Table 12.4, which suggests that poor academic achievement is the leading cause for dropping out of junior high, is drawn from that survey. In fact, however, as the letter to the editor cited above indicates, a declining interest in study is often related to a realization that economic success is independent of educational level or academic achievement. A recent and detailed sample survey of Beijing's urban and rural individual laborers likewise shows the relative unimportance of education to income. As the study noted, "A multi-approach analysis of individually owned rural businesses shows the following relationship between income and other factors: Educational level has the *least* effect on income, followed by length of operation, then age; factors that affect income most are length of business hours and initial capital (or scale of operation). This is similar to what we found in the urban areas [emphasis added].[35] Similarly, an utter lack of interest in furthering their basic education was common to the new military recruits and female textile workers discussed above.

CONCLUSION

At the outset, we suggested two aims for this chapter; one methodological, the other substantive. Methodologically, despite obvious weaknesses, survey research has become an important tool in the analysis of Chinese social change. It is likely to increase in importance as it matures and becomes more widely accepted. For example, one weakness—the lack of time series data—is already being remedied. Until recently, studies which concluded that a decline in political commitment distinguishes 1980s youth from their counterparts in the 1950s and 1960s were based only on the assertions of the researchers, since no survey evidence was available for the earlier period. But we are now seeing quasi-longitudinal studies on a variety of questions, such as job preferences of high school students and the behavior of only children in school.

Substantively, survey research has provided valuable data on youth attitudes, some of which has confirmed information available from other sources. On a number of issues, such as the motivations of soldiers and young women workers, the surveys have gone further, providing information on attitude and behavior patterns seldom discussed in the Chinese press or available though formal interviews in China.

In sum, what do these attitude surveys tell us about the nature of the post-Mao transitional society? First, the transitional society presents many more alternatives for Chinese youth than did its predecessor. In this more open society, investment options can be taken relatively quickly. For example, if one has not been able to enter a key junior or senior high, continuing one's schooling may be considered to be a poor investment, since the likelihood of entrance to a good university is remote. On the other hand, dropping out and finding a well-paying job, or helping one's family prosper, become attractive possibilities. The introduction of a nine-year compulsory education law in 1986 is an attempt to reduce or at least delay some of these options, but it is too early to predict the effectiveness of this measure.

Second, the freedom to invest has become possible in part because of a clear decline in the state's ability to control social change. Efforts to stimulate the economy and regularize political and personal life have created an environment which supports a privatization of values. Moreover, the post-Mao ideological vacuum, which offers little policy justification beyond the development of the economy, has contributed to the use of money as a standard for success. The encouragement of private entrepreneurship, the daily floating population in virtually all Chinese cities, and increased opportunities for labor mobility, are all products of the economic reforms, while the large numbers of school leavers, increases in juvenile delinquency, premarital abortions, divorces, and so forth all reflect the decline in social control.

Third, institutions that have long been established as the major conduits for social mobility and as measures for success—the party, the military, state enterprises, the schools—are being forced to adjust under the new socioeconomic conditions. For the party and military, there are questions of whom to recruit, and how to socialize them. For example, peasant youth are becoming more economically independent and no longer look to the military as a possible escape route from a backward countryside. Rather, they often see military service as a necessary price to pay to protect their wealth (through party membership) or to expand their wealth (by learning a valuable skill). Should the military recruit these new rich peasants and seek to convert them into political reds, socializing them to support communist values? Is is possible that the institutions themselves will be resocialized away from such values, following an influx of these new recruits?

Fourth, concern with politics has inevitably declined. Before the Cultural Revolution it was common for Chinese youth to adopt strategies that led them either to seek academic/professional success (the expert path) or to engage in political activism (the red path).[36] During the Cultural Revolution, of course, concern with politics was necessary for all youth who sought upward mobility. Now, political interest *follows* success in other areas. New rich peasants will seek party membership or military entrance after economic success. Students who apply for party membership do so only after achievements in their academic and professional careers. The declining interest of young people in politics is not surprising. What is ironic, however, is the party's own contribution to this decline. While the media continues to emphasize the crucial importance of fostering a communist value system, party recruitment in recent years has been concentrated heavily on the achievers, i.e., those with university degrees, professional positions, and so forth. With the party reaching out to the expert, those who are only red have nowhere to go.

NOTES

1. This section draws from Stanley Rosen and David S. K. Chu, *Survey Research in the People's Republic of China* (Washington, D.C.: United States Information Agency, December 1987).

2. For Taiwan, see Sheldon Appleton, "Survey Research on Taiwan," *Public Opinion Quarterly*, vol. 40, no. 4 (Winter 1976–1977), pp. 468–481.

3. See, *inter alia*, William A. Welsh, ed., *Survey Research and Public Attitudes in Eastern Europe and the Soviet Union* (Elmsford, N.Y.: Pergamon Press, 1981); Walter D. Connor and Zvi Y. Gitelman, *Public Opinion in European Socialist Systems* (New York: Praeger Publishers, 1977); Alexei Yakushev, "Are the Techniques of Sociological Surveys Applicable Under the Conditions of Soviet Society?" *Archiv. europ. sociol.*, vol. 13, 1972, pp. 139–150; Darrell Slider, "Party-Sponsored Public Opinion Research in the Soviet Union," *Journal of Politics*, vol. 47 (February 1985), pp. 209–227; Ellen Mickiewicz, "Policy Applications of Public Opinion Research in the Soviet Union," *Public Opinion Quarterly*, vol. 36, no. 4 (Winter 1972–1973), pp. 566–578; Vladimir Shlapentokh, *The Politics of Sociology in the Soviet Union* (Boulder, Colo.: Westview Press, 1987); Valdimir Shlapentokh, "Two Levels of Public Opinion: The Soviet Case," *Public Opinion Quarterly*, vol. 49, no. 4 (Winter 1985), pp. 443–459.

4. The authors of one study on young workers' outlook toward life felt it necessary to state that the workers filled out the questionnaire "honestly." As they put it, only a small number (at most 10 percent) had been warned by their parents not to be deceived, that the survey could be used to catch rightists. See *Qingnian yanjiu*, no. 12, 1982. Some informants were very skeptical about the reliability of surveys, arguing that in political surveys no one will be honest, while in nonpolitical surveys, about 30 percent would fill in answers randomly, since they assume that such surveys will have no effect on governmental decision-making or their own lives.

5. Zhang Wenrui, Yang Yuwen, and Liu Bangguo, "Budui bingyuan chengfende da bianhua ji xin tedian" [The great changes and new characteristics in the composition of our troops], *Qingnian yanjiu*, no. 6 (June 1986), pp. 19–23. A translation appears in Stanley Rosen, ed., "Youth Socialization and Political Recruitment in Post-Mao China," *Chinese Law and Government*, Summer 1987, pp. 102–117.

6. This observation is based on a preliminary comparison of the questionnaires used by the State Economic Structural Reform Commission (*tigaiwei*) and its subordinate body, the Chinese Economic Structural Reform Research Institute (*tigaisuo*).

7. Mao Peilei, Zhang Xuezhen, and Weng Xianzhen, "Tigao xiaoxuesheng daode renshide yanjiu" [Research on raising the moral understanding of primary school students], *Jiaoyu keyan qingkuang jiaoliu*, no. 1, 1985, pp. 11, 19–22.

8. See Welsh, *Survey Research*.

9. JPRS-CPS-86-070, September 4, 1986, pp. 68–70 (*Zhongguo qingnian bao*, June 11).

10. Some of the survey data cited in this section will also appear in Stanley Rosen, "The Impact of Reform on the Attitudes and Behavior of Chinese Youth: Some Evidence from Survey Research," in *Communist Dialectic: The Political Implications of Economic Reform in Communist Systems*, ed. Donna Bahry and Joel Moses (New York: New York University Press, forthcoming); more recent survey data is presented in Stanley Rosen, "The Impact of Reform Policies on Youth Attitudes," in *Social Consequences of Chinese Economic Reforms*, ed. Deborah Davis and Ezra F. Vogel (Cambridge: Harvard University Press, forthcoming).

11. Zhang De and Zhou Liangluo, "Dangdai daxueshengde sixiang zhuangkuang yu tedian" [The conditions and characteristics of college students' thinking today], *Qinghua daxue jiaoyu yanjiu*, no. 2, 1986, pp. 35–47. Despite these responses, over 60 percent of the sample expressed an interest in joining the party.

12. Tao Chounian, Sun Binggang, and Yu Chunxian, "Daxuesheng zai xiang shenme?" [What are college students thinking?], *Wengao yu ziliao*, no. 3, 1985, pp. 29–34. This is a publication of the Shandong provincial party committee school.

13. Song Daoquan, "Bu liyu daxuesheng xuexi Mao Zedong sixiangde jige yinsu" [Some obstacles to the study of Mao Zedong Thought by college students], *Weidinggao*, no. 6, 1986, pp. 20–24.

14. FBIS Daily Report, March 31, 1987, pp. K18–19 (*Ming Bao*, Hong Kong, March 28). For a detailed survey this institute jointly conducted with *China Youth* magazine, see Bai Nanfeng, "Young People's Attitudes and Aspirations: Will They Welcome Reform?" in *Reform in China: Challenges and Choices*, ed. Bruce L. Reynolds (Armonk, N.Y.: M. E. Sharpe, 1987), pp. 161–187. An extensive survey of university students in Beijing appears in *Xin shiqi daxuesheng sixiang zhengzhi jiaoyu yanjiu* [Research on ideological and political education of university students in the new period] (Beijing: Beijing Normal University Press, 1988).

15. Sources for this and the following paragraph include Daily Report, February 28, 1989, pp. 45–47 (*Renmin ribao*, February 20); Daily Report, March 2, 1989,

pp. 47–50 (*Zhongguo tongxun she*, March 1); Daily Report, March 14, 1989, p. 34 (*Hong Kong Standard*, March 13); Daily Report, December 14, 1988, pp. 29–30 (*Jiefangjun bao*, November 27); Daily Report, June 2, 1988, pp. 52–57 (*Jiefangjun bao*, May 17); *Cheng Ming* (Hong Kong), December 1988, p. 27.

16. Zhang, Yang, and Liu, "Budui bingyuan," n. 5.

17. Zhu Minghe and Liao Youlin, "Jingji fanrong dui nongcunji zhanshi fuyi taidude yingxiang" [The influence of economic prosperity on soldiers from the countryside], in Nanjing junqu zhuanji, *1984 budui qingnian yanjiu lunwenji* [A collection of studies on military youth in 1984], pp. 205–214.

18. Huang Guoqing, "Qingnian zhanshi wuzhi xuqiude yanjiu," *1984 budui qingnian yanjiu lunwenji*, pp. 191–204.

19. Wu Xingzhong, "'Wanyuanhu' zhanshi sixiang tezheng diaocha" [An investigation of the ideological characteristics of soldiers from "Ten thousand yuan households"], *Qingnian yanjiu*, no. 3, 1985, pp. 16–23. A shorter version is in *Tuanxiao xuebao* [Journal of the Communist youth league school], no. 2, 1985, pp. 31–35.

20. The surveys discussed here are drawn from a large collection of surveys and other documents published in China on the political, economic, and social status of Chinese women today. This collection has been translated in four separate issues of *Chinese Sociology and Anthropology*, Fall 1987, Winter 1987–1988, Spring 1988, and Spring 1989; they will also appear, with additional material, in Stanley Rosen, ed., *Chinese Studies on Chinese Women* (Armonk, N.Y.: M. E. Sharpe, forthcoming).

21. Daily Report, September 20, 1988, pp. 45–46 (*Xinhua*, September 17).

22. Daily Report, October 25, 1988, pp. 38–39 (*Xinhua*, October 22, citing *Liaowang*).

23. Zhuang Jianguo, "Shanghai shiqu daiye nu qingnian jiuye wenti diaocha fenxi" [Analysis of an investigation into the problem of job-hunting among young unemployed women in Shanghai], *Laodong kexue yanjiu ziliao* [Research materials on labor science], no. 21 (November 5, 1985). For a recent survey conducted among 15,000 women in eleven provinces, municipalities, and autonomous regions, see Liu Jixin, "Nuxing yuanyi gan shenma gongzuo?" [What kind of work do women want to do?], *Zhongguo funu bao*, March 14, 1988.

24. For examples, see Wu Jikang, "Nu qingnian weihe buyuan jin fangzhichang?" [Why are young women unwilling to enter textile mills?], *Qingnian yanjiu*, no. 5, 1986; Zou Naixian, "Qingnian fangzhi nugong shenghuo fangshi xuqiu bianhuade diaocha" [Survey of changes in young female textile workers' demands on life], *Qingnian yanjiu*, no. 10, 1985; Youth Work Group under Wuxi Textile Industry Bureau, "Fangzhi hangye nu qinggong teshu jiaoyu wenti chutan" [A preliminary investigation of special educational problems among women workers in light industry], *Shanghai qingshaonian yanjiu* [Shanghai youth research], no. 8, 1984.

25. Wu, "Nu qingnian"; Liu, "Nuxing yuanyi."

26. Zou, "Qingnian fangzhi."

27. Youth Work Group, "Fangzhi hangye."

28. Zou Ping, "Beijingshi bufen weihun qingnian rengong liuchan qingkuangde diaocha" [An investigation of abortion among some unmarried youth in Beijing], *Qingnian yanjiu*, no. 10, 1985, pp. 57–61. On sexual attitudes of college students, see Tong Zhiqi, "Gaige xinchao yu dangdai nu daxuesheng" [The new tide of reform and female college students today], Qingnian yanjiu, no. 10, 1986, pp. 12–17. On premarital sex in a rural setting, see Zhong Weiqiao, "Yingchengxian Langjunqu qingnian hunqian xing guanxi diaocha" [An investigation of premarital sex among

young people in Langjun district, Yingcheng county], *Qingnian yanjiu*, no. 2, 1987, pp. 40–44.

29. *Qingnian bao*, February 22, 1985, p. 2; July 12, 1985, p. 5; and December 21, 1984, p. 5. *Beijing qingnian bao*, June 18, 1985, p. 1. Also see *Tianjin ribao*, April 18, 1986, p. 1; and *Wenhui bao* (Shanghai), January 7, 1986, p. 2.

30. *Qingnian bao*, December 21, 1984, p. 5.

31. *Qingnian bao*, July 12, 1985, p. 5.

32. *Beijing qingnian bao*, June 10, 1986, p. 1; July 14, 1985, p. 1.

33. Wang Yuren, "Wenzhou jiating gongye gugong jingyingzhongde tonggong xianxiang" [The phenomenon of hiring child labor in family enterprises in Wenzhou], *Weidinggao*, no. 8 (April 25, 1987), pp. 18–22; Zhu Qingfang, "Qianlun geti jingjide fazhan bianhua ji duice" [A preliminary discussion of the changes in the development of the individual economy and how to deal with them], *Jingji yanjiu cankao ziliao*, no. 66, 1986, pp. 33–40.

34. *Guangzhou ribao*, June 9, 1986, p. 1.

35. Chen Jian, "Laodong jiuyede youxiao tujing" [An effective way to increase employment], *Jingji yanjiu cankao ziliao*, no. 114 (July 26, 1985), translated in Stanley Rosen, ed., "The Private Economy," Part 1, *Chinese Economic Studies*, vol. 21, no. 1, Fall 1987, p. 52.

36. Susan Shirk, *Competitive Comrades* (Berkeley and Los Angeles: University of California Press, 1982); and Stanley Rosen, *Red Guard Factionalism and the Cultural Revolution in Guangzhou* (Boulder, Colo.: Westview Press, 1982).

Chronology

1949

Before a large gathering in Beijing's Tiananmen Square on October 1, Mao Zedong officially proclaims the establishment of the People's Republic of China.

1950

Promulgation of land reform law, mandating confiscation of land from landlords and rich peasants and its distribution to poor peasants. Initiation of massive, sometimes violent campaigns to implement land reform.

Promulgation of marriage reform law, banning arranged marriages, concubinage, polygamy, and interference in the remarriage of widows, and establishing equal rights for both sexes.

Entry of China into Korean War. Campaigns to "wipe out hidden counterrevolutionaries."

Initiation of efforts to make institutions such as Protestant and Catholic churches and schools sever ties with foreign supporters and become self-governing, self-supporting, and self-propagating.

1953

End of Korean War.

Accusations in *People's daily* of "imperialist elements hiding in the Catholic Church."

1955

Beginning of massive drive for agricultural collectivization.

Political campaign against the literary critic Hu Feng and "all Hu Feng elements" throughout the country—one of the first widespread persecutions of dissident intellectuals.

1956

Completion of socialist transformation of industry from private to public ownership.

Based on Colin Mackerras, *Modern China: A Chronology from 1842 to the Present* (San Francisco: W.H. Freeman, 1982), and the Asia Society's *China Briefings* (Boulder, Colo.: Westview Press, 1980–1988).

Mao Zedong calls for greater intellectual and artistic freedom with the slogan, "Let a hundred flowers bloom, let a hundred schools of thought contend."

1957

"Hundred flowers" campaign reaches its climax with many open criticisms of the Chinese Communist party (CCP) from all sectors of society. Beginning of an "anti-rightist" campaign (initiated by Mao but led by Deng Xiaoping) against intellectuals deemed to have spoken out too forcefully. Hundreds of thousands of intellectuals publicly disgraced, imprisoned, or otherwise punished.

Formation of the Catholic Patriotic Association.

1958

Beginning of the Great Leap Forward—immense effort to achieve quick economic development through mass mobilization. Formation of people's communes in countryside.

Pope Pius XII issues encyclical condemning the policies of the Catholic Patriotic Association.

1959

Failure of the Great Leap Forward, compounded by widespread natural disasters. Beginning of three years of famine in which 15 to 25 million people die.

Victory by Mao over challenge to his authority by Defense Minister Peng Dehuai.

1960

Beginning of open polemics between China and the Soviet Union.

Gong Pinmei, Catholic Bishop of Shanghai sentenced to life in prison for "counter-revolutionary" crimes.

1962

Mao's speech calling for greater emphasis on "class struggle" is the beginning of the "socialist education movement" in the countryside.

1965

Attack by literary critic Yao Wenyuan on a drama written by Wu Han marks the beginning of the Cultural Revolution.

1966

Cultural Revolution—"a great revolution that touches people to their very souls"—goes into full swing. Power struggles among Chinese leadership and rise of "red guards and revolutionary rebels" among Chinese youth. Enormous rallies in Tiananmen Square. Closure of universities. Attacks on intellectuals. Violent ransacking of bookstores and private homes. Destruction of temples and churches and all other signs of traditional culture.

1967

Most violent phase of the Cultural Revolution. Public denunciation of China's premier, Liu Shaoqi, for "taking the capitalist road." Deng Xiaoping and many other high leaders also fall from power. Bloody fighting among various red guard factions. Eventual takeover of control by People's Liberation Army (PLA).

1969

Border clashes between Chinese and Soviet troops on the Ussuri River.

1971

Henry Kissinger visits Beijing secretly and holds talks in preparation for a visit to China by President Richard Nixon the following year.

Lin Biao, Mao's second in command and officially designated successor, is killed in a failed attempt to assassinate Mao.

China is admitted into the United Nations, displacing the Nationalist government on Taiwan.

1972

The Shanghai Communique signed at the conclusion of Nixon's visit in February establishes a framework for eventual normalization of U.S.-Chinese relations.

1973–1975

Many top leaders purged in Cultural Revolution, including Deng Xiaoping, are returned to power.

1976

Premier Zhou Enlai dies on January 8. In April, thousands of people gather in Tiananmen Square to commemorate his death. Mourners make speeches criticizing some of Mao Zedong's closest associates. Police clash with mourners, killing some, arresting many. Two days later, government issues an official announcement branding the Tiananmen Incident a counterrevolutionary event and blaming it on Deng Xiaoping. Deng is stripped of all his posts. Hua Guofeng is elevated to a position next in line to Mao.

Mao Zedong dies on September 9. On October 6, under orders from Hua Guofeng, Mao's four closest associates—including his wife, Jiang Qing—are arrested. Beginning of a massive campaign to celebrate "smashing the Gang of Four" and to purge all of their followers.

1977

Deng Xiaoping is once again appointed to the standing committee of the Politburo, China's top leadership body.

1978

In December, the Third Plenum of the Eleventh Communist Party Central Committee is dominated by supporters of Deng Xiaoping, even though its formal leader is still Hua Guofeng. The meeting officially launches a program of Four Modernizations, in science and technology, education, agriculture, and the military. In line with this policy, massive reforms begin to take place throughout Chinese society. Higher education is restructured to emphasize intellectual "expertise" rather than political "redness." A large program of sending students for advanced study abroad is launched. Policies that will lead to the decollectivization of agriculture are initiated.

1979

On January 1, the United States and the People's Republic of China formally establish diplomatic relations.

In February, Chinese troops stage a brief invasion of Vietnam, "to teach a lesson" to the Soviet-leaning Vietnamese.

Throughout the year, dissidents in Beijing and elsewhere put up wall posters arguing for a "fifth modernization," democracy. This Democracy Wall period also marks a flowering of experimentation in literature and art. After a springtime of intellectual ferment, Wei Jingsheng, a leader of the movement for democracy, is arrested. In the fall, he is put on trial, charged with transmitting state secrets to foreigners and purveying counterrevolutionary propaganda. He receives a long prison term. Political dissent is silenced.

The Religious Affairs Bureau is revived, and temples and churches begin to be reopened. The government issues a document distinguishing between religion [organized Buddhism, Taoism, Islam, Catholicism, and Protestantism] and feudal superstition [folk religion]. The former is to be permitted, under careful government supervision; the latter is to be discouraged.

1980

The party forbids the public display of wall posters, in order to prevent people like Wei Jingsheng from emerging in the future.

Deng Xiaoping reaffirms the party's traditional stance that literature and art cannot be divorced from politics. Censorship of writers and artists increases.

Opinion polls, a new feature on the Chinese scene, report widespread dissatisfaction with wages, housing, leader privileges, dullness of life, factionalism, and education.

In September, Deng Xiaoping retires from active government duties but retains a major amount of power behind the scenes. Hua Guofeng also retires from his post as premier, but because he is being forced out of power. Zhao Ziyang is chosen to succeed Hua as premier.

In November, the Gang of Four and six of their close associates are put on trial. Jiang Qing (Mao's widow) and Zhang Chunqiao receive suspended death sentences with possibility of commutation to life in prison. The others receive lengthy prison sentences.

1981

The Communist party issues an official reevaluation of Mao's place in Chinese history, criticizing his role in the cultural revolution.

Hu Yaobang formally replaces Hua Guofeng as head of the Chinese Communist party.

1983

Campaign is launched against "spiritual pollution." Advocates of intellectual freedom and democratic reform are criticized.

1984

"Spiritual pollution" campaign winds down. Economic reform moves forward, with decisions about decentralizing foreign trade structure and giving enterprises more autonomy.

1985

Queen Elizabeth II signs agreement ending term of British rule over Hong Kong on July 1, 1997.

A new educational reform policy stresses more autonomy for colleges.

Rural people's communes formally abolished. Replaced by small towns and township governments.

1986

In December, student demonstrations begin in Hefei and Wuhan and quickly spread to other cities.

1987

In January, student demonstrations continue to grow. The party responds with a campaign against "bourgeois liberalism." Several leading intellectuals, including the journalist Liu Binyan, the astrophysicist Fang Lizhi, and the writer Wang Ruowang are dismissed from the party. For not responding firmly enough to student demonstrators, Hu Yaobang is forced to resign his post as party general secretary. He is replaced by Zhao Ziyang. Li Peng takes over as premier.

Protests in Tibet turn violent. Up to 10 policemen and at least 9 demonstrators are killed. At least 60 demonstrators arrested.

1988

Inflation produced by the economic reforms perceived as a serious problem. Attempts made to reimpose political control over the economy.

The TV series *River Elegy* severely criticizes China's "feudal" political culture.

1989

In April, Hu Yaobang dies. Thousands of students turn out on Tiananmen Square to mourn him and to protest the policies that had led to his dismissal. A Beijing Spring of democratic ferment begins. Student movement rapidly spreads. Demonstrations spread to Shanghai and other cities. Deng Xiaoping gives a speech emphasizing the need for the party to suppress disorder at all costs.

In May, Mikhail S. Gorbachev arrives in China to normalize Sino-Soviet relations. Some students begin a hunger strike, which further galvanizes the movement. One million demonstrators, now including workers as well as students, fill Tiananmen Square, calling for freedom and democracy, an end to government corruption, and the removal of Li Peng from office. Government declares martial law. Zhao Ziyang is removed from office for encouraging the demonstrations. Demonstrators erect a statue of the Goddess of Democracy in Tiananmen Square.

On June 4, on orders from Deng Xiaoping, the PLA crushes the demonstrations, killing hundreds, possibly thousands, in Beijing. Similar violence by the army against demonstrators occurs in a number of cities throughout China. Widespread arrests and executions take place. Jiang Zemin is appointed new Party general secretary.

Suggested Reading

Barme, Geremie, and John Minford, eds. *Seeds of Fire: Chinese Voices of Conscience.* New York: Hill and Wang, 1988.

Chan, Anita, Richard Madsen, and Jonathan Unger. *Chen Village: The Recent History of a Peasant Community in Mao's China.* Berkeley and Los Angeles: University of California Press, 1984.

Cheng, Nien. *Life and Death in Shanghai.* New York: Penguin Books, 1988.

Davis-Friedmann, Deborah. *Long Lives: Chinese Elderly and the Communist Revolution.* Cambridge: Harvard University Press, 1983.

Frolic, B. Michael, ed. *Mao's People: Sixteen Portraits of Life in Revolutionary China.* Cambridge: Harvard University Press, 1980.

Gao, Yuan. *Born Red: A Chronicle of the Cultural Revolution.* Stanford: Stanford University Press, 1987.

Goldman, Merle. *China's Intellectuals: Advice and Dissent.* Cambridge: Harvard University Press, 1981.

Honig, Emily. *Sisters and Strangers: Women in the Shanghai Cotton Mills, 1919–1949.* Stanford: Stanford University Press, 1986.

Honig, Emily, and Gail Hershatter. *Personal Voices: Chinese Women in the 1980s.* Stanford: Stanford University Press, 1988.

Johnson, David, Andrew J. Nathan, and Evelyn S. Rawski, eds. *Popular Culture in Late Imperial China.* Berkeley and Los Angeles: University of California Press, 1985.

Kleinman, Arthur. *Social Origins of Distress and Disease: Depression, Neurasthenia, and Pain in Modern China.* New Haven: Yale University Press, 1986.

Laing, Ellen Johnston. *The Winking Owl: Art in the People's Republic of China.* Berkeley and Los Angeles: University of California Press, 1988.

Link, Perry. *Mandarin Ducks and Butterflies: Popular Fiction in Early Twentieth-Century Chinese Cities.* Berkeley and Los Angeles: University of California Press, 1981.

————, ed. *Roses and Thorns: The Second Blooming of the Hundred Flowers in Chinese Fiction, 1979–80.* Berkeley and Los Angeles: University of California Press, 1984.

————, ed. *Stubborn Weeds: Popular and Controversial Chinese Literature After the Cultural Revolution.* Bloomington: Indiana University Press, 1983.

Liu, Binyan. *People or Monsters? and Other Stories and Reportage from China After Mao.* Bloomington: Indiana University Press, 1983.

MacInnis, Donald. *Religion in China Today: Policy and Practice.* Maryknoll, N.Y.: Orbis, 1989.

McDougall, Bonnie, ed. *Popular Chinese Literature and the Performing Arts in the People's Republic of China, 1949–1979.* Berkeley and Los Angeles: University of California Press, 1984.

Madsen, Richard. *Morality and Power in a Chinese Village.* Berkeley and Los Angeles: University of California Press, 1984.

Pickowicz, Paul G. *Marxist Literary Thought in China: The Influence of Ch'ü Ch'iu-pai.* Berkeley and Los Angeles: University of California Press, 1981.

Schell, Orville. *Discos and Democracy: China in the Throes of Reform.* New York: Pantheon Books, 1988.

Siu, Helen F. *Agents and Victims in South China: Accomplices in Rural Revolution.* New Haven: Yale University Press, 1989.

Siu, Helen F., and Zelda Stern, eds. *Mao's Harvest: Voices from China's New Generation.* New York: Oxford University Press, 1983.

Thurston, Ann F. *Enemies of the People.* New York: Knopf, 1987.

Vogel, Ezra. *One Step Ahead in China: Guangdong under Reform.* Cambridge: Harvard University Press, 1989.

Zhang, Xianliang. *Half of Man Is Woman.* Translated by Martha Avery. London and New York: Viking, 1986.

Zhang, Xinxin, and Sang Ye. *Chinese Profiles.* Beijing: Panda Books, 1986.

Zweig, David Stephen. *Agrarian Radicalism in China, 1968–1981.* Cambridge: Harvard University Press, 1989.

About the Editors
and Contributors

R. David Arkush, a specialist on modern Chinese history for many years at the University of Iowa, has recently joined the faculty of Indiana University. He is the author of *Fei Xiaotong and Sociology in Revolutionary China* (Harvard, 1981) and "'If Man Works Hard the Land Will Not be Lazy': Entrepreneurial Values in North Chinese Peasant Proverbs," *Modern China*, no. 10 (1984). He has also, with Leo O. Lee, compiled and translated *Land Without Ghosts: Chinese Impressions of America from the Mid-Nineteenth Century to the Present* (University of California Press, 1989).

Deborah Davis teaches at Yale University. She is the author of *Long Lives: Chinese Elderly and the Communist Revolution* (Harvard, 1983), and is currently completing a study of occupational mobility in urban China. This is her first effort to write about popular culture.

Thomas B. Gold is Associate Professor of Sociology at the University of California–Berkeley, where he has taught since 1981. He is author of *State and Society in the Taiwan Miracle* (M. E. Sharpe, 1986). He is currently writing a book on the private sector in China.

Emily Honig is an Associate Professor of History and Women's Studies at Yale University. She is the author of *Sisters and Strangers: Women in the Shanghai Cotton Mills, 1919–1949* (Stanford University Press, 1986) and the co-author (with Gail Hershatter) of *Personal Voices: Chinese Women in the 1980s* (Stanford University Press, 1988). Her current research concerns the history of Subei people in Shanghai from the nineteenth century through the present.

Ellen Johnston Laing has held the position of Maude I. Kerns Distinguished Professor of Oriental Art at the University of Oregon since 1979. Her research interests focus on traditional painting in sixteenth- and seventeenth-century Suzhou, paintings by Chinese women, and contemporary art in China. In addition to many publications on traditional art in scholarly journals, she is the author of *The Winking Owl: Art in the People's Republic of China* (University of California Press, 1988).

Perry Link teaches modern Chinese language and literature at Princeton University. His earlier publications on popular Chinese culture include *Mandarin Ducks and Butterflies: Popular Fiction in Early Twentieth-Century Chinese Cities* (University of California Press, 1981); *Stubborn Weeds: Popular and Controversial Chinese Literature After the Cultural Revolution* (Indiana University Press, 1983); and "The Genie and the Lamp: Revolutionary *Xiangsheng*," in Bonnie S. McDougall, ed., *Popular Literature and Performing Arts in the People's Republic of China* (University of California Press, 1983).

Richard Madsen is Professor of Sociology at the University of California–San Diego. He is co-author of *Chen Village* (University of California Press, 1984) and *Habits of the Heart* (University of California Press, 1985), and author of *Morality and Power in a Chinese Village* (University of California Press, 1984).

Paul G. Pickowicz is Professor of History and Chinese Studies at the University of California–San Diego. He is author of *Marxist Literary Thought in China: The Influence of Ch'ü Ch'iu-pai* (University of California Press, 1980), and co-author of *Chinese Village, Socialist State* (Yale University Press, forthcoming). His current research is on the relationship between cinema and society in late Republican China.

Stanley Rosen teaches political science at the University of Southern California. He is the author of *Red Guard Factionalism and the Cultural Revolution in Guangzhou* (Westview, 1982), the co-author of *Survey Research in the People's Republic of China* (United States Information Agency, 1987), and has co-edited *On Socialist Democracy and the Chinese Legal System* (M. E. Sharpe, 1985) and *Policy Conflicts in Post-Mao China* (M. E. Sharpe, 1986). He edits the journal *Chinese Education*.

Helen F. Siu teaches anthropology at Yale University. Her earlier publications on contemporary China include *Mao's Harvest: Voices From China's New Generation* (co-editor Zelda Stern, Oxford University Press, 1983); *Agents and Victims in South China: Accomplices in Rural Revolution* (Yale University Press, 1989); and "Socialist Peddlers and Princes in a Chinese Market Town," *American Ethnologist*, vol. 16, no. 2, May 1989.

Zhang Xinxin is a native of Nanjing and a graduate of the Central Drama Institute in Beijing. She is co-author of *Beijing ren* (Beijing: Renmin wenxue chuban she, 1985; published in English as Chinese Profiles [Beijing: Panda Books, 1986]), which contains portraits of one hundred ordinary Chinese. In 1989 she was a Visiting Scholar at Cornell University.

Index

Abortion, 68, 208, 212
ACLS. *See* American Council of Learned Societies
Actresses, 42, 43
Advertising, 5
Aesthetic preferences, 5. *See also* Housing space
Agricultural collectivization, 44, 47
All-China Women's Federation, 206
"Alleyway news," 22
American Council of Learned Societies (ACLS), 2
Ancestor worship, 90, 108, 124, 125, 157. *See also* Household altar
An'er brings rice (*An'er song mi*) (opera), 79, 80, 81
Anhui, 142
Annihilation of the underground stronghold, The (underground literature), 21–22, 26, 27–28, 30, 31, 32
Anthropologists, 1, 3, 89, 111, 121, 123
Anti-Rightist movement (1957), 42, 44, 113
  on film, 41, 42, 46, 47, 49
Aristocratic groups, 5, 6
Arkush, R. David, 4, 9, 10, 11, 72
Art, 94. *See also* Housing space, decorations; Rural homes, decorations
At middle age (film), 40, 43, 48, 50
Authority, 73
  in fiction, 27–28, 32, 33

Backyard furnaces, 124
Bai Hua, 41
Behavior, 8
Balanced symmetry, 156, 158
Bats (as symbol), 159
Beidouzhai, 115–116
Beijing, 200, 207
  abortions, 208
  bishop of, 114
  getihu, 181, 186
  markets, 181
  opera, 145
  schools, 210, 211
  scroll exhibition, 163
Beijing Legal Affairs Institute, 60
Beijing Spring and massacre (1989), 1–2, 51
Beijing University, 202
Benedict XV (pope), 112
Binhai county, 149
Bitter love (film), 41, 42
Black (color symbol), 30
"Black materials," 195
Boat people, 110
Bond, James (literary character), 30
Bourgeois humanism, 47
Bourgeois liberalism, 19, 41, 42
  anti-, campaign (1981), 44, 51
Boy Holding a Goldfish (New Year's print), 160(illus.)
Boy holding carp (New Year's image), 159–160, 162–163
Buddhist monastery and temple, 125, 128

Bureaucracy, 185, 186–187, 188–189
Butterflies (as symbol), 159, 163
Buzhengtong (unorthodox), 2

Calendars, 159, 162
Calligraphy, 157, 163
Capitalists. *See Getihu*
Carnegie, Dale, 65
Case of the Nanjing Bridge, The
  (underground literature), 22, 25,
  27, 30
Catholic church, 106–107, 108, 112–
  117
  government-sponsored. *See* Catholic
  Patriotic Association
  See also Rites Controversy
Catholic Patriotic Association (1956),
  105, 111, 112, 113, 114, 115, 116,
  118
  and celibacy, 113–114
Catholics, 6, 11, 103–104, 107
  ascriptive patterns of association, 110,
  111
  beliefs, 107–108, 109, 118. *See also*
  Rites Controversy
  and CCP, 112–116
  communities, 110, 111
  identity, 109–110
  number of, 105
  rituals, 110, 111, 112, 113, 114, 116
  survival of, 105–106, 116–117
  "uprising" (1966), 104–105
Cats (as symbol), 159, 163
CCP. *See* Chinese Communist party
Census, 139
"Centerpiece Pictures" (scroll
  exhibition), 163, 170(n20)
Centerpieces. *See* Scrolls
Central Intelligence Agency (CIA)
  in fiction, 21, 26
Centralized symmetry, 156, 158, 163
Chan, Anita, 8, 9
Changchun Film Studio, 41, 43
Changzhou, 139, 147
Chen, Matthew, 2
Chen Dewang, 149
Chengwang temple, 125
Chen Naishan, 151, 152
Chen Rong, 43
Chiang Kai-shek, 202
Chicago (Ill.), 89

China, 96
  defined, 6
  north, 72, 73, 82
  Republic, 17, 138, 139. *See also*
  People's Republic of China
China Film Association, 51
China News Analysis (Hong Kong),
  107
China youth daily, 199
Chinese archives, 1, 180
Chinese Catholic Bishops Conference
  (1986), 114
Chinese Catholic Church Administrative
  Commission, 114, 115
Chinese Communist party (CCP)
  (1921), 38, 43, 44, 45, 51, 52,
  179, 185, 212, 213
  attitude toward, 178, 186, 187, 188,
  193, 200–201, 202, 203, 206
  censors, 40, 42, 50
  Central Committee, 44, 45, 194
  and family household, 90, 94
  on film, 40, 41, 43, 46, 47, 48, 51,
  52, 121
  and labor, 185
  membership, 98, 100(n15), 189,
  200, 206, 213
  and reform, 43–44, 45, 47, 51, 122,
  133, 152, 175–176, 177, 178, 179,
  190, 193, 194, 206
  and religion, 103, 104, 105, 112–
  116, 118, 163, 169
  Thirteenth Party Congress (1987),
  176, 187
  United Front Work Department, 114
  See also State intervention
Chinese Profiles (Zhang Xinxin), 10, 59
Chinese Women's Association, 66
Chrysanthemum festivals, 124, 133
Church, defined, 106
Church of Our Lady of Sheshan, 110
CIA. *See* Central Intelligence Agency
Cinema. *See* Film
Ci Xu, 167(caption)
Class conflict, 5, 143, 194
Class consciousness, 5
Co-habitation, 208
Cohen, Lizbeth A., 90, 93
Collectives, 187, 188
Collectivization, 44, 47, 90, 178, 179

"Combat Revisionism" slogan, 26
Commander-in-Chief Zhu De in the Taihang Mountains (portrait), 166, 168(illus.)
Committee on Scholarly Communication with the People's Republic of China (CSCPRC), 180
Communism, 176, 198, 202, 213
Communist Youth League (CYL), 187, 189, 200, 206
Communization movement, 126
Competition, 176, 186
Condoms, 68
Confucianism, 27, 72, 81, 95, 159
Confucius, 181
Conservatism, 65
Consumer revolution, 92
Continuities, 8, 11
Cooperatives, 187
Corner forgotten by love, A (film), 40, 42–43, 46–47, 49–50
Corruption, 175, 186, 189
Counterhegemonic culture, 5
Cranes (as symbol), 156, 159, 163, 166
Cremation, 125
CSCPRC. *See* Committee on Scholarly Communication with the People's Republic of China
Csikszentmihalyi, Mihaly, 89
Cui Guangrui gathers firewood (*Cui Guangrui dachai*) (opera), 76
Cultural Affairs Bureau, 145
Cultural artifacts, 8, 9–10
Cultural pollution, 35(n30)
Cultural Revolution (1966–1976), 17, 22, 24, 26, 28, 32, 33, 40, 44, 45–46, 47, 58, 64, 126, 152, 153, 188, 195, 213
  fiction, 18, 19
  in film, 37–38, 46, 48
  films. *See* Film, 1950s–1970s
  official pronouncements on (1980s), 37
  and religion, 105, 113, 114, 125
  and tradition, 94–95, 125–126
Culture, defined, 111
Culture change, 122
CYL. *See* Communist Youth League

Dalian, 208
Danwei, 179, 182, 183, 185, 187

Daoist priests, 125, 127, 134
Daoting men (opera), 79, 80
Davis, Deborah, 2, 4, 5, 8, 12, 88
Decentralization, 94, 95
Democracy, 2, 5
Democracy Wall, 37, 40, 43
Deng Liqun, 35(n30)
Deng Xiaoping, 1, 38, 94, 202
Department of Civil Administration, 59
Detective stories, 17, 19, 20–21
Dialects, 141, 142, 143–144, 145, 146, 148, 149, 150
Ding County (Hebei Province), 4, 73, 74
  divorces (1929), 78
Ding deng (opera), 81
Dinglang seeks his father (*Dinglang xun fu*) (opera), 79, 81
Ding Qiao, 40
Dingxian plays, 74
Ding zhuan (opera), 81
Divorce, 4, 5, 57, 58, 59, 60, 67, 68–70, 212
  incompatibility grounds for, 57
  number of, 59, 66
  in operas, 78–79, 81
  third party problem, 59–60, 61–64, 68, 69
Dominican missionaries, 109
Dongguan Brigade (Zhuoxian), 163
Door gods, 158, 166
Doyle, Arthur Conan, 19
Dragon (as symbol), 162
Drama, 10, 179
Drinking Horses (painting), 166, 167(illus.)
Dual price system, 187
Duck pairs (as symbol), 156, 159

Economic decentralization, 94, 95
Economic development, 47, 200, 210
Economic System Reform Commission Research Institute, 203
Economy, 176, 178–179, 186, 193, 196, 203, 204, 206, 211, 212
  Stalinist model, 178, 188
  See also Private entrepreneurship
Education, 5, 39, 65, 66, 151, 193, 205–206, 208, 212
  compulsory, 212
  and income, 211
  See also School dropouts

Egalitarianism, 6
Eight Steeds (scroll), 164
Einstein, Albert, 202
Emei Film Studio (Sichuan), 42
Employment, 178, 179, 184, 193,
    209–211, 212. *See also* Women, in
    work force
Eternal regrets in love (underground
    literature), 24, 29, 32
Ethnic groups, 5
    prejudice, 5, 11, 12, 143. *See also*
    Subei people
European imperialism, 111, 112
Extramarital sex, 57, 69, 193

Family life, 4, 5, 12, 88, 90, 95
    and CCP, 90, 94, 103, 129
    English, 73
    See also Funerals; Rural areas, rituals;
    Weddings
Family planning, 94
Famine (1959), 42, 44
Fanshen (Hinton), 104
Fan tang (opera), 81
Fashion, 94
Father-son ties, 73, 157
Fei Xiaotong, 73
Fiction, 8, 10, 20, 28, 149, 151, 179
    officially approved, 18
    See also Underground literature;
    under Cultural Revolution
Field observation, 8, 9. *See also*
    Participant-observation
Filial piety, 78, 157
Film, 5, 8, 10, 148, 179, 190
    audiences, 37, 39, 40, 43, 49, 50
    genres, 39, 40, 49
    1930s and 1940s, 49
    1950s–1970s, 38, 40, 49
    1980s, 39, 40, 41–52
    and popular political thought, 39,
        40–41, 45–52
    preferences, 49, 52–53(n3)
    serious, 39, 45, 50, 52–53(n3)
    social criticism in, 40
    survey (1983), 52–53(n3)
Film Bureau, 40
Film directors, 40, 41, 49, 50, 51
Filmmakers, 39, 40, 45, 48, 51
    Fifth Generation, 51
Fish (as symbol), 159–160, 162–163,
    164, 165(illus.)

Fish Playing in a Lotus Pond (scroll),
    164, 165(illus.)
Five Classics, 81
"Five relations," 157
"Flying book," 18
Folk culture, 5
Folk literature, 74
Foreign settings
    in fiction, 28–29
    in film, 50
Foreign thrillers
    films, 39
    literature, 28–29. *See also* Spy
    thrillers
Four Basic Principles, 45, 191(n1), 200
Four Books, 81
"Four cardinal principles." *See* Four
    Basic Principles
Four Cleanups campaigns (1964), 126
Four Modernizations, 7, 150, 176, 196,
    198, 200, 201
"Four olds," 125
Foxiang Ge, 161
"France in Chekiang," 112
Franciscan missionaries, 109
French missionaries, 111–112
Fudan University, 147, 149–150, 203
Fujian Province, 73, 181
Funerals, 95, 121, 125–126, 127, 129–
    131, 133, 134
    banquets, 130–131
Funing, 142
Fu Tieshan, 114

Gang of Four, 43, 44, 45
    on film, 46
Gao Daquan (literary character), 18
Gao Wenju sits in the courtyard (*Gao
    Wenju zuo huating*) (opera), 78,
    81
Gauze skirt, The (*Luo qun*) (opera), 79
Getihu (urban private entrepreneurs),
    175, 178, 181, 182
    attitudes of society toward, 189–190,
    191
    attitudes of state toward, 188–189,
    191
    attitudes toward state, 185, 186–188
    defined, 176
    field research, 180–183
    films about, 190

lifestyle, 185–186, 190, 191
as marginal element, 179, 182, 190–191
motivation of, 183–185
tests, 184
wealth, 186, 187–188, 190
"Girl from Subei, The" (Wang Xiaoying), 149
Girls of the Sea (scroll), 163
God of Longevity, 157, 162(illus.), 163
Gold, Thomas B., 5, 8, 9, 175
Golden rooster, 132, 134, 136–137(n23)
Gong Pinmei, Ignatius, 112, 113, 116
Good and evil
in film, 46
in literature, 29–30, 31, 32
in opera, 80–81
Goode, William J., 73
Good sister-in-law, The (Xiaogu xian) (opera), 78, 80
Grain rationing, 96
Great Leap Forward (1958), 42, 44, 47, 124, 126
Guandao, 187
Guangdong Province, 18, 110, 115, 118
delta, 9
Guangzhou, 19, 115, 200, 202, 211
Guangzhou Evening News, 20
Guomindang. See Kuomingtang
Guo Yanjun, 60–61, 65, 66, 68–70

Haimen, 141, 142
Hanson, Eric O., 112
Harbin, 207
Hegemonic culture, 5
He lineage association, 127
Heroes
in fiction, 31–32
in film, 48
He Xiaoshu, 42
Hibiscus town (film), 51, 190
Hierarchy, 32, 130, 139
High culture, 5
Hinton, Carma, 104
Hinton, William, 104, 109
Historians, 1, 3, 138
Hitler, Adolf, 202
Holmes, Sherlock (literary character), 19, 30
Chinese. See Huo Sang

Holy Spirit Study Center, 118–119(n8)
Hong Kong, 8, 93, 114, 115, 121, 127, 132, 133, 178
bishop of. See Wu, John
Honig, Emily, 5, 8, 11, 12, 138
Horror stories, 19
Horse Square village, 104, 109
Household altar, 90, 127, 156, 157, 162(illus.), 163, 169
Household registration (1955), 96, 97–98
Housing allocation, 96–97
Housing shortage, 161
Housing space (interiors), 4, 88, 89–90, 98
decorations, 93, 95–96, 156, 157–160, 161–163, 164
furnishings, 92–93, 94, 95, 156, 157, 158(illus.), 160, 161
hallways, 91–92, 157, 158
and private interest, 88, 90, 94, 95
size, 91, 92
and social class and status, 91, 98
survey area, 91
walls, 92, 161
See also Rural homes
How to Win Friends and Influence People (Carnegie), 65
Huai'an, 142, 144, 150
Huai Army, 143
Huaibei, 142
Huai Opera Troupe (Shanghai), 144, 145, 148
Huating Road (Shanghai), 181
Huiyou, 131
Hundred Flowers era (1956–1957), 195
Hundred Flowers film competition, 41, 42, 43
Huo Sang, 20, 30
Hu Qiaomu, 35(n30)
Hu Yaobang, 41
Hu Zhongming, 64–65, 66
Hypergamy, 82

Idealism, 65, 71
Incense, 157
Industrial and Commercial Administration and Management Bureau, 186
Industrialization, 90

Inner Mongolia, 58
Intellectual ferment, 94
Intellectuals, 4, 5, 10, 40, 43, 48, 52,
    59, 62, 113, 183, 194, 199
Interviews, 4, 8–9, 180
    émigré, 8, 180
    "guerrilla," 180, 182, 183

Japan, 93, 143, 153
Jesuits, 107, 109
Jesus, 202
Jiangbei. See Subei region
Jiangbei shack settlements (Shanghai),
    142, 152
Jiangnan, 138, 139, 141, 142, 147,
    149, 150, 153
Jiang Qing
    in fiction, 28
Jiang Shichuang divorces his wife (Jiang
    Shichuang xiuqi) (opera), 78, 81
Jiangsu Province, 73, 95, 139, 141,
    142, 143, 147
Jinan military district, 205
Jin Jiang Hotel (Shanghai), 186
Jinji Film Award, 41, 42, 43
Jin Luxian, 110
Job allocation system, 179, 184, 185
Juvenile delinquency, 212

Khrushchev, Nikita, 44
Kissinger, Henry, 202
Kitchen god, 159
Kligman, Gail, 2
KMT. See Kuomingtang
Knight errant fiction, 17, 23, 29, 31
Korean War (1950–1953), 95
Kundera, Milan, 65
Kuomingtang (KMT), 95
    in fiction, 30

Labor market, 179, 207
Laing, Ellen Johnston, 5, 9, 10, 11, 12,
    156
Lam, Paul, 115
Land reform (1950–1952), 104, 124,
    126
Lawyers, 60, 61
Legend of the Anqi Bridge, The
    (painting), 166, 171(n34)
Legend of Tianyun Mountain, The
    (film), 10, 40, 41, 42, 43, 44, 45–
    46, 47, 49, 50, 52

Lei Feng (literary character), 18
Leisure, 94
Leninism, 188
Lettuce (as symbol), 132, 134, 136–
    137(n23)
Liberation daily (Jiefang ribao), 190
Licenses, 181, 184, 186
Lido Holiday Inn (Beijing), 186
Li Jinghan, 74
Lin Biao, 44
    in fiction, 22, 27
Link, Perry, 2, 5, 6, 9, 10, 12, 17
Literary scholars, 3
Liu Xiu zou guo (opera), 81
Liu Yulan visits the temple (Liu Yulan
    shang miao) (opera), 77
Li Yalin, 40
Longbao si jiangxiang (opera), 80
Long Bow village, 104, 109
Longmu Temple, 128
Long runs the Pearl River
    (underground literature), 29
Lotus (as symbol), 164, 165(illus.)
Love, 4, 57, 72–73
    marital, 73, 83
    Western, 73
    See also Operas, and love and
        marriage
Love stories
    on film 39, 49
    See also Romances
Low culture, 5
Lu, Luke, 115
Luo qun ji (opera), 80, 81
Lu Xun portrait, 163, 164, 166, 169
Lu Yanzhou, 41

Macao, 114
Ma Chang (Shanxi Province), 110
Machiavelli, Niccolo, 65
Macroprocessing, 1
Madsen, Richard, 2, 5, 6, 11, 103
Maiden's heart, A (underground
    literature), 20, 24–25, 28, 29, 31
Mandarin (language), 139, 144, 150
Mandarin duck and butterfly genre, 20
Maoism, 43, 44, 48, 121, 122, 126,
    130, 133, 175, 179, 188, 191
Maoist mobilization, 88, 94
Mao Zedong, 11, 18, 43, 44, 45, 58,
    202

death (1976), 40
in fiction, 22, 26, 27
Mao Zedong Thought, 45, 191(n1),
  202
Marriage, 4, 50, 57, 66
  arranged, 73, 95
  French peasant, 82–83
  introduction bureaus, 146
  license, 58, 59
  modern, 70
  number of (1987), 59
  registration records, 139–140, 146
  traditional, 70, 90
  See also Love, marital; Operas, and
    love and marriage; Women, and
    marriage and divorce
Martial-arts adventures, on film, 39
Marx, Karl, 176, 202
Marxism, 5, 6
Marxism-Leninism, 45, 194
  -Maoism, 191
Mass culture, 5
Mass Education movement (1930s), 74
Mass media, 5, 179, 190
Maximum Illud (encyclical), 112
May Seventh Cadre School, 60
Mazu, 110
Meeting at the blue bridge, The
  (*Lanqiao hui*) (opera), 75
Meishu (art journal), 163, 164
Miaojin gui (opera), 79, 80, 81
Middle class, 98
Military. *See* People's Liberation Army
Ministry of culture, 43
Minnan region (Fijian Province), 181
Missionaries, 105, 109, 111–112
Mixed economy, 176
Modernization, 5, 6, 44, 122, 194
Moonlighting, 177
Morality, 190, 207, 208
Movies. *See* Film
Mukerji, Chandra, 3
"My mother's house," 89, 90, 95

Nanjing, 142, 147
  bridge, 161
Nanjing military district survey, 205
Nantong, 141, 142, 147
  ren, 141
Nanxi (pseudonym for market town),
  122, 125, 126–132, 134

Napoleon, 202
Nationalist party. *See* Kuomingtang
National People's Congress (NPC)
  Seventh (1988), 177, 187
Native place identity, 138–139, 143,
  147–148, 150, 152
New England, 90, 93
New Fourth Army, 144, 150
New Year's prints, 156, 157, 158–160,
  161, 164, 166, 169
Nietzsche, Friedrich, 65
Ningbo people, 147, 149
Ningbo/Shaoxing region (Zhejiang
  Province), 139, 147
Niu Zhongyuan, 165(caption)
Novitiates, 105
NPC. *See* National People's Congress

One-child family, 94
One embroidered boot (underground
  literature), 30
Opening to the West, 1, 3, 11, 60,
  176, 179, 180
Operas, 4, 8, 11, 72, 73–75, 141, 142,
  144–145, 148
  audiences, 74–75, 80
  characters in pictures, 161
  comedies, 81
  and love and marriage, 72, 75–77,
    78, 79, 80, 82, 83
  official attitude toward, 74
  performers, 74
  revival, 74
  separation anxiety plot, 77–80
  and sex, 75, 76
  suicide in, 80
  texts, 74
  See also under Women
Opium War (1840–1842), 141
Oral network. *See* "Alleyway news"
Ordinary life, 4
Ouyang Hai (literary character), 18
Overseas Chinese, 123, 130

Painting, 8. *See also* Housing space,
  decorations; Scrolls
Pan Hong, 43
Parent-child (vertical) relationships, 72,
  73, 77, 78–79, 82
Parker, Jason, 2
Participant-observation, 4, 9, 180, 181

Party bureaucrats, 10, 51
Patriarchy, 90, 130
Patronage, 132
Pearl River delta, 122
Peasants, 4, 5, 11, 59, 73, 83, 122,
    193, 204, 205, 213
  comments on scroll exhibition, 164,
    166, 169
  See also Operas; Rural areas
Peng Ning, 41
Peonies (as symbol), 159, 162, 166
Peonies and Two Doves (painting), 166
People's daily (Beijing), 44, 199, 203,
    206
People's Democratic Dictatorship,
    191(n1)
People's Liberation Army (PLA), 95,
    97, 203, 204, 212, 213
  attitudes toward, 204, 205, 206
  General Political Department survey,
    195–196
People's Republic of China (PRC)
    (1949), 38, 44, 94–95, 96, 124,
    139, 144, 193
  chronology, 217–222
  See also Opening to the West
Per capita income, 206–207
Pickowicz, Paul G., 2, 5, 9, 10, 37
Pine and Cranes (painting), 166
Pines (as symbol), 156, 159, 163, 166
Pius XI (pope), 112
Pius XII (pope), 112
PLA. See People's Liberation Army
Poetry, 19
Political culture, 194, 195
Political leaders, 2, 35(n30), 38, 94,
    176
  in fiction, 18, 22, 27
Political paintings, 88, 95
Political protest movements (1978–
    1979), 40
Political reform, 2, 38, 43, 95. See also
    Chinese Communist party, and
    reform
Political scientists, 1
Political system, 2, 5, 6, 94. See also
    Chinese Communist party
Politics, 37, 38, 213
  in film, 37. See also Film, and
    popular political thought
  in literature, 26–27

Pomegranates (as symbol), 156, 159
"Poor Street, The" (Chen Naishan),
    151, 152
Pop psychology, 65
Popular cinema (magazine), 39, 41
Popular culture, 1–2, 3
  defined, 3–4, 5, 6
  methodology, 4, 5, 7–12, 179–183,
    193, 194–200
  traditional, 122, 124
Pornography, 17, 19, 24–25, 28, 31
Portraits, 163, 164, 168(illus.)
Poultry-Raising Girl (scroll), 163
PRC. See People's Republic of China
Press
  official, 40, 41, 44
  See also Mass media; Professional
    journals
Prince, The (Macchiavelli), 65
Private entrepreneurship, 5, 175, 176,
    177–178, 179, 188, 212
  rural, 177, 178, 179
  See also Getihu
Private interests, 94, 95, 212. See also
    under Housing space
Professional journals, 200
Professionals, 39, 183, 213
Proletarian dictatorship, 45, 191(n1)
Propaganda, 5, 7
Propriety, 11, 12, 156–157, 164, 169
Prostitutes, 142
Protestants, 107
Public Security agents, 31, 96
  in fiction, 21, 26
Puns, 159, 162, 166

Qinghua University, 202
Qing times, 11, 17, 20, 138
Quanzhou, 181
Quan Zhuming, 168(caption)
Qufu (Shandong Province), 181
Qu Junong, 74

Reagan, Ronald, 27
Rebus. See Puns
Red Guards, 185
Refrigerators, 92
Religion, 5, 11. See also Catholics;
    under Chinese Communist party;
    Cultural Revolution
Religious Affairs Bureau, 114

Religious revival, 94, 106
Renmin ribao. See *People's daily*
Repression, 1, 51
"Research on Improving the Moral
 Education of Primary School
 Students" (1985), 196–197
"Resist America, Aid Korea" campaign
 (1953), 21
"Resolution on Certain Questions in
 the History of Our Party Since the
 Founding of the People's Republic
 of China" (1981), 44–45, 46, 49
Revolutionary art, 17
Reynaud (bishop of Ningpo), 112
Ricci, Matteo, 109, 111
Rice-planting songs. See Operas
Rites Controversy, 11, 108–109, 111,
 112
Rituals. See under Catholics; Rural
 areas
Rive Coffee Shop (Shanghai), 186
Rochberg-Halton, Eugene, 89
Romances, 17, 19, 22, 27, 35(n23).
 See also Triangular love stories
Roosters (as symbol), 156, 162
Rosen, Stanley, 5, 11, 193
Rural areas, 121–122, 179, 196
 and education, 193, 209, 211
 family, 90, 94
 on film, 42, 47
 1930s, 73
 and private enterprise, 177, 179
 and regime values, 200
 rituals, 121, 122–124, 125, 127–128,
  133. See also Nanxi
 socialization, 178
 See also Operas
Rural homes, 156, 160
 decorations, 156, 161, 162, 163–164,
  166, 169
 furnishings, 156, 157, 161,
  162(illus.)
Rural-urban migration, 96, 152, 184

Saint Jerome, 73
Sang Ye, 10
Scar literature, 45
School dropouts, 193, 209–211, 212
Schudson, Michael, 3
Science, technology, and gadgetry in
 fiction, 31

Science fiction, 19
Scrolls, 157–158, 169
 exhibition (1983), 163–164, 166
Second handshake, The (Zhang Yang),
 18, 20, 29, 30
Secrecy and deception in fiction, 30–31
Sect, defined, 106
Secularizing trend, 132, 133
Segalen, Martine, 82–83
SELA. See Self-Employed Laborers
 Association
Self-Employed Laborers Association
 (SELA), 187, 189
Self-interest theory, 103, 106
Seminaries, 105
Sex, 64–66, 68, 69, 73, 193, 208–209.
 See also under Operas
*Sexual experiences of a high school
 girl, The.* See *Maiden's heart, A*
Sexual revolution, 60, 66, 208, 209
Shandong Maritime Institute, 202
Shandong Province, 83, 84–85(n16),
 142, 181
Shang gao ceremony, 131
Shanghai, 9, 11, 12, 200
 abortions, 208
 Catholics, 111, 112
 CCP secretary, 144
 dialect, 141, 143, 144, 148, 150
 elite, 138, 139, 144
 getihu, 186
 immigrants, 138, 139, 141, 142, 144,
  153
 markets, 181
 mayor, 144
 pornography survey (1983), 19
 red light district, 142
 slums, 142, 151–152, 153
 See also Housing space; Subei people
Shanghai Film Studio, 41
Shao Mujun, 51
Shaoxing operas, 145
Sha xu (opera), 80
Shen Fan (Hinton), 104, 105, 109
Shenzhen University, 202–203
Sheren Miao (temple), 129
Shooting a bird (*Da niao*) (opera), 75,
 76
Shouchaoben. See Underground
 literature, hand-copied
Sichuan Economic Reform Office and
 Economic Research Center, 199

Sichuan surveys, 199, 202
Silent thought, 8
Sister Xia (underground literature), 28, 35(n27)
Siu, Helen F., 5, 8, 9, 11, 121
Small garden, A (Xiao huayuan) (opera), 77
Small Town Called Hibiscus, A (film). See Hibiscus town
"Smash the iron rice bowl," 185
Social change, 209, 212. See also Popular culture; Youth, value changes
Social control, 195, 212
Social differentiation, 193, 194
Socialism, 176
Socialism with Chinese characteristics, 176, 191(n1), 194
Socialist modernization, 44, 194
Socialist road, 45
Social sciences, 193, 194, 197–198, 200
Sociologists, 3, 74, 88, 139, 150, 209
Soldiers, 5, 97, 144, 203, 211
    surveys of, 203–206
Song dynasty, 74
Southwestern University of Finance and Economics, 199
Speculators, 188
Spiritual pollution, 19
    anti-, campaign (1983), 40, 50, 51
Spy thrillers, 17, 21–22, 30, 34(n15)
Stalin, Joseph, 44
Stalinism, 44
State enterprises, 179, 186, 188, 212
State farms, 178
State intervention
    accommodation to, in rituals, 121, 123, 124–126, 128, 129, 130, 132–133, 134
    in homes, 88, 90, 95, 96
    and labor, 151
    resistance to, 207
Stone, Lawrence, 73
Stone Group, 187
Stories of Chinese women in love and marriage (Zhu Weiguo), 61
Story of the earrings, The (Erhuan ji) (opera), 79, 81
Strange encounter with a wandering brave (underground literature), 23, 29–30, 31, 34–35(n21)

Students, 19, 39, 97, 126, 193
    film survey (1984), 49
    protesters, 1, 2, 51
    on regime values, 200, 201, 202–203
    surveys of, 196–197, 199, 201(tables), 202, 203
    value changes, 200–203
    See also School dropouts
Subei dialect, 142, 144, 145, 146, 148, 149, 150
Subei people (ren), 5, 11, 110, 138, 139, 143–144
    attitudes of, 140, 141, 146, 147–150
    attitudes toward, 140–141, 142–143, 144–147, 148, 149, 150, 152, 153
    concept, 141–143, 150
    education, 151, 152
    information about, 139–140
    occupations, 142, 144, 150, 151, 152, 153
    political prestige, 144, 150
    residence, 142, 151–152, 153
Subei region (Jiangsu Province), 139, 140, 142, 144, 149, 150, 152
    opera, 142, 145, 148
Sugar cane (as symbol), 132, 134, 136–137(n23)
"Sunday engineers," 177
Sun Yu, 40
"Survey of the People's Views on Reform" (Sichuan), 199
Surveys, 5, 8, 11, 139, 146, 179, 193, 194–200, 212
Suzhou, 207
Suzhou Creek, 91

Tabloids (unofficial), 20, 126
Taiping Rebellion (1848–1865), 143
Taiwan, 114, 121, 132, 133, 178, 181, 194
Taixing, 142
Taiyuan, 104
Talent-and-beauty stories, 32
Tangwu, 157
Taxes, 178, 186
Teachers, 39, 199, 211
Television, 40, 148, 179
    sets, 92
Temple to Lord Guan, The (Guanwang miao) (opera), 75

Terrifying footsteps (underground literature), 20–21, 25, 26, 29, 31, 32
Textile workers, 207–208, 211
Thought levels, 7–8
"Three differences," 175
Thurston, Anne, 8, 9
Tiananmen Square (Beijing), 51. *See also* Beijing Spring and massacre
Tianjin, 200
Tigers (as symbol), 159, 161–162, 163
To borrow and pawn (Jie dang) (opera), 81
Tong, John, 115
To Taste a Hundred Herbs: Gods, Ancestors, and Medicine in a Chinese Village (film), 104, 105, 109, 110
Tradition, 5, 6, 90, 95, 121
   and business, 188, 191
   in fiction, 27, 29, 32, 33
   in film, 49
   in homes, 156. *See also* Housing space; Rural homes
   in marriage, 70
   reconstitution of, 122, 124, 125–126, 128, 132–134
   See also under Cultural Revolution
Transitional society, 212–213
Triangular love stories, 17, 20, 23–24, 29, 33
   films, 49
Tripod (Hong Kong quarterly), 118–119(n8)
Troeltsch, Ernst, 106
Troubadour tradition (medieval Europe), 73
Two locked chests, The (Shuang suo gui) (opera), 75–76, 77
Two lovers visit a cemetery (Shuang hong da shangfen) (opera), 78, 80

UCLA. *See* University of California–Los Angeles
Underclass. *See* Getihu; Subei people
Underdogs, in fiction, 32–33
Underground joke, 35(n24)
Underground literature, 5, 6, 12, 17
   covers, 20
   genres, 17, 19, 20–25
   hand-copied, 17, 18–25
   quality, 25
   readership, 19–20, 25
   recorded, 19
   themes, 17, 19, 20, 26–33
Under the Bridge (film), 190
United Nations, 198
University of California–Los Angeles (UCLA), 2
University of California–San Diego, 2
Urban areas, 4, 139, 161. *See also* Youth, urban
Urbanites, 38, 39, 40, 43, 45, 48, 51, 52, 59. *See also* Getihu; Housing space
"Uterine family," 73, 81

Values. *See* Modernization; Students, on regime values; Tradition; Youth, value changes
Van Gulik, R. H., 157
Vatican, 105, 109, 112, 113
Verbal expressions, 7–8
Verne, Jules, 19
Vocational schools, 207

Walder, Andrew, 8, 9
Wang, Jiu, 67–68, 71
Wang Mingyue divorces his wife (*Wang Mingyue xiuqi*) (opera), 79
Wang Qimin, 40
Wang Tingmo, 104
Wang Xiaoying, 146, 149
Washing machines, 92
Watson, James, 123
Weddings, 95, 121, 127, 129, 131–132, 133, 134
Weixin group, 107
Wenyi bao (publication), 41
Wenzhou, 185, 187, 210
Wenzhou Labor Service Company, 187
White Pagoda, 161
White snake. The (Bai she zhuan) (opera), 79
White tiger legend, 132, 134, 136–137(n23)
Whyte, Martin, 8
Willows (as symbol), 159
Wolf, Margery, 73
Woman in the Tower (Wumingshi), 18

Women, 4
    in fiction, 28
    as *getihu*, 185
    and housing space, 88
    intellectuals, 61
    and marriage and divorce, 66–68,
        71, 207
    in operas, 80–82, 86(n40)
    in paintings, 161, 163
    surveys of, 206–208
    in work force, 185, 193, 206–208,
        210, 211
    See also Parent-child relationships
Woodside, Alexander, 2
Workers, 5, 20, 126
    flat, 161(illus.)
    protesters, 1, 2, 51
Work units, 96, 97, 185
Wu, John, 110, 115
Wu dialect, 141, 142
Wuguanfang (unofficial), 2
Wuhan, 207
    survey, 199
Wumingshi, 18
Wuxi, 207
Wuxi/Changzhou area (Jiangsu
    Province), 139, 147
Wu Xiaojiang, 63, 70

Xiamen, 181
Xiao Wenyan, 145
Xie Jin, 40, 49, 50, 51
Xue Jinlian ma cheng (opera), 81
Xu Guangqi, 111
Xu Shiyou
    in fiction, 22, 27
Xuzhou, 142

Yamaha Fish Stall (film), 190
Yancheng, 142
    ren, 141
Yang, Martin C., 83

Yang Ershe reduced to begging (*Yang
    Ershe hua yuan*) (opera), 77
Yang Fulu visits his fiancée's family
    (*Yang Fulu tou qin*) (opera), 77
Yangge. See Operas
Yang Wen taofan (opera), 81
Yangzhou, 140, 142, 149
    ren, 141
Yangzi River, 139, 141, 144
    bridge, 161
Yankou ceremony, 128
Ye (bishop), 115
Yen, Y.C. James, 74
Youth
    labor, 178
    rural, 204, 205, 213
    "sent down" (in countryside), 19,
        20, 64
    surveys (1980s), 200–202
    urban, 38, 39, 40, 45, 209, 211
    value changes, 193, 200–211, 212,
        213
    See also Students
Yu Taijun guan xing (opera), 81

Zhabei district (Shanghai), 88
Zhang Chunqiao
    in fiction, 27
Zhang Ji, 40
Zhang Shiwen, 74
Zhang Xian, 42
Zhang Xinguo, 168(caption)
Zhang Xinxin, 4, 5, 9, 10, 57
Zhang Yang, 18–19
Zhejiang Province, 96, 139, 142, 210
Zhenzhen's Hair Salon (film), 190
Zhou Enlai, 144, 150, 202
    in fiction, 22, 27
Zhou Naxin, 60
Zhu De portrait, 163, 166, 169,
    169(illus.)
Zhuge Liang (literary character), 30
Zhuoxian (Hebei Province), 163
Zhu Weiguo, 61, 65, 66